To Mike Loxton
with best wishes

Tony Pawson

April 1993

Two Game Fishermen

TWO GAME FISHERMEN
An Hereditary Passion

TONY and JOHN PAWSON

Methuen

First published in Great Britain in 1993
by Methuen London
an imprint of Reed Consumer Books Ltd
Michelin House, 81 Fulham Road, London SW3 6RB
and Auckland, Melbourne, Singapore and Toronto

Copyright © 1993 Tony and John Pawson
The authors have asserted their moral rights

A CIP catalogue record for this book
is available from the British Library
ISBN 0 413 66380 9

Typeset by CentraCet, Cambridge
Printed in Great Britain
by Clays Ltd, St Ives plc

Contents

Acknowledgements   vii
Foreword   ix

PART 1 – Highlights of a Season
Alaskan Adventure   3
Antipodean Adventure   14
Lochstyle Competition   30
Bank and River Competition   44

PART 2 – Accidents and Anecdotes
Caught Young   63
Chapter of Accidents   86
Chapter of Anecdotes   99

PART 3 – Tackle, Tactics and Thymallus
Grayling: A Really Game Fish   135
Lake Tactics   153
Tackle and Flies   172

PART 4 – World Championships
Success in Spain   183
Triumph in Tasmania   206

PART 5 – The Master Angler
Celebrating Walton   231

Appendixes   247

Index   267

Acknowledgements

My grateful thanks to my father, Guy, who instilled me with the fishing passion and to my mother, Helen, who gave me every opportunity to indulge it; to brother Philip for his ready support in fostering that passion and to my wife, Hilarie, and all my family for abetting it. It has, of course, been a special pleasure to me to fish so much with my son, John, and see him become so much more expert than I have ever been.

My thanks go also to the many fine fly fishermen who have not only taught us more about our sport, but whose friendship has helped us enjoy it to the full. It is possible to mention only a few, but my gratitude to all of them. Outstanding in their assistance to me and the sport in general have been Peter Cockwill, Charles Jardine, Bob Church, Chris Ogborne, Brian Peterson, the sculptor David Hughes and Brian Thomas. Of special help also in developing John's great talents have been the World Cup team of 1987 including manager Geoff Clarkson, double world champion Brian Leadbetter, who showed him so much in practice, and Dennis Buck. Other outstanding fishermen to contribute to his enjoyment and knowledge include Chris Howitt, Clive Perkins, Jeremy Lucas and Jeremy Clarke, and the rest of the Bath and District team, who bring fun as well as skill to competitive fishing.

That expert all-round angler, Moc Morgan, has also been an inspiration, as have many overseas fishermen. Among those to contribute greatly to John and my enjoyment of European fishing have been Belgians Paul Vekemans, Christian Fouvez and many times world champion caster, Guido Vinck. In

Acknowledgements

France, Bertrand Kron and Robert Taillandier have been good fishing friends, and I have had special help from Spain's Rafael de Madariaga Giraldo.

In Tasmania, John was given the time of his life by Noel and Lois Jetson, whose wise guidance contributed to his World Cup win. Among Australian friends also were that very special fisherman, the late John Sautelle Snr., and his son, as well as Robert Sloane and John's fishing partner, John Rumpf, while Patrick Neville made outstanding contribution to my enjoyment of New Zealand's marvellous fishing.

Poland's Jozef Jelenski gave us new insights into fishing, especially for grayling, as did Austria's Reinhard Resch. It is a pleasure to include some of Jozef's passages from his letters to me. Sincere thanks also to Jeremy Herrmann for his individual contribution on bank fishing.

I was fortunate to have permission to reproduce photographs by masters of the art such as Peter Gathercole (nos. 15, 16 and 19 among the black and white illustrations and nos. 5 and 6 in the colour section) and, also in the colour section, Bill Bachman (1 and 2), Bob Church (18), Peter Cockwill (10, 11 and 13), Mike Oliver (17) and Roy Westwood (3, 4 and 23). I am grateful, too, to the *Angling Times* for their permission to reproduce no. 21 in the colour section.

My appreciation goes also to Canada's Jack Simpson for his supportive work in transforming the suspect organisation of the world fly fishing body, FIPS Mou, and to the remarkable Czech world champion, Slavoj Svoboda, who partnered John on Grafham in 1987.

My thanks also to the *Observer* and my colleague Hugh McIlvanney for use of his article, and to the *Observer* magazine for that of Doctor Collee on fishing's health-giving properties.

Finally, my special thanks to Marguerite Maynard who typed the manuscript as she has for most of my fourteen books, starting with the official centenary history of the FA Challenge Cup.

Tony Pawson

Foreword

In my youth I used to pore over a book by A. H. Chaytor entitled *A Salmon Fisher's Letters to his Sons*. The mixture of anecdote and instruction fascinated me, and it was that memory which prompted me to embark on this book with my son, John. There is, of course, a great difference. Chaytor was instructing his sons whereas, ever since John was 18, I have been learning from him as the technical expert of the two of us.

Between us, we have almost a hundred years of weekend and holiday fishing, with John no doubt anxious that it should be clear that sixty-eight of those years are my fishing lifetime. Both of us started aged 4 and both of us qualified immediately under Lord Grey's requirement:

> Fly fishing is an earthly paradise, and there is but one quality that is necessary to make us fit to enter into and enjoy it. We must be born with an intense desire to catch fish with a rod and line.
> Fly fishing is but one form of angling, and to enjoy it to the full a man must be born an angler. The passion may be latent, for years it may not discover itself owing to lack of opportunity but, if it is not revealed when opportunity comes, it is not there.

Lord Grey also gave excellent advice on how a work such as this should be approached, and that too we have tried to follow:

> If, then, a book is written about a pursuit like fishing, it should be not to preach, or to convert, or to dogmatise. Books about

sport and country life should be written and read, partly perhaps for the sake of hints, information, and instruction, but much more in the hope that the sense of refreshing pleasure, which has been felt by the writer, may slide into a sympathetic mind.

Chaytor, too, wrapped up his hints in stories and anecdotes which certainly touched sympathetic nerves in my mind. Such technical hints as there are will come mainly from John, while my main contribution is in anecdotes and stories, many of which I hope will illustrate the supreme pleasure which I have always had from my fishing.

Fishing is a fascinating mixture of skill and luck, and that is no doubt why we have been such an ideal combination: I have the luck, John has the skill. That contrast may help to find some sympathetic understanding from every type of angler as may our very contrasting approach. I have always been a happy-go-lucky, impatient angler, always wanting to be casting or on the move and living up to the early instruction of Scottish gillies that the prime principle in catching fish is to 'keep your flies in the water'. John has always been the methodical, technically correct, exceptionally patient fly fisherman.

On a Hampshire stillwater I am forever on the move, forever casting blind to test out new places, forever trying to find new hot spots. John only enjoys himself on such waters when he can spot and stalk individual fish, no matter how long it takes him. If he wants to learn a new method he will go on through a succession of blank or unsuccessful days until it is mastered. Typical was his approach on Austria's Gmundener Traun with its huge grayling. For three days he concentrated on a difficult nymph technique with limited success. Typical of mine was that, after one day, I decided I was not enjoying it and went back to dry fly on which I was sure to do reasonably well. By day four, John could catch equally well on dry fly or the nymph floated thirty yards downstream without drag and inches above the bottom after a parachute-type cast. Not surprisingly, he was soon catching three to my one.

Methodical or happy-go-lucky, in our different ways we have both caught well and, more importantly, enjoyed ourselves immensely. We have had success in competition, but even more pleasure in the ordinary fishing which has been 99 per cent of our experience, and which has taken us to many delightful waters and countries. If this book passes on a small part of our own enjoyment, and maybe a few hints as well, that will be our real reward.

To simplify it for the reader, and keep a uniform format, all John's many contributions are put in bold quotes while the rest is mine.

Tony Pawson

PART 1

Highlights of a Season

Alaskan Adventure

For myself and my more expert son, John, it enhances the fascination of your season's fishing if you combine the familiar with the unknown. It is a comfortable feeling setting out on known waters where you are sure of good sport and confident in your method. But there is a special thrill in trying new fisheries with new challenges, different scenery, new techniques required, and with success uncertain. As a 70-year-old, the familiar now holds the greatest attraction for me, though it needs to be topped up by the occasional venture into the unknown. For the young and adventurous, there is nothing so exciting as being confronted with strange waters in far-off lands with no certainty about the fish you will find or whether you will be skilful enough to catch them.

In 1991, each of us found the spice of exploring distant waters. For John, his first trip to Alaska was a memorable experience, later aptly summed up in a single sentence: 'You can have a lifetime's salmon experience here in just a week.'

It was in July that he set off with Peter Cockwill in a party which included other fishing friends such as Paul Weiss and Chris Tarrant. A delay in the flight from Heathrow to Anchorage meant that they were stranded for the night at Bethel, a short hop away from their journey's end, the Chosen river. Of the dreary little town Chris Tarrant made the caustic comment: 'We spent a month in Bethel one day.' Yet at least the chance to sleep there let them arrive at the Chosen fit and full of anticipation, while the contrast heightened the pleasures to come.

As soon as the weather cleared, a small plane took them to the river mouth and the waiting guides. Some of these loaded the baggage on their motor boats to take to the camp fifteen miles upstream, while the remaining six each took a pair of anglers to fish. John had Chris Tarrant as his partner, and both were immediately impressed with their guide, Danny, as John recounted to me:

'I reckon to be very good at spotting fish, but he was exceptional, as some of the others also proved. As we surged upstream at full throttle, he would spot a king salmon here, a shoal of chums or sockeye there, when I found them hard to detect at the speed the boat was going. With the chum salmon turning so swiftly from silver to pink and green, and the sockeye to bright red, once in the river, many did stand out very clearly, but a lot needed keen eyes to locate. Such spotting as they raced up and down the river, with the salmon undisturbed by the boats, enabled the guides to locate concentrations of fish where good sport was guaranteed.

All our fishing was to be from the bank, but the boat was vital when one of the huge king salmon was hooked. When a virile 30lb-plus fish takes off down those fast currents, 150 yards of line is stripped off in a flash. The king is soon out of control as the backing continues to race out, unless the boat is powering you downstream too. With many rootwads and branches in the river, the only hope is to leap into the boat and follow as fast as you can. Most of the guides were highly expert and had the boat ready for instant launch, apart from one who was not so experienced and kept parking some way upstream with a shallow to cross by hauling before he could reach you. By the time he did, the king was usually long gone, and your fly with it.

The first stop on that first morning was a moment of high excitement. The wild and beautiful scenery was barely noticed as our whole concentration centred on catching our first Pacific salmon, with Danny saying there were many chums and sockeye in the deep eddy close to our feet. As we fished out from the shingly shallow neither of us could quite believe *any* salmon would be easy to hook. We knew the sockeye would not be, since they feed on plankton in the sea and are not often attracted to the gaudy flies we had been told were fancied by the chums and massive kings. But the chums were said to be easy quarry.

Within a few casts we knew this was indeed very different from salmon fishing in Britain, where it may take you a week or more to hook a couple, and blanks are more frequent than red-letter days. Both of us were soon battling with chums of over 10lb, and others followed fast. As always, it was that first fish in a new environment, that first heart-fluttering pull on the line, which brought a particular thrill, a special sense of pleasure. With it went a compulsion to land the fish and see a Pacific salmon close-up for the first time. So those first two were cautiously played, then admired for their bright colours before being gently released. To my surprise, a sockeye soon followed, already beginning to change colour, but not yet a vivid red.

Another surprise was the way the salmon took. Fishing in Britain or Ireland I had given the salmon time to hook themselves, merely tightening when everything had gone solid. With these, however, it was more like nymph fishing for large trout. As soon as there was a gentle check, you needed to strike hard, hoping it was a salmon rather than a snag.

That eddy was indeed packed with chum, and soon we were hooking them so fast that the sport was as continuous as if catching small wild brown trout on the prolific Altnacealgach lochs in Sutherland. There was rarely a quiet moment when one or other of us was not playing a chum. There was also an entertaining variety in the colour of these salmon which ranged from around 6lb to about 15lb. Those which had just come into the river were sparkling silver. Those which had been up only a few days already had red and green stripes. The cocks near to spawning had begun to develop a kype and had bumps inside their jaw. Those in which transformation was complete sported a ferocious set of teeth, as the beautiful silver fish became a fierce multicoloured specimen on its way to spawn and die.

With our minds fixed solely on chum, we began to play them ever harder. There was then a cry of surprise from Chris as his line was suddenly ripped out, and a massive salmon vaulted high into the air before hitting the water with a reverberating splash amid cascades of iridescent spray. The boat was instantly ready, but as the king continued to strip line he became more difficult to master. His surging run finally pulled out the hook, but there was no question of the rod suddenly snapping straight. Until Chris reeled in, it remained bowed by the weight of the endless yards of trailing line and backing.

There was only momentary disappointment at the loss. We had seen a 25lb salmon at full power and knew for certain now that both of us would battle with many more. The brief encounter had whetted our appetite and increased our respect for the fish they appropriately called kings. They did indeed fit Edmund Blunden's lines:

> Not brainless, puny, darting things
> But wise important water kings.

The urge now was to catch one of them, and Danny took us to another lie where he had seen a gathering of big fish. What a gathering that was! By the end of the day, I had hooked close on twenty, the majority of which shook free or fouled impossible snags as they tore through or past the hazards such as tree branches stranded in midstream. The third king I hooked tried different tactics. For a time he sulked immovable, or perhaps not deigning to notice he was hooked. Then he took off upstream in a defiant dash. Next to his leap, the most thrilling sound and sight was the line vibrating and singing as it sliced upstream through the current at unbelievable speed.

There was no regret for me when I lost a king, provided I had seen it. But there was a feeling of desolation when the line went slack before there was any clear indication of the size of a hooked king. You were left wondering, was it just a 20 plus-pounder? Or perhaps 40 or possibly 50? Or might it be even closer to that rod-caught record of 97lb? One of our party, Sean, who concentrated solely on the kings, finally landed one of 50lb, which was the largest of our stay. Practice improved his catch rate until he was close to landing one in two despite the problems. But, with the kings, there were days when they were in sulky mood, and ten hours of fishing for them might only result in a couple hooked. How different were the chums. ,There was one day when I spotted a stream of them running in shallow water only a few yards out. Instead of my usual relaxed fishing I set out to see how many I could beach, unhook and return in an hour. Hooked so close in without current to help them, you could hold them under the rod tip and beach them in two or three minutes. So continuous were the takes that over a dozen were returned in just over the hour.

There were times, of course, when the chums, like the kings if to a lesser extent, were not in taking mood. The sockeye, however, were always difficult to catch, and different methods and flies were required to have much hope of landing many of them. The main chance was to spot a shoal in one of those swirling backwaters which produce clear windows of sight down to the fish. Then it was like trying to spot and catch difficult trout on a clear stillwater with a small fly worked close to the fish's nose. This was best done with a short line and a very short cast. There were also occasions when a shoal of sockeye running upstream in shallow water could be more easily taken on small white flies fished across them. This was part of the fascinating variety in the Chosen river fishing, with its abundance of large fish and its range of techniques required to deal with the different species. The July weather was unusually cloudy and often wet with only rare gleams of sunshine. So there were few occasions when you could see well enough into the water to fish for a particular salmon and watch him take. For me, there was one such enthralling experience as a line of trees at my back made it easier to see clearly into a shoal of chum and watch the flash of the mouth as the target fish quietly intercepted the fly.

My good friend Peter Cockwill is an outstanding practical angler and very knowledgeable about tackle. So I had gone to his shop in Godalming to get kitted, as there was no point going on an expedition like this without suitable equipment for every type of fishing and fish you would encounter. For the kings, you need an exceptionally strong rod. Peter had found the best suited to this fishing were the specialist American rods, with Loomis preferred to Sage. More expensive they may be, but they are wonderfully light as well as immensely powerful. For kings, a 9ft with a 9 line was sufficient with a 7 line adequate for chums.

For the reels, it was essential to have a good drag mechanism, and System Two reels proved more than adequate.

American lines developed for such fishing were also a great asset. For kings, you need a Teeny T300. This has a fast sink tip some eight yards long with another twenty-plus yards of floating line before the endless yards of backing. The kings lie on the bottom in deep water, and the way to catch them was to cast upstream above the lie, then let the fast sink line fall free. The leader nylon had to be a mere couple of feet at most, so that the fly was close to the line down on the bottom and not working higher up above the fish. Once the line was right down, the fly could be played round with the current.

For chum, a weight 7 Teeny line with much shorter fast sink tip and a similarly short leader kept the fly at the right depth for fish which preferred to run and lie in shallower water. The best flies were Teeny nymph patterns from size 4 for kings to 8 for sockeye. Shocking pink proved the lethal colour for chums and was also good for kings, as was black. For sockeye, smaller flies were needed, with black or white effective colours.

The fly-tying kit was in action most nights, for a day's fishing here absorbed many a fly. You might be broken by a king, or in the many snags. Then the flies that survived those hazards would be chewed to bits by the numbers hooked. Those numbers, and the strength of the chums when played at distance, as well as of the huge kings, made powerful tackle imperative. Yet even such strong tackle was powerless to control the kings, until you had followed them down half a mile or more. Sean's great fish took him an hour and a half to land and was finally beached three miles from where he was hooked.

On that first day when Chris Tarrant and I had tired ourselves with too much fishing, and too many fish, Chris determined to get tough with his next king. After it had taken him down a short way, he decided to make Tarrant's last stand on the bar on which he stood. "We finish it *here*," he announced to the world. A minute later, he was scrambling for the boat with the backing racing out. There were three other shingle bars and three more such defiant pronouncements before he did finish it. "Here" was then at least a mile further downstream!

The excitement of these battles had the adrenalin flowing too fast to notice aching arms, and there was a fine sense of achievement when a fish was finally landed. There was also awe at the size and power of these kings, and even at times a tinge of fear when you tried to free a snag in the midst of the main current. The guides were expert at holding the boat still over the snag even in the fastest stream. Yet, with the line still tearing out, it was precarious work leaning over the side of the swaying boat to haul up the branch or disengage the line.

There was also the danger of the line cutting your fingers. That happened to me on the bank when one careless moment nearly cost me dear. My guide, Ted, had let me try his expensive weight 7 Sage, which made an average chum feel like a large king. I had thought one fish was played out and was holding the rod in one hand as I looked round for a suitable beaching place. Suddenly, the salmon took off and, instinctively, my fingers closed on the line to slow him down. The intense pain as it burnt into my flesh drew an involuntary "Bloody hell!" and made me open my hand. I felt like saying something stronger and so, I imagined, would my guide as his rod and £350 of tackle went surfing away at speed behind the bolting salmon. Ted took it calmly: "I know where his lie is. He'll go back there, and we'll recover it shortly." Later, he worked the boat slowly over the lie and soon spotted the coils of brightly coloured line. That was hooked with a spinner, and the salmon was still on. Ted was taking no second chance with his rod; ripping out the hook he made sure of recovering it without further alarm.

That was a lesson painfully learned. On that first day there was another to absorb. My high loss rate of kings was in part due to failing to set the hook hard enough, so that it was often torn out in the force of that initial rush. With the sizeable rainbows I had been catching just days before in English reservoirs, it was enough to tighten and play them hard. With the kings, it was necessary to strike really hard as soon as you felt them as well as keeping maximum pressure thereafter.

For some of us, the kings were an irresistible fascination but, for one at least, their power was too awesome. After he had hooked and lost several fish, I noticed he spent much of his time sitting on the bank watching. Gradually, we realised he was now apprehensive rather than eager, for the moment a king took hold and he had to steel himself for a tiring fight he was resigned to losing.

In a way, I could understand the feeling. When Chris and I

went on too long that first day we were apt to groan, "Not another king," as strained muscles and tired arms were forced to endure another struggle. But it was the desire for constant variety rather than fear of kings which concentrated much of my fishing thereafter on other species. Chums in particular provided splendid sport. Coming over on the plane I had tied up a multitude of flies, only to find that I had ignored the crucial colour, as chums appeared to fancy anything pink. So I had pink fly-dressing sessions most evenings, though you could probably catch your fill on any colourful pattern.

There were excitements apart from the fishing. Grizzlies abound in the area, and it was with a tremor that from time to time I came across footprints the size of a dinner plate on ground which had been unmarked as I passed an hour before. The guides told us that soon the grizzlies would concentrate on the spawning salmon, and then steer clear of all humans. But now some were hungry enough to ignore their apprehensions about man, with one in particular snuffling round the camp. Grizzlies are a protected species but, for an unarmed human, it is an unequal contest to take on something standing ten foot on its hind legs! So the guides had a variety of guns and thunderflashes to scare away any that became too inquisitive, though these had been needed only once in the previous fifteen years. There were also baited traps like the aerosol can covered with honey and peanut butter just outside the camp. In the early hours one morning, the bear did indeed get a shock snack from chewing the aerosol and was sped on his way by a noisy barrage, which frightened us as much as the grizzly. What with tiger snakes in Tasmania and grizzlies in Alaska, the best of fishing has brought me in contact with some of nature's most dangerous species as well as some of the most delightful.

For me, the most delightful in that Alaskan river was the Arctic char. They figured largely in one magic day I spent with Peter Cockwill. We found a shoal of these delicately coloured fish averaging around 2lb and ready to rise freely to large dry flies. Even when the current dragged them – or especially when they dragged – the char sailed quietly up to take the flies with a satisfying swirl. We also took time out that day to photograph the chum in its various colours. "Catch me a silver one," Peter demanded and, sure enough, the first to come out a few casts later was burnished silver, straight in from the sea. "Now one ready to spawn," and, by similar coincidence, the next out had a big kype and long teeth which made me wary as I unhooked it for return after it had posed for photographs. Peter confused me for a moment when he said later, "I'm dead." Seeing my surprise he added, "Well, this is paradise, isn't it?" With the sun for once sparkling on the water and the soothing sound of the stream to complement such fishing, he had a point.

That day, Peter had chosen an ideal stretch of river. For a start, there was a deep hole well stocked with kings. This time we each landed the first two we hooked. My third was also under control, and I was powering him towards the shingle when the hold gave and the fly flew out. "You prat," said Peter. "That's a silly way to lose a fish." "You have to play them hard," was an excuse which Peter rapidly dismissed. "There's hard and hard. When you have him beat, there's no need to look as if you are trying to throw a 25lb salmon over your shoulder." He was right, of course. While they are in the current and fighting hard, you have to exert maximum drag on the reel and maximum pressure. But, once they are under control, being too hard on them can pull out the hook.

With Peter, there was usually something new to learn and, despite the ease with which salmon were hooked, the week was never boring because playing so many fish taught you so many valuable lessons in a very short time. The variety of experience was the other enchantment. Peter's cleverly chosen stretch also included a long wide shallow only a few inches deep in places. "Put on a floating line and this Grey Duster dry fly, and let's fish this for Arctic char," he suggested. So I went ahead and waded out until I could fish into reasonable depth of water. When I looked back, Peter was barely above ankle deep and into a fish. Thinking it a one-off fluke I watched for him to go deeper. Instead, he soon caught another. Looking back towards the bank I then saw flashes of silver in the really shallow water and realised I had waded unheedingly through the best place. When Peter's Grey Duster finally disappeared in a tree, I found that a couple of size 10 Roman Moser Buck Caddis dry flies, left by chance in my box, proved even more effective, ending the day pulled to pieces but still taking fish.

Another pleasure was listening to the stories of the guides. I asked about the absence of any but a few rainbows. "They'll come in shoals later when the salmon start to spawn and they can banquet on a limitless supply of salmon eggs. It's fascinating to watch them work in pairs to outwit the chums despite their fearsome teeth. One will swim in front to distract the salmon. Then the other will charge the hen fish from behind, hitting her with such force and accuracy that the eggs spurt out to be greedily devoured." Fishy battles of wits on the spawning beds have apparently been matched on occasion by human confrontation along the river. The native Innuit, dressed now in jeans and baseball caps rather than traditional Eskimo costume, still retain their volatility of character. This erupts at times when something happens to upset them or banned liquor is consumed. My guide recounted one such occasion when an unusually small run of salmon led to a protective order stopping commercial fishing. Sport fishing, however, was exempted since the anglers return the salmon to go on to spawn.

Despite being well paid for allowing anglers to reach the state-controlled river over their land the Innuit took out their frustration on the fishermen. They drove their motor boats straight at any angler wading deep, swerving away at the last moment to leave him shaken and with the waves from the boat cascading down his chest waders. The owners of this fishing concession are the Duncan brothers, all of whom are tall, powerful and very tough. They decided it was time to put a stop to this. Knowing the river much better than the Innuit, Brad Duncan fished kneeling down on a shingle bar well out from the bank. His appearance was of a man deep in the river and up to the top of his waders – a tempting target at which an Innuit boat was soon pointed. Too late for it to stop, he suddenly rose to his full height, revealing how shallow was the water just before the boat stranded itself on the bar with broken propeller. Brad was said to have recounted with glee the look of total surprise on Innuit faces as he stood up. Each side having made its point, normal good relations soon resumed.

The chum and char did not wholly distract me from the kings and, on average, I hooked five or six more each day. The largest landed was over 30lb, but the loss rate was still high in these fierce fights. Fish lost always seem to remain more vividly in the memory, and there were two which caused me some disappointment despite my knowing exactly how large they were. Indeed, it was an illogical reaction because both would have been released in any case moments later.

The first was, so far as I know, the largest of my hooked kings. As soon as he bolted downstream, my guide Kirk, brought the boat and, for once, there were no problems as I followed the king down, realising how big he was when he made a thunderous leap. Half an hour later, I had manoeuvred him out of the current into a still backwater between two shingle bars over a mile from where he was hooked. Without the stream to aid him, the king was close to giving up, his tail flipping the surface and his huge body clearly visible as he rolled on his side. "A great fish. Forty pounds or more," said Kirk. But the flipping of the tail or my presence on the bar disturbed a shoal of chums which dashed past, upsetting the king and niggling him into a final run out into the current again and straight at the only snag in sight. The run was quickly checked and the branch finally broken but, as the king was played towards the next shingle bar, the hook finally pulled out, loosened by the pressure applied to break the snag. As compensation I was soon into a king of around 30lb, which was played out in as many minutes. As I was leading it on to the shingle, a final swirl pulled out the knot of the cast, and he too went free a minute or two before he would have been properly released.

A week on the Chosen river is indeed the experience of a lifetime, but not one to repeat too often; otherwise, ordinary fishing can be made to seem dull by comparison. Certainly the four weekends following my Alaskan trip were the only ones all summer when I did not go fishing. The mind needed a rest as well as the muscles before adjusting and enjoying again the trout fishing at Bewl Water.'

Antipodean Adventure

New Zealand was even further for me to travel in November of that year, but it was a pleasure to change English winter for spring sunshine. Or so we thought until, at the end of a long and tiring flight, the plane was diverted to Fiji because of wind and rain closing in on Auckland. November is usually a fine and settled month in this country, but the weather had been surprisingly stormy and spring more than a little late. Still, the sun soon brightened my visit and encouraged the trout, which had been lying so low that even on rivers the fast-sink line was a preferred technique – indeed the main one, offering real chance of success in the faster, deeper streams.

Ever since Zane Grey publicised New Zealand as the eldorado of fishing and O. S. Hintz wrote so evocatively of catching huge rainbows in Lake Taupo and the feeder rivers of this vast lake, it has been a dream place for many anglers. Even little townships such as Turangi on its southern shores have signs proudly claiming to be the Trout Capital of the World. That, unfortunately, is over the top, even allowing that distance lends enchantment. There are bigger and more prolific trout from Alaska to Argentina, from Canada to Chile. Yet there is still splendid fishing despite increased angling pressure and large-scale poaching, which defeats protective legislation such as that forbidding the sale of trout. But in many places the fly fishing can be hard, particularly for those wedded to one technique. Overall, though, New Zealand has attractions which are hard to match anywhere else for those anglers who agree there is more to fishing than catching fish.

Much of the scenery is breathtaking with its volcanic domes, some rounded by time, many still sharp-pointed pinnacles, its lush North Island pastures and the countless rugged mountain ranges of the South Island. There is also the fascinating variety of flowering shrubs and trees, such as the dark red flowers of the flax and the bottle-brush tree, or the delightful pohutukawa with its creamy white buds opening to become another cascade of red as the filaments dance in the breeze. But the predominant spring colour is yellow, with many riversides ablaze from broom and gorse and wild lupins. The national tree, the kowhai, circles Taupo with its yellow radiance and paints much of the countryside with that bright colour. The native trees colour the forests a dark green giving them a slightly sinister aspect as if to remind the vistor of the times when the Maori from Polynesia wiped out the even earlier settlers, the Moriori, then themselves battled between their tribes or against the British.

The harshness of the indigenous varieties is now softened in most areas by the delicate greens of imported species. Above all are the ferns in infinite variety with the sturdy black, silver and golden tree ferns, the ponga, covering whole hillsides, together with the silver ferns, another of the country's emblems.

The special attraction of the fishing is not so much the size and condition of the wild trout, impressive as those are. The true delight is in the variety of the free fishing and the quite different challenges you meet, and in the different techniques you need in the various waters. The starkest contrast is in the choice between sophisticated fishing in high-powered boats setting out from civilised townships such as Taupo or Rotorua, and genuine wilderness fishing not many miles distant.

My three weeks in New Zealand were related to the Commonwealth and World Cup competitions, so my base was Rotorua, but with freedom to roam within a hundred-mile radius. The experience of myself and the England Commonwealth team covered only a fraction of the available water, yet each member found a quite different type of fishing as their own personal highlight. For me, it was the small streams which have always had a fascination from the time, aged four, I first dropped a worm into a Scottish burn. Three of the best I fished were indeed reminiscent of such burns, except that the water was so startlingly clear, the fish much larger and easier to spot, but a little harder to catch.

My kind host was Pat Neville, with whom I had often fished at Rutland before he returned to New Zealand a few years ago to be its Chief of Air Staff. He had also fished the Test on many occasions, finding it a most enjoyable experience but commenting that, compared to New Zealand streams and rivers, it was a clouded water full of stocked fish. A day with him on the Rautawiri and Torepatutahi emphasised that this was not just a tongue-in-cheek remark, but one with much truth. The Torepatutahi's alternative name, the Blue stream, evokes its clarity. It cuts deep into a narrow gully whose sides are covered with a tangle of ferns, brush and toetoe grass, another cortaderia, like pampas grass, with tall reed-like stems and a plume of feathery white filaments.

The best way to fish the Blue is to walk along the top peering into the water up to forty feet below. Only when you spotted two or more sizeable fish in one of the little pools was it worth creeping down to cast for them. On our first brief visit, Pat made it easy for me by spotting them from above and directing the cast. Fishing upstream with a floater and one of Jeanette Taylor's weighted yellow-head Caddis flies, the second cast saw the floss marker disappear and the instant strike connected with a lively rainbow of about 1½lb. So lively was it that it hurdled over a wire across the stream and nearly released itself prematurely.

This visit was in the nature of a reconnaissance, so there were only a couple more pools fished and a couple more caught before Pat took me to a special pool on the Rautawiri stream, known as the Brown because of the colour of the river bed, rather than any lack of clarity in the water. The test of this particular pool was in reaching the point where a small brook flowed in on the far bank. That favourite lie was a difficult cast against the wind, since the combination of water depth and pumice silt on the stream bed made it impossible to wade close and the near-bank vegetation provided an impenetrable barrier. With a light line and rod, it was just out of my range casting against the strong wind from a promontory overlooking it. The problem was solved by paying out yards of the floating line and letting the Caddis fly drift down before being slowly retrieved. For several casts, the main current veered the fly away at the crucial moment to send it sailing wide of that tempting inflow. But once the fly dropped within inches of the far bank at maximum range it floated straight into the killing area with three nice rainbows hooked in quick succession, the largest about 2½lb.

The short visit whetted the appetite and, a few days later, we were back. Virtually all fishable water in New Zealand is covered by the 'Queen's Chain' legislation which gives anglers who have acquired the appropriate cheap general licence the right to fish free and walk within twenty-two yards of the water margin. Where access to that chain is over private land, the friendly people of the country will nearly always allow fishermen over their land, but their permission must be sought. Jim and Elva Robinson uniquely hold riparian rights over the streams bounding their property. They could not have been kinder in allowing us to drive down to the river at the back of the farm, although Jim's long friendship with Pat put back our start time by half an hour's entertaining chat. This time, Pat pointed me straight to the Brown stream, Rautawiri, below the junction with the Torepatutahi where the fish tended to be bigger. Looking down on it from above, a small pool soon caught my fancy with the water frothing and swirling in the dark run-in before smoothing into a shallower glide under an overhanging tree. Even though it was impossible to spot any fish in that deep rippled headwater, there just had to be trout lying there. It called to mind the evocative verse:

> Water brown, water bright
> Pearls and swirls that sever
> Running water's my delight
> Always and forever.

17

This was the type of pool I had to investigate. The climb down in chest waders was far from easy, but second cast I saw a good rainbow cruise down into the quieter water where he was clearly visible. Only as he turned did I realise he had followed the Caddis fly down, and the strike was only just in time to start a splashing battle with a 2lb trout. We planned to leapfrog each other but, from above the next pool, Pat called to me to come up and look down at a couple of good rainbows he could see. They were lying well out, easy to spot, and just above a weed bed which provided a good mark. Easing down well behind them I cast several yards ahead to give time for the fly to sink down to their level which, as usual in this clear water, was deeper than it looked. The Caddis bumped past their noses but drew no reaction. A couple more casts a yard further up were similarly ignored. Since trout's eyes focus outwards, perhaps this was too straight? So several casts drifted the fly past the bigger trout's right eye. Not a flicker of movement. Well, many trout, like many humans, are monoculars with single-eye vision. Perhaps the left eye might trigger a response? After all, I thought to myself, a lot of nonsense is talked about how difficult wild fish are. They may be warier, but they are also hungrier, feeding machines with one eye on survival, one on anything edible. So perhaps a cast taking the fly past that other eye might stimulate the taste buds?

Such thinking is typical of the way you can remain optimistic while targeting a reluctant fish. If it works, you congratulate yourself, although perhaps it is only persistence and the trout's unpredictable instinct which has dictated its reaction. Whatever the truth, on this occasion there was a particular thrill as the largest rainbow now fixed its eye on the Caddis and followed it back towards me. The mouth flashed white, the sinuous body turned, and the strike started a thrashing fight close to the bottom of the pool where the water raced away under a tunnel of trees.

My rule is always to fish with strong enough leader not to risk getting broken. Better to hook one fish and catch it, than three which depart with your fly. So the 6lb Drennan double-strength leader held him there and finally worked the 3½lb fish over a weedbed close to the bank when played out. Intending to put every fish back I had no net, but Pat had asked me to keep two over 2½lb for his son-in-law to smoke, so I eased it out by hand. The next little pool was identical to the first and, again, out of the swirling water at the head a good rainbow cruised into view following and taking the fly before using the stream to keep the reel singing. The first of those two had turned out to be stuffed with brown fern beetles. These are real delicacies for the trout as are the green variety, falling from the many manukas, or tea-trees, which early settlers were able to use to make a passable cup of tea. But this one's food had been a couple of kouras, or small freshwater crayfish, whose hard shells were still far from digested. Pat had commented, 'If you catch a trout which has been feeding on koura, its flesh will be bright red.' This one's was an extraordinary vivid scarlet.

So it continued as we fished back up the Rautawiri and the Blue, the Torepatutahi, with frequent sorties down the valley sides in pursuit of spotted fish and with a high ratio of success for both of us. Indeed, the feeding machines seemed to be motivated more by appetite than survival instincts. But, now that I had the two 'keepers' required, the further seven which came my way were all returned. To complete a delightful day, my last catch was the first brown trout I had from these streams. As I peered over a clump of toetoe grass I seemed to be eyeball to eyeball with it on the fin high in the water. No sooner was the Caddis flicked in front of it than it surged in, a two-pounder whose hunger was clearly dominant over caution. Yet the fine condition of these trout made me wonder why they should act hungry. Perhaps they had such a wide range of food that nothing made them suspicious. Certainly they liked that Caddis, with only one fish taking the small flashback nymph on the dropper.

The pleasure of fishing such streams was enhanced by the setting and by the other wildlife. As I played that final brown, a pukeko bird made a colourful flight past me, its blue feathers glinting in a way which explained why they are used in the

Scotch Poacher, a night fishing fly whose luminous blue attracts the trout. As it flew away, the white circle at its tail indicated why hunters find it such a tempting target.

That had been a guided and assisted venture on streams rarely fished. For another happy day on a similar small stream, it was a case of exploring on my own. 'Highway 30 crosses a prolific little river whose name escapes me,' said Pat. 'It begins T–A–A, and you can't mistake it because it has nearly as many letters as some of those Welsh villages.' The sign on the bridge duly identified it as the Taahunaatara, with the pool below the bridge revealing a large and uninterested rainbow who, no doubt, had seen it all before.

'Cross the shallows at the bottom of the first meadow and walk up the far bank high up to spot the trout, then work back along the far side fishing your marked spots,' had been the advice. It sounded easy, and there were signs of a track through the trees to the first pool below the crossing. Nothing came in the promising run-in but, as the current smoothed off into a glide, there was a violent take. That was a brown of over 1lb and, next cast, an even fiercer take came from a rainbow double that size. So far, very good. But the stream was too deep and fast to wade down and it disappeared now between two steep hillsides, the far bank totally overgrown with impenetrable brambles, the near trackless and with thick scrub, toetoe and ferns. It looked unfished for a year at least, the advice outdated. So it was a case of fish when you can.

Progress was difficult and occasionally hazardous, as the scrub and dead grass concealed unexpected deep gullies or sudden potholes. On a sunny day in chest waders, this was suitable only for the young, agile and adventurous, or the old, keen and crazy. At least I was not crazy enough to proceed without great caution, whether forcing my way along the bank or wading parts of the stream. We had one grave warning already of the wading dangers in an area where there is so much pumice stone. It takes you by surprise to see large pumice 'boulders' float by, but it is the pumice silt on the bottom which is the real hazard. One of our Commonwealth team had already stepped out on what looked like firm gravel only to find himself sinking over the top of his chest waders, to be rescued just in time and with much difficulty by helpful Australians fishing nearby.

This was now true wilderness fishing, though only a quarter of a mile from a main highway. But whenever I could edge down to one of the little pools, each with its own characteristic of deeps and shallows, runs and rocks, eddies and glides, the rewards were swift. The Caddis had attracted ten mixed browns and rainbows before I finally emerged to easier going. There had been one deep and inviting pool which could only be fished from a high rock. To do so I had gone up to 8lb double strength, a prudent precaution as two rainbows had to be lifted some ten feet to be released! Pleased not to have lost my fly in them or on the back cast amid toetoe or the tall flax or other obstacles, I now threw a long line without looking behind. That lost me the magic fly on a wire over the river. Perhaps because I had no identical replacement, perhaps because the fishing was now easily accessible from a nearby farm, two good-looking pools yielded nothing. It had been a stimulating three hours, but time to stop before exhaustion set in.

True wilderness fishing in New Zealand is a very special experience but it also needs special precautions. Even the Rangitaiki river, which figured prominently in the World Championship, has to be treated with respect when the multitude of competitors and controllers are not there. In the midst of the vast Kaingaroa forest, stretching for mile after mile after mile in every direction and with side roads and tracks which have only the rare vehicle down them, it can be a very lonely place. Run out of petrol here, and you have many hours' walking ahead of you with the real risk of becoming lost. Get a puncture, and you may be in real difficulty. The track surface is usually pumice, and a jack will simply break through the crust and bury itself ever deeper unless you first spread the weight by putting a large spade or a wide hubcap under it. So it is a wise precaution to take not only something on which to rest a jack but survival rations as well when you fish in such places.

On a previous visit to New Zealand, I had found the Rangitaiki a pleasant and prolific river. But that was near the end of summer, when the water was low and upstream nymphing or small dry flies made for entertaining fishing and good catches. After a wet winter, the Rangitaiki was coloured and high, the big fish – and it does have double-figure trout – well down. So the only successful method was downstream with fast-sink line, nor was there anything elegant about the most effective flies.

The New Zealand World Cup team had put in much practice on the venues and had settled on a variant of the Black Woolly Worm and the Black Woolly Bugger (yes, that is a standard New Zealand pattern) as the fly which won them the event. The England team, which finished third but caught several more fish than any other country, used similar tactics, and their more varied flies included Tadpoles and the like. Brian Leadbetter, in becoming the first person to win the individual World Championship for the second time, combined his knowledge of coarse and game fishing to flush out the fish, with a variety of different methods on the various locations in a stunning performance.

The catch rate on the Rangitaiki and the lakes round Rotorua made it clear that, in New Zealand, you may expect big fish, but that big bags are not easily achieved on many of the well-known waters. A 1990 official report based on a limited survey is given in condensed form in the booklet *Rotorua Lakes: Rainbow Country*. In its own words, 'Rotorua on its wild volcanic plateau is gateway to a group of fascinating lakes, each with a beauty of its own and twelve of them fishable. All contain rainbow trout. Brown trout are found in Rotorua and Rotoiti.' While the study was anything but comprehensive it was consistent in its finding that, even with the majority of anglers trolling, these lakes have an average catch rate of less than one fish every four hours. The international competitions in the area pointed to the same figure. The England team of five, each fishing eighteen hours, caught a total of thirty-six sizeable trout, one every two and a half hours, more than any other team. The winning New Zealand team, well practised on these waters, caught thirty, or one every three hours, and the overall average of the seventeen national teams was just under one every four hours, exactly the average of the survey.

The England team excel in lake fishing, and their relatively high total was due to good catches in the one session on Lake Aniwhenua. Many of these were big fish, with the largest caught in the competition weighing 12lb, a trophy trout that was kept while all the rest were returned. But that meant the catch rate on the four other venues, the Rangitaiki river and the associated Whaeo Canal and Flaxy Lake, averaged only one every seven hours! There are always vast individual variances within such 'averages'. But New Zealand fishing is not a numbers game except in some places on some occasions. What makes it special, apart from the size of its wild trout, the whole ambience, and the friendliness of the helpful New Zealanders, is the remarkable variety of the free fishing so easily accessible. For me, the small streams were the fascination. But each of my successful Commonwealth party found different fly fishing highlights.

For Bob Church, the big wild rainbows in the lakes were a prime target after his first brief sortie on Lake Rotoma had been well rewarded. Driving back from Aniwhenua, where prolific weed growth had spoiled the bank fishing in a water which fished so well from anchored boats, he stopped at Rotoma. The bay looked delightful. With the crystal-clear water glinting in the bright sunlight, the fishing prospect looked less inviting with his companion, Dennis Buck, betting any odds against his catching in the half-hour he could spare. Wading out a long way in the shallow margin Bob tried a variant of the salmon tactic of backing up. Casting long, and with a white Cat's Whisker on a size 10 hook as his lure, he walked several yards to the side before beginning his retrieve. Once he started to draw in the line, the fly inevitably pursued a curved path at accelerating speed. Within minutes, that attracted a hard take and a somersaulting rainbow soon made it clear he was into a good fish. When finally played out it proved to be in exceptional condition and was estimated at around 6lb.

That set Bob up for the subsequent day on a trophy trout lake, Tarawera, where big fish abound and anything under 4lb is an unpleasant surprise. Pat Neville took him out in his boat, using the depth recorder to anchor on various drop-offs where the bottom dropped sharply down from the edge of a shelf some fifteen feet deep. Casting into the deeper water and retrieving back past the ledge soon proved profitable. The rainbows' main food at this time comes from the shoals of small smelts which only swim close inshore on calm days such as this. The standard flies for smelting rainbows are size 8 Grey Ghost, Jack Sprat, or Silver Dorothy, though New Zealand patterns such as Parson's Glory, Killwell (with white stripe), Hamill's Killer, or the Mrs Simpson are effective on most lakes. Those whose sensibilities are offended by English fly names such as Dog Nobbler would be unlikely to use another New Zealand pattern which often catches well, namely the Red-Arsed Bastard. For those who take the Shakespearian view of 'What's in a name?' the tying of this on a long shank 8 is:

Tail: Thick clump of bright red floss silk.
Body: Mixed bright and dyed cock hackle with a furnace cock hackle and tied in together.

Bob's choice of a White Tinhead, one of Jeanette Taylor's popular patterns, was a happy one as the smelting rainbows liked the look of it. Using a Hi-D line Bob had three large fish of a total weight of 16lb – all coming within a lively period of an hour shortly after noon. When the trout dozed off, there was other entertainment. The boat shifted to new water near a cliff face, and Bob was at once attracted by the whistling of a tui bird perched on a tree high up above him. Having been told that the tuis were good mimics, like the myna birds, Bob whistled back. The tui then kept hopping lower and trying to imitate Bob, finally giving a passable rendering of 'Pop Goes

the Weasel'. The tui also has a less admirable human characteristic. Its preferred food is nectar and, when the red flax is in
flower beside the streams, it will take more than its fill, finally
rolling around in a drunken stupor and unable to fly.

There is a special attraction about this beautiful Tarawera
Lake, with so many of the surrounding hillsides covered with
giant tree ferns. But it has its darker side. Jeanette Taylor also
hooked three large trout there, landing one of over 4lb. But
then a sudden storm blew up on the exposed part of the lake,
and the race to shelter over the wind-lashed water was not
without its moments of anxiety. But that was a minor tremor
compared to the disaster which once befell the lake. The whole
of the Rotorua area is still volcanically active with ten major
eruptions over the past 40,000 years, the latest that of Mount
Tarawera as recently as 1886. The neighbouring village of Te
Wairoa was then a main centre of tourism because of the
remarkable Pink and White Terraces, formed over centuries
from the silicate leaching out of the ground, on nearby Lake
Rotomahana. These were visited in excursions by whale boat
and canoe before being destroyed in that eruption which sliced
the mountain in half, raised the lake level 30 feet, spread ash,
lava and mud over some 5000 square miles and buried also the
village of Te Wairoa with most of its inhabitants.

For Jeanette, the highlight was when the Commonwealth
party visited King Country and another of the small streams
which so appealed to me. Under the expert guidance of Lindsay
Lyons, the party fished its small clear pools with upstream
nymphing tactics. Jeanette delighted in finding brown trout as
well as rainbow in the run-ins and the tail of the glides. Using
a strike indicator at the end of the cast for the first time she
found this speeded reaction so that she caught regularly
throughout an enjoyable day.

For Paul Canning, who was to do so well in the Commonwealth competition, following his win in Wales by being
runner-up in New Zealand, the highlight was quite different.
With Dennis Buck and Brian Thomas, he went off for several
days' exploration, included in which was some fly fishing in

the Bay of Plenty, renowned for its quantity and variety of sea fish. The sport began when flocks of diving gannets pointed the way to a shoal of kahawai. Fly fishing with white Minkies, Paul was soon catching well and finding the kahawai fought harder than any fish he had encountered previously. With stormy petrels joining in to locate the fish, which averaged around 3lb, it was for him a marvellous experience.

Paul is a studious and intelligent angler who likes to work out everything about the fish he stalks. So it was an added bonus for him when, on our way back, I took the party to one of Auckland's main attractions, Kelly Tarlton's Underwater World. There you can walk down tunnels watching through the clear sheeting as sharks and many other species swim above your head. Paul was able to study in detail the behaviour of the kahawai as they cruised above and beside him in the same kind of shoals he had encountered in the open sea. On the landing stage outside, with a walk-way far out into Mission Bay, I also watched Europeans with expensive tackle aiming to catch the same kahawai. A group of Maori was similarly intent, but many of them were without rods and were cleverly manipulating yards of nylon tied to their fingers. At my best count, they were ahead 65–nil as I walked by! That prompted the reflection that expensive tackle is not necessarily a passport to success.

After the Underwater World we all visited another of Auckland's showpieces, the War Museum. It is worth remembering that the written Maori language was devised at Cambridge University in 1820 by a professor working with the Maori chiefs, Hongi and Waikato; until then their language had been verbal only. The Maoris' physical history is well recorded in the Museum. They were fighters by tradition and most of their games and dances, staged there every day, were aimed at giving them suppleness and strength for using their primitive weapons. The huge building also reminds one of the high percentage of New Zealand's small population who gave their lives in two far off World Wars. Among the exhibits are Spitfires and evocative pictures of the Gallipoli campaign in the First World War and of the campaigns in North Africa and Italy in the Second.

Brian Thomas had one especially memorable evening and another thrilling fifteen minutes. While touring round, fishing at random, he and two companions came on Lake Waikare-moana. Stopping at a motor camp they enquired about the fishing and were told there were plenty of trout in Home Bay by the camp site. He and Dennis Buck tested that comment by catching a couple of rainbows, then waited until late afternoon before putting in three hours of serious fishing from the bank. Using New Zealand flies, such as the Mrs Simpson and various coloured Tadpoles, they caught so well that, as dark closed in, they had returned sixteen rainbows averaging between 2 and 3lb. The other memorable experience for Brian was the excitement of playing a 7½lb rainbow on Lake Okataina.

The late spring had left the waters high and cold, which was primarily responsible for Dennis's comment that, for him, the highlight would be when he saw a natural rise! But what fascinated him was a quite different experience. Lake Rotorua is a large expanse of water surrounded by hills formed as the molten lava was squeezed up from beneath the ground with the huge depression, which geologists call a caldera, then filling with water to form the relatively shallow lake. Rotorua differs from the more famous Taupo in being only an eighth of its size and having only a few short streams to support the vast spawning activity, as opposed to Taupo's twenty-three rivers and feeder streams. These short streams, however, are easier to police and protect and, like Taupo's Waitahanui stream mouth, Rotorua has its 'picket' lines too when the trout congregate there. At the end of November, I looked over the Waiteti stream mouth, and from the bridge it was easy to see large trout cruising in all directions. No one was fishing because that stream is protected until 1 December. But, come that day, up and down from the bridge will be so lined with fishermen that it will be difficult to squeeze in, and eight-fish limits will for a time be commonplace as at some other stream mouths. Bank fishing at Rotorua, however, is much affected by the wind. In England, it is usually good tactics to fish from the shore into which the wind is blowing. That is often a waste of time in

Rotorua and the surrounding lakes when the wind is strong. First, in the shallow lakes the stirred-up silt will muddy the water. Then the smelt on which the trout feed will not come in close when it is rough. Finally, only when the wind is blowing offshore will the alternative food of beetles and other terrestrials come drifting out from the fringe of trees to entice the trout close in.

Trolling on lakes is the most favoured method of fishing for many, with the local experts well aware of the shelves and drop-offs most popular with the trout. Lead-cored lines are currently banned on Rotorua, but Dennis Buck was fascinated with the expertise involved when his guide demonstrated a technique in use on some other lakes like Tarawera, Okataina and Rotoma. Highly coloured lures, like the aptly named Traffic Lights, were trolled at the precise speed of three kilometres an hour along a promising shelf close to the large island in the middle of the lake. To keep the lure at forty-five feet, the rig was thirty yards of nylon, then fifteen yards of Deep Water Express lead-cored line, then 100 yards of Hi-D ST 20. The trolling line was a different colour every ten yards to aid precise control. The echo sounder in the boat picked up the depth of fish and bottom, with the boat speeded or slowed to reach fish in a deep pocket. Very effective it proved.

Dennis's comment about lack of natural rises reflected the fact that it was too early and too cold for the fish to be up on top. It was a great regret of mine, however, that I could not fit in an evening on the Whaeo Canal. Mike Oliver, who guided me so well in the Rangitaiki area on a previous visit, had thus described for me the type of fishing I might have expected:

'On the Rangitaiki do not try to match the hatch. In my experience, they take more freely on terrestrials, i.e. yellow-bodied grasshoppers or caddis and on Royal Wulffs. The hatches are generally too irregular to be of any use. Weighted nymphs are highest takers.

'On the Whaeo canal during the day, pheasant tail nymphs and such weighted flies sunk ten feet will sometimes snatch the bottom-hugging rainbows, and unweighted green weed-coloured small nymphs will take the edge-feeding browns. Rarely will you be able to get them to sup a dry until darkness is almost on you, but a very lightly hackled nymph sometimes entices them. I use a nymphy-looking Tupps as the first risers begin on the edges.

'The browns show half an hour before the rainbows. Then, as darkness comes, it will begin to rain as the whole area comes alive. Royal Wulffs are favoured for a while but, as darkness really sets in, splashy risers will be heard. Deerhair Caddis in brown dubbed bodies, and sometimes green, are best.

'You can catch well after dark by casting a few feet in front of the sound. As the tension of the current pulls the hook home, you will feel the fish on and secure. Six trout can be caught in thirty to forty minutes. They are hard fighters, so I use a minimum 4lb tip. The current flow does not seem to affect the fishing, but wind will put them down. Low-level water ruins the edge feeding. Stalking is imperative to get within a bull's roar of the edge feeders.'

Such different opportunities point to the real attraction of New Zealand. Within a short distance you can sample a wealth of varied waters with large wild fish, and you may need to use a dozen different techniques to enjoy them to the full. So they are a real challenge and a real pleasure to the true fisherman.

Was it worth the long flight to get there? On the way back we did the sensible thing and broke the journey for a night's sleep in Los Angeles. It proved to be the eve of Thanksgiving Day. All the Americans I spoke to knew it was time to hurry home to Mum and consume turkey and pumpkin pie. My own private thanksgiving that day was to have been privileged to enjoy New Zealand's delightful country, waters, and people.

Lochstyle Competition

A sport as popular as fishing is bound to encompass a wide variety of people and a wide variety of opinions. More and more are finding enjoyment in periodic competition, but that is something each individual has to decide for himself. The pleasures of fishing are so varied that each has a wide range of choice involving a range of disciplines and methods. The conventions, too, are varied, but the only ones that matter are those laid down by official bodies such as the Salmon and Trout Association, or in official codes such as the Game Angling Code reprinted at the back of this book. If you fish in accordance with those precepts and the rules of the particular fishery, then choose as you will and do not let anyone try to put you down. As Lord Grey, that great philosopher of the sport, wrote: 'The gift of the power to enjoy has various forms and diverse objects. There is no need for those who have one form of this gift to look askance at those who enjoy another form.' That is perhaps too idealistic, true as it is. Whatever fishermen do, there is always another group who look askance at it, and competition is no exception. Make your own judgements.

My own enjoyment of occasional competition derives from the intense interest I have found in it both as a learning experience, and as a social experience in meeting a host of friendly anglers, many better informed and more expert than myself. In a letter to *Trout Fisherman* Pat Quinn recently wrote this of his own impression: 'My son, David, and I are recent converts to fly fishing competitions, and I have to write to say how much more fun we have had from our fishing than ever before. It has brought us in contact with so many delightful people, and among these anglers I have met more true sportsmen, in every sense of the word, than in any other sport. The friendly atmosphere is outstanding, and we have been so impressed by the number of people who have so readily assisted us to improve our fishing and enjoy it more.'

Pat Quinn is the happy and ebullient type of man who evokes a similar response in those he meets, which may account for his euphoric reaction. But, for many others, the camaraderie has been as important as the learning experience and the opportunity to test oneself against some of the best.

Again I am of like mind with Lord Grey when he summed up the attraction of competition: 'We improve year by year, and take pride in the increase of our own prowess. Then from understanding we pass to an artistic admiration; we become judges of how the thing should be done, and we are critics of style. Competition is then desired, not solely for the excitement it provides, but as a stimulus to good performance.'

To that excellent summary I would add that not only does the learning aspect sharpen your skills, but it also enhances the thrill of hooking a fish. Reading some eminent writers describe their youthful enjoyment of many aspects of fishing and how they 'matured' to taking pleasure in only one, I am left with the sneaking feeling that that is another way of saying they became world-weary of fishing in old age and lost many of the pleasures which they had once enjoyed. Having competed for the first time when aged 57 I can confirm that it has helped me to enjoy fly fishing in the round as much at 70 as I did when 7. The challenges and pressures of competition may exaggerate the disappointments of failure, but also enhance the joy in success. The contrast, too, increases the satisfaction to be had from quiet fishing on one's own with no time- or performance-pressure to mar the solitary and sometimes selfish pleasure.

The competitive and the withdrawn have always battled with each other within me. At my prep school, there was a playtime tradition that you could play boisterous games, but with the understanding that at any time any individual could cry *'pax'* and withdraw without being considered a spoilsport. That suited me ideally. Competition has proved a stimulus in fishing, but long exposure to it would soon bring the need to cry *'pax'*, just as it did in my decision to give up county cricket after three successful years. So occasional fishing competition followed by many leisurely hours on my own, or with a friend, exactly suits my nature.

The happiest aspect of fly fishing competition for me is that it has been something I can do together with John. There is nothing better for a father than to share an interest and see your son get better than you have ever been. In that sense, 1991 was a magical fishing year, not just in watching John's remarkable performances, but in sharing with him the pleasure of making it through the eliminators to the England team of five for the first-ever home river international. Between us we make a good pair of competitors. For fishing is a splendid mixture of skill and luck and, while I have the luck, he has the skill. Well, he has luck, too, but as Gary Player used to say, 'The more you practise the luckier you seem to get.'

The *Angling Times* Classic, the champion-of-champions match, provides one of the season's main challenges. All those involved are 'winners', including some of the best of the Welsh and the Scots, with around a hundred involved each year. John already had a consistent record, coming third in 1988, its inaugural year, and in the top ten again the following year. That was one reason for his feeling hopeful when I met him in the Rutland car park. The other was that Rutland Water is a favourite of his, and he had already had outstanding success in another big event there at the start of the season.

Helping him through his pre-match drill of stretching the different types of lines on his four reels I asked his advice, as it was my first day on a reservoir that season. The flies he gave me proved effective. But was he pulling my leg when he suggested that the South Arm was fishing best before himself winning the event on the unfancied North Arm? Not so.

Most competitors, like myself, begin with a preconceived

plan and a starting place they hope to reach first as they roar away at the gun. On five-mile-long Rutland, such decisions can be crucial. If you go up one arm and find it fishing badly you cannot then waste an hour motoring round to the top of the other. Apart from his technical expertise, John is a cool and calculating competitor, always thinking, always adjusting. As my boat raced across towards the South Arm, I was surprised to see him hanging back and wondered if he had a problem with his motor. Instead, he was studying the pattern of the other boats. As he told me later:

'The fish were mainly in small shoals, and most of these were up the South Arm, but I knew there were a few such pockets up the unfancied North Arm. When I saw the mass of boats head for Fantasy Island or South Arm and only a couple turn up the North Arm I reconsidered my initial plan. It was now obvious the pockets up the South Arm would be hammered by many expert anglers and that, if I could find one up the North Arm, it would be possible to fish with less interference.

So I decided to give Barnsdale Creek a try, as it was still close enough to Whitwell Lodge that I was not totally committed to North Arm if it proved unproductive. With the weather cold and the May wind blowing strongly, Barnsdale was also one of the most sheltered spots. When I arrived I could see another competitive boat with that outstanding angler, Dave Grove, and an uninvolved boat anchored in the middle of one of the best lines of drift. That still left plenty of room and many undisturbed areas.

Before the start, those whom I had talked to agreed that ten fish might be a winning total since it had turned so cold. So I was cheered when a fish took on the hang as soon as I had cast long enough and controlled the flies to my satisfaction.

My partner was Jim Collins, who had been my captain in the previous year's international in Ireland. Jim is a very experienced Rutland angler and was kind enough to endorse the desirability of staying in Barnsdale when I kept picking up the odd fish most drifts.

My successful flies were a Green Palmer on the bob and a pink mini-lure on the tail. The fish were quite deep, but I was using a Wetcel 2. This doesn't sink so fast as a Hi-D, but Barnsdale was sheltered enough that we could drift quite slowly even without a drogue. So, when cast long, the flies had plenty of time to sink. The great advantage of the Wetcel 2 is that you can fish with it anywhere from close to the surface to down deep, and make quick adjustments as the fish change their depth. That proved invaluable when the trout suddenly came on to feed near the surface around midday. By retrieving as soon as the flies were in the water, the Wetcel 2 kept them high enough and I had two fish while Jim was changing from Hi-D. In the end, those two made all the difference between winning and being an also-ran.

For some forty minutes, the trout were really active and the action was hectic. You often get one short spell like this in an eight-hour stint and, in a competition of this quality, you have to take full advantage when the chance comes. That means intense concentration and playing your fish hard even at the risk of breaking. I did indeed lose one good fish by bringing him to the net before being played out. At the last second, he came to life and dived down, catching the dropper in the net for an inevitable break. But, by the time the rise petered out, I had six more trout in the boat.

My original aim had been to stay in Barnsdale only for a couple of hours, and other boats were now beginning to crowd in. But that meant they had not been finding fish elsewhere, and each time I looked outside Barnsdale the wind was too strong for good drifting. So we stayed there throughout. With over two hours to go, I had caught fourteen which proved just enough to give success in a match of a winner-take-all nature as opposed to national finals which are all about getting in the top twenty to qualify for the next home internationals. In those two hours I lost a couple, perhaps because I could no longer sustain the intense level of concentration of the first six hours, perhaps because the fish were now shy with more boats about, as well as off their feed.

It was a satisfying end to an enjoyable day to find that my catch was half a pound heavier than runner-up Graham Pearson's. Graham had eleven fish up the South Arm, including one of 3lb 10oz, as became such a noted catcher of big fish.'

Different tactics and different methods were needed for John's national qualifier at Bewl. With thirty anglers involved, some twenty of them internationals, it was clearly going to be no easy day for getting into the top five, who would go through to the national final. John was also uncertain about best method and areas.

'Bewl is my "home" lake and also, with the very different Rutland Water, one of my two favourites. It has the advantage that it warms up quickly and you can catch well with floating lines almost from opening day. Equally, to do consistently well there you need to master all the techniques from Hi-D to fishing small dries. That variety is one reason why so many southern anglers have come to prominence in competition because, on whatever other water a competition is held, the good Bewl anglers will have practised the required technique in their "home" fishing. Bewl is also one of the prettiest reservoirs, and its many bays not only make fishing more interesting, but ensure that you can always find a sheltered spot whatever the wind. It is also small enough that you can change to different areas without too much loss of time.

On this occasion, I had caught reasonably in practice, but with no particular pattern. So I had not sorted out to my own satisfaction what flies to use, or where to start. The best starting options seemed to be the dam area or the Nose. Most chose the dam, and my choice of the Nose proved unfortunate. After an hour and a quarter, the only thing my partner and I had caught was the rope round the propeller, which wasted time but fortunately did not break the sheer pin as it might well have done.

By then, there was a mass of boats around the dam. This was clearly one of these times when it pays to join the mêlée, especially when it is obvious many are catching well. As we motored over, my partner and I could see several bending rods to confirm that fact. The conditions of gentle breeze were ideal for top-of-the-water fishing, and one of those into a fish was Jeremy Lucas. "That's one place gone," I commented. "In these conditions Jeremy is unbeatable as a nymph fisherman, even without the head start we've given him."

Soon my partner said excitedly, "That was a hard take." A

few casts later, he hooked one but lost it. Then he caught one 'on a Hare's Ear', he told me. We were now nearly two hours into the match and I had not had a pull, while clearly several others already had three or four fish or more. So it needed a rapid change of method. I put two Hare's Ears on and a maximum permitted size 10 Orange Hopper on the dropper, as the wind was now rising. With the waves beginning to build, I also changed from long casting to a much shorter length which gave total control in the working of the flies in the rougher conditions.

I was aiming to keep the flies stationary under water, with the retrieve merely recovering line at the exact pace of the boat's drift. Then, finally, I was lifting up and hanging the dropper, holding it on the wave crest. The fish took mainly on the hang, occasionally on the lift. Happily, that worked so well that in no time I had three in the boat. So confident was I now in the method that I was murmuring aloud at the hang, "One, two, three, *take*," as a fourth fish did indeed take when I said the word. So I was now back in with a chance, confident of more fish if the rough conditions continued. Yet, even as I played that fourth trout, the wild wind began to die as suddenly as it had risen and, as the surface of Bewl smoothed to a near flat calm, that method ceased to work any more. After another fruitless three-quarters of an hour, it was time for another complete change. But where to go? Chingley Wood, or the Nose again? My partner commented that he had seen a number of fish at Chingley the previous day and, as the Nose had been so disappointing earlier, we settled for that and left the throng at the dam.

That looked a good decision as we soon saw fish coming along with noses right on the surface film as they sipped nymphs. One of the first times I fished Rutland, my father and I were being taken out by that most generous, competent and optimistic angler, Brian Thomas. At every new spot we reached Brian would say with infectious enthusiasm, "We will have fish here." That was always cheering, though not always justified by results. So it became something of a family quote, and I was happy to repeat it with total confidence as I saw those risers.

A change of method again was clearly required, and I now tried a team of small dries. But, slowly, the confidence and trembling expectation began to evaporate. The fish were erratic in course and so choosy that, after another hour, I had only one more rise, one more fish, and my partner was finding it equally hard going. So, rather than fish on mechanically, hoping for the best as it is so easy to do, I spent a couple of minutes on a complete rethink. If there were so many difficult ones on the surface, might there not be even more easier ones below? If chasing them was proving so difficult, and as there were clearly a lot of fish around, might it not be better to let *them* find the flies, rather than trying to make the flies find them? So I changed yet again to fishing a couple of feet down, with the team of nymphs kept stationary by a retrieve only at the snail's pace of the boat drifting so slowly in the calm.

By now many other boats were crowding round, but happily this proved the killing method while the vast majority of the other anglers remained intent on those elusive top risers. From five in six hours I went to the limit of twelve in the next hour and a half, well before closing time. That qualified me comfortably enough, as the only others with maximum catch were Jeremy (inevitably, and long before me) and Chris Reeve, who had done as I so often do and ignored the crowd. He had fished all day close to the cages and apart from his twelve had lost several of the large "golden" trout which provide such sport at Bewl. The first one I ever caught there earlier in the season took me well down the backing in its first wild run and before it came to the net it had me imagining a trout much larger than its 7lb, exciting and satisfying as that was. As for Jeremy, I marvelled again that, in the middle of a crush of good anglers, he could be counted on to outscore them three or four to one when conditions were even half-suited to his preferred nymphing method – a marvellous angler.

That, for me, was one of the most challenging and pleasurable day's competition I have ever experienced. It needed recovery from a bad start and the working out of the right method in the very different conditions of a gentle breeze, then squally wind, and finally near flat calm, fishing all the catching time in the middle of other boats with equal chance, and having to work out at the end that the right method was not the obvious one which had been suggested by the misleading rises.'

That qualifier in June was followed by a very different challenge for John in the September final back at Rutland. Before the start, the knowledgeable ones such as Bob Church and Chris Ogborne, who had been in so many finals before, told me this should be one of the fairest ever. The eliminator system is ideal for home internationals as it broadens the opportunity for many competent anglers to enjoy these events at least once. But there is the same sort of luck in fishing as in bridge. If Rixi Marcus and Terence Rees had taken on a couple of novices and the deal of cards favoured them, the novices could have won the first two rubbers. But, over ten, the luck would have evened out, and the novices would have been left trailing far behind. So it is with eliminators in fishing. Luck in the choice of area, luck in not losing any fish, luck in having an expert boat partner to guide, luck in other ways too, good or bad, always leads to some capable, but less expert, anglers getting through, while some of the best are eliminated along with most of the less good. I recall Bob Church telling me of one of the occasions (few indeed!) on which he had not qualified for the final and was acting as boatman. While it was the sort of day on which it was difficult not to catch, and one of his pair was hauling in the fish, the other caught only one all day, which he proceeded to hang over the side in a plastic bag with a hole in it so that even his one fish was missing before the end.

'Excuse me,' said the mystified Bob late in the day, 'but would I be unfair in thinking you were lucky to qualify?'

'Not at all. I know I'm not really good enough, but I went in for the qualifier for experience and to learn from better anglers. It proved a hard day when very few fish were caught. After my first cast, I put the rod down to light a cigarette and, when I picked it up, a fish was on. At the end of the day my partner said, "Reel up now," and as I was reeling in I caught the second fish, which was enough to qualify me!'

For this final, however, it was generally agreed that nearly all the leading anglers had qualified with many fewer casualties along the way. The fish were also widely spread and most of those being caught were of roughly similar size. So the conditions were as fair and challenging as possible. When I saw John in the car park, he was relaxed but not over-hopeful. That trip to Alaska had left him so sated that he had fished only once in the past five weeks, a day at Rutland the previous weekend. His intended practice on the day before the final had to be cancelled because of a rush of work. As a great believer in practice John was not optimistic about his chances, particularly as the rest of his season had been so successful that he was bound to have an off-day or two. Perhaps because he was not as keyed up as usual, he was in fact to have his most enjoyable competition day ever and, for the second time in the season's two major individual competitions, to catch more fish than the other ninety-nine finalists. This was his account of it.

'Fishing the weekend before I had done well on the South Arm, but been told that the main hot spots were regarded as Fantasy Island or the North Arm. I had a preliminary plan to try Fantasy Island for a couple of hours and then go up South Arm as that was the only one on which I had practised. You are unwise to believe everything you may be told before a major event, as those who have spent hours of practice working out the right flies, methods and places can hardly be expected to reveal their hard-won secrets to someone who may then deprive them of a place in the international. However, a chat with my Bath team colleague, Jeremy Clarke (whom I knew as a generous purveyor of information and a top-class angler whose information could be trusted on all counts), confirmed that there were still fish up the South Arm.

My boat partner, Lee Henfrey, told me this was his first final and that he had never fished Rutland before. The advantage of that was that he was ready to let me choose where to go throughout the day. The disadvantage was that I could not expect any advice or guidance from him about how Rutland was fishing. Happily, he proved an entertaining companion, a good angler, and a quick learner who was to qualify in the top twenty himself by taking sensible advantage of what he saw to be successful.

My original plan was a very provisional one. Hanging back to observe what others did, I found a main mass of boats heading for Fantasy and nearly all the rest for North Arm. The Fantasy fleet looked too thick to me, so I followed Jeremy right to the top of South Arm, which we found almost deserted. I had fixed on a floating line to start with, while Jeremy had told me he was going for Wetcel 2. Not expecting much, or in the mood for intense competition, I was surprised to net a fish within five minutes. That first fish is so important, and at once the adrenalin was flowing. My godfather, the cricketer Colin Cowdrey, maintains that for success in any sport the ideal is that almost impossible combination of intense concentration and relaxation. To be too tense limits the physical skills. He instances that more slip catches tend to be dropped in Test matches in the first few overs, more batting mistakes made in those tense first overs at the crease, than when, later, players are still intent but more relaxed. Yet the tension that heightens awareness is essential to top-class performance. That mixture of intense concentration on my fishing and total relaxation to really enjoy a day's outing certainly worked for me. With such a good friend as Jeremy close by, we were able to chat and exchange information whenever we drifted close to each other. That good start was soon maintained with another trout on the floater. I was using a very slow figure-of-eight retrieve and a team of nymphs, as mini-lures had been totally ineffective when tried the previous weekend.

So far Jeremy had not scored, but now I saw him take two in a drift. He then had a third some hundred yards from the bank. On a similar drift I had no take until my final cast, almost on to the shore, brought a third. That trout took in only a couple of feet of water, and I reasoned that Jeremy's success further out indicated the fish were in fact down a few feet. So even though I had caught on that last cast on a floater I immediately changed to a Wetcel 2, with good results.

We each continued to catch at intervals with Jeremy keeping just ahead of me. Knowing that it would not be a particularly easy day we had estimated six fish as almost certain to get us in the top twenty and qualify us for next season's home internationals. When I reached that figure in early afternoon as we continued to drift the shallow Hideaway Bay I was totally confident we had both done enough. With that main object certain of achievement, the rest of the day was a relaxed and delightful fishing experience. Even the fact that boats now began to thicken up in our area was a sign that others were not finding it easy, and that was confirmed when one of the bailiffs, touring round the competitors, told us that even such a pair of experts as Chris Ogborne and Dave Shipman, fishing together up the North Arm, were struggling, as were most of the competitors who had chosen to go there.

Fishing became more difficult as the boats crowded in, but Jeremy and I continued to pick up the odd one by changing down in nymph size from 14s to 16s. The difference now was that the press of boats made it harder to drift the best line and also made the fish more scary. Previously, they had taken so confidently that all my first six came to the net. Now they tended to snatch at the fly and several came off, two in my final drift. By then I had ten to Jeremy's nine, but only as we motored home in happy companionship did we begin to think one of us might have won, rather than just qualified. In the event, Jeremy's nine weighed two ounces more than my ten, which was a momentary disappointment. But I reflected that Jeremy had been first to discover the correct method and had so freely given me information and advice that I was delighted for him. That was a fine end to a magic day.'

That was probably a good lesson for John that, while practice is often invaluable, if you know a lake well enough you may succeed without it. When he won the national championship two years earlier it was, however, practice that made perfect. He had fished Rutland for several weekends and was aware that the fishing was very hard. For practice on the day before he asked me to team up with him, though I fish very rarely on reservoirs now and was not competing in the national. He believed from previous experience that a Wetcel 2 was the best method and was happy with his team of flies, a Cat's Whisker as point and two Green Palmer flies as droppers. He asked me to try a floater while he concentrated on that. From the top of South Arm to near Yacht Bay he had two to my one, but that proved nothing as there was also the difference in expertise to take into account. But four hours' fishing had confirmed that it was indeed going to be hard on the day. At that point,

John said, 'Hi-D has not been working, but I must give it a try, so will you change to intermediate?'

As we started to drift towards the yachts, John suddenly got excited commenting, 'A good follow there.' The fourth time he said it, I asked, 'Can't you catch one for a change?'

'I could have caught at least two of those if I'd wanted by dropping the fly back on them. But I know now there are plenty of fish here, so why pull some of them out now rather than coming back for them tomorrow?' When I caught one on the intermediate by the yachts, that confirmed it for him, and we drifted off elsewhere with John finding more fish where the streams from one of the boils smoothed out.

That intelligent practice paid off since, the following day, he headed straight for the unfancied yacht station, fishing an unfancied method; within a couple of hours he had caught four fish before others crowding in drove him away to catch a few more elsewhere and become national champion. That may have been 'easy ball' for him, but his over-cool approach certainly had me worried. When I arrived at Rutland I was given the news that John was well ahead and at least certain to qualify for the international. Mike Childs then asked me to be the judge of whether at the finish the boats had all passed the notional line across from the Whitwell headland. No sign of John as the boats crowded in. With less than a minute to go, only one boat appeared to be far outside but heading in fast. There was John sitting cheerfully at the motor and crossing the line only fifteen seconds before I would have had to judge him disqualified. I told him his nerves might be ice-cool, but mine were not, and it seemed very stupid to take such a risk when the main object of qualifying had long since been achieved!

On the question of luck, there was one incident which amused him. After catching three he was just starting a new drift and had made his first long cast with a Hi-D, which fortunately had not sunk too far, when he saw his only natural rise of the day. With one fleeting chance with the tackle he had, he lifted the Hi-D out with maximum force and landed the flies as delicately as he could at the exact point he judged the fish now to be. As the flies hit the water, the fish took. 'That was the best bit of fishing I managed that day or, in view of the difficulties involved, probably that season. All my boat partner said was, "You lucky so-and-so to catch one first cast of the drift!"'

Many anglers, in theory practising for a major event, get carried away when they start catching and stay there enjoying themselves instead of continuing to practise properly. That is a mistake John was taught to avoid when he joined the World Cup team in 1987. The well-organised Geoff Clarkson told his team in practice to keep quartering Rutland Water, even the areas not currently fancied. If they found fish they were to move on at once. Local knowledge was that the North Arm was not fishing well, but that there were fish aplenty along the Normanton bank. The England team, however, also identified some hot spots up the North Arm while competitors from most of the other twenty countries stayed to enjoy themselves along the Normanton bank. As a result, that area was hammered too hard and did not fish well on the first competition day. England had been hoping for three to be drawn that first day on Rutland and two on the less productive Grafham. In the event, only John and Brian Leadbetter were drawn on Rutland and by going to the unfished, uncrowded hot spots up the North Arm they caught so many fish that, with Chris Ogborne, Bob Church and Dennis Buck also doing well on Grafham, by the end of the first day it was clear the England team could all be blank the next day and still win. As it was, they all continued to catch well, with John winning the runner-up's individual trophy for this team event, behind Brian Leadbetter.

Bank and River Competition

For John, there were also two quite different competitive challenges in 1991. The first was one which I could share with him in a couple of my only five days of competition that year. In 1990, with help from some of the expert fishermen on the Yorkshire Wharfe, a sponsorship from Yorkshire Electricity, and the energetic support of the then minister for sport, Colin Moynihan, Geoff Clarkson had organised a national river final. A main object was to provide better information when selecting Drennan England teams for the World Championship. The venues for these are chosen by the host countries, and the four in which I had fished were all on rivers, as were most of the others to be. Success in boat fishing is some pointer to competitive ability, but not necessarily to river fishing ability. So this was a useful addition to selection knowledge and an opportunity of trying out 'possibles'.

That year was almost entirely by nomination and mainly with the World Championship in mind. However, its success led to the event being given a broader and more organised base and an additional, and now main, purpose. It is now run by the Confederation of English Fly Fishers as a qualifier for a new series of home river internationals which started in 1992, with the top five in the 1991 final making up the England team for that event.

Obviously, as a CEFF event, the aim was for everyone to qualify for the final via regional eliminators. Equally clearly, it was too early to expect some regions without suitable rivers to arrange such eliminators, and there was still a World Championship interest. So several regions merely nominated a couple of contenders without an eliminator, and several other finalists were put in direct as part of their trial for selection for the World Championship. Tongue in cheek, I enquired whether as a 70-year-old soon finishing with competition, and as the only Briton to win a World Championship on a river, I might be nominated. That was treated as the poor joke it was intended to be!

So John and I both entered the South of England eliminator, to be fished on that delightful moorland stream, the Teign, with only three to qualify. Bob Preston made a good choice taking us down there rather than in Hampshire's prestigious waters. I had never realised what a vast resource of delightful and not over-fished streams there are in that area. Dave Grove is an outstanding river fisherman and revels in that wide choice of attractive streams, as I found when I stayed with him for my day's practice. 'For an annual Duchy of Cornwall permit I pay £84, which gives me access to around a score of small Dartmoor streams and rivers; with such countless miles of fishing you are spoilt for choice. Wild moorland trout are an entertaining challenge if you forget the modern mania for big fish and adjust to a pounder being a monster and enjoy the rushing streams, and scenery as wild and beautiful as the trout.'

Dave and his wife, Lucy, another very good angler, were able to advise me and were very hospitable hosts. But I was to find one drawback in Dave's keenness. Getting my day ticket at the Anglers' Rest Inn, courtesy of the Upper Teign Anglers Association, I was soon entranced with the stream, which reminded me of those Scottish burns which had captivated me when at the age of four I first learnt to worm fish. The small fish could be taken fishing downstream wet fly, but more certainly fishing upstream with the size 14 brown hackled flies Dave had tied for me, or with weighted nymphs.

Many of the gravelly pools were fast and shallow, but then would come deep runs where wading was difficult on the slippery rocks. The river was now narrow, now expanding suddenly into a salmon pool (and some salmon do run up), now to the equivalent of a small lake. The endless variety kept enticing me forward, and I needed to learn the river as well. A full day in chest waders was an always enjoyable, but ultimately tiring experience at my age. Driving back to Dave I had thoughts of a large dinner and early bed. Dave had other ideas.

'Just time for a quick meal, and we are off to the Totnes Weir pool on the Dart. Might be good tonight, and the big sea trout have begun to run.' Ill-equipped with light rod and line, but game to the last, I was still sleep-casting well after midnight. Dave and a friend had each had a 3lb sea trout and I missed one, with many a loud splash to keep me just awake in that mysterious night light to which the eyes finally adjust. A few days later, Dave rang me to say some of his friends had caught forty sea trout there in a night up to 6lb. Well, you never do hit it quite right, do you, but that eighteen hours of fishing underlined the profusion of river opportunity in the area where small is beautiful, and large even more delightful for those who prefer big fish.

John had time for only a brief half-day practice before eliminator day. The local association had kindly provided a controller each and, with some seven miles of river at our disposal, we could choose where to fish provided we did not interfere with others. The best water was said to be below the Anglers' Rest, and that was where John and most competitors headed. Having spotted a good pool well above it I decided to head upstream instead. That seemed a good decision when, after just fifteen minutes of searching the shallow current close to my bank, three trout had already been measured, recorded as counters, and returned.

Impatient fisherman as I am, that spurred me to further efforts, and trying to stand on a slippery rock in midstream to cast under some overhanging bushes I was soon flat on my back on the bottom. That is normal for me and usually no problem. But it was an exceptionally cold April, with the water cold, the wind bitter, myself soaked, and five and a half hours left. I cannot say they were the most enjoyable of my life, particularly in the last hour when I claimed my chattering teeth and shivering hands contributed to two larger than average trout getting off.

Still, I caught enough to finish third. John, displeased with himself for losing or missing several he ought to have caught, finished second, and Bob Preston was an easy winner using weighted nymphs instead of the dry flies we preferred.

So both of us qualified for the final on the Wharfe. To fish an eliminator for small wild trout on a small wild moorland stream and then tackle a much larger river with sizeable wild grayling and stocked trout from 1½lb to 3lb was a double challenge. The developing system meant at that stage that the majority of the forty participants had been nominated direct without having the challenge of an eliminator on a different river at a different time of the season. Still, the evidence of the day was that, far from being a handicap, it was a help to have sharpened up before, as all three of us from the Southern qualifier finished in the top six.

Happily, the Wharfe is a river I had often fished in its upper reaches above Burnsall. Whenever cricket reporting took me to Headingley, I had taken the opportunity to spend Sunday at least fishing this delightful water. John had fished there only twice before and was ecstatic about the look of the river, the type of fishing and particularly the unspoiled woodland and countryside. The one practice day we had together before the event therefore proved a rude surprise for him, though not for me. The final was on a Tuesday in July (generally noted as one of the worst months for river trout and too early for good grayling fishing), and no practice was allowed on the Monday. So we fished together there on the Sunday, and John was horrified at the difference. Now the whole of Leeds, indeed most of Yorkshire, seemed to be tramping the riverside encouraging their dogs to swim in the river and their children to paddle in it or throw stones into it. Every back cast had to be watched to avoid hooking a couple of hikers.

Practice on the Dee for a World Championship had made John very expert in fishing weighted nymphs upstream for grayling, oddly not a method most of the expert treatises on grayling fishing mention much, though the renowned Oliver Kite developed it to a high degree. The Wharfe grayling thicken up in numbers the further down from Burnsall you go, but the start of July is anyway too early for them to be caught in quantity. We worked hard on a very hot day leapfrogging each other over the whole stretch from the Devonshire Arms past Bolton Abbey, through the remarkable Strid Wood section and up to Barden Bridge. The Strid Wood water is extraordinary, as a wide river narrows itself to channel its whole force through a narrow crevice in the rocks. There the water boils and bubbles, and anyone incautious enough to fall in is almost certain to be dragged down to the bottom of the whirlpools and unlikely to be seen again alive. But, typical of this day, there were scuba divers active there as we passed upstream in search of quiet water.

Daytime fishing in July is relatively hard anyway, and the thousands lining the banks and disturbing the water did nothing to help. As I came out of Strid Wood into the open fields above Barden Bridge, the milling crowd grew ever thicker. John dropped off at one nice-looking pool where he soon had a fine grayling. Above him, I was defeated by some of the few rising fish I had seen. Experimentally, I tried everything from tiny flies to large Wulffs, from casting upstream to casting across with enough slack to avoid drag, to floating the fly down to the rise. With grayling particularly, that last is a method which makes hooking them much more certain, apart from the advantage that they see the fly before they see the cast as they flash up from the bottom. The disadvantage, of course, is that if you don't float it over them precisely the first time, they see *all* the cast and the disturbance as you lift off, which is likely to spook them.

A couple who were fishing in the final were out reconnoitring the river and saw John. Having asked him about his success and peered at his flies they then watched my unrewarded efforts as I waded in midstream. 'How nice it would be if we had a few incompetents in the final like that old buffer out there', remarked one. 'Even a novice could fish better than him.'

Containing his laughter John replied, 'Dad's not always *that* bad,' which led to embarrassed apologies and much entertainment for John.

The final is run on the basis of five different sections, each with eight anglers. You can go where you please in the two- or three-mile sections, and your catch is recorded every two hours of the six-hour event. Your 'placings' *in your own sector* are added up for each of the three periods, and the winner is the one with the lowest total, with most fish as the tie-break provision. That is as fair as possible, as you are not tied to one short and perhaps barren stretch, and it reduces the differential between being drawn on a good sector, or a poorer one. There is, however, still an advantage in being drawn on the most prolific sector, as a blank in any of the three sessions means you are automatically accorded eight place points, virtually ending any chance of being in the top five. The points on which these placings depend relate to numbers caught and the length of each rapidly measured fish since, happily, it is a catch-and-release event.

With no fishing on the Monday, we walked the whole river, John pointing out places where he had done well above Barden Bridge, while I showed him the best lies I had found in the upper water with which I was familiar. That was fortunate since, by Murphy's Law, I was drawn on the sector he knew well, and he was drawn on the sector I knew well. In my sector, there were also two of the best World Championship fishermen, Chris Ogborne and Chris Howitt, while John had two others in Dennis Buck and John Lindsey as well as a local Wharfe expert, Oliver Edwards. John also had the most challenging sector, as the river above Burnsall was exceptionally low with hardly any current in most of the now shallow, weeded pools and a very long stretch of water, some three-quarters of a mile, in the middle, which was out of bounds for the championship.

Dropped off with the other seven at Barden Bridge on a very

windy day, I was slow putting up my second rod and a few minutes late in starting. That was a worthwhile delay for me, as I was now totally prepared to fish dry fly or nymph as I felt inclined. To my surprise, no one had started on the long inviting pool above the bridge. So I began there hopefully with dry fly and soon came on a few risers in mid-pool. Failing to tempt them I changed to a weighted nymph with a size 14 Snipe and Purple as dropper. Suddenly, the floss marker disappeared, the strike was firm, and I was launched with a good brown. At the start of the second session, I was surprised to see that first pool still vacant and came back to try those risers again. This time, interest was immediate as I changed to a size 14 Double Badger. But two rises were missed, one large trout hooked and lost. The rises had not looked that confident so I went down to an 18, and immediately had two good trout of around 45cm. As I landed the second I remarked to my controller, 'There are three more still rising and I've got them taped now. No problem.'

Yet a problem there was. The day was windy with the odd shower, but as I turned round I was amazed to see the quiet current was now a fast race, the clear stream suddenly muddy with branches, twigs and leaves whirling past as the water climbed up my waders. An unseen downpour in the hills had created a flash flood, with the river roaring up several feet in as many minutes. So coloured was the water, so violent the flood, that I hardly bothered to fish at the start of the final session. Most of the others in my section also congregated round the bridge to take a breather, with Dave Shipman very disconsolate. He had left his spare rod on a small island just before the flood and, when he looked round, the island had gone and so had some very expensive tackle. Fortunately, like most sensible anglers, he had insured it.

Looking without hope for a quiet backwater, I passed another of my section anglers who told me he had just caught one. That changed me to eager action. So I put on two weighted Hare's Ears and worked them right in under the bank. Even so, a fierce pull took me by surprise, and it was with thumping heart that I finally manoeuvred my biggest trout of the day towards the net. That proved an anxious moment. The sensible Yorkshire area rule is that you may only use knotless nets. That is also especially important in a catch-and-release event to avoid damaging the fish. As mine had knots, John had lent me the knotless one his team used in the World Cup in Tasmania. Designed to take up little space in the baggage this was a special one where the net shot alarmingly out of its tube and, needless to say, had a very soft front rim. Since I always prefer a hard rim to the net, in the racing current I made a couple of miscues before the trout was safely in.

When we had all chatted at the bridge before the final session, it was clear I had finished second of the eight in the first session and first in the second. With the odds against catching in this flood, I could appreciate the comment of Chris Ogborne fishing close by: 'That could be a very important fish.' In fact, it made me equal first on placings with Martyn Adams, but runner-up on the tie-break of most fish caught.

John's section above the Dub, a tributary which had enough water to raise the level below, had been the hardest. It was much too low at the start and the first to be swamped by the flood. John had gone straight to a pool where we had spotted rising fish, and he caught a couple within an hour and a half, using size 20 dry flies. Because a twenty-minute walk past the out-of-bounds water then faced him, he stopped half an hour early in order to walk to a promising pool above a suspension bridge, since it was vital to catch in each session. That he did, despite the flood coming down soon after he had restarted. With John Lindsey also catching in each session, they both qualified for the team of five as did Ian Greenwood, an experienced Dee angler and several times an international.

To complete a remarkably consistent season on boat, bank and river, John was also in the top ten in the three-leg European Grand Slam. He had a record of consistency in these European events going back to the first unofficial French Open on Lac du Chateau in Normandy in 1981, to which Bob Church and I were invited to take two teams of three. With over 100 anglers from fifteen different countries, John Wilshaw won the event with son John coming third in his first international match. That success owed much to his usual careful observation. He soon found that most of his takes were on the drop, or the first few pulls of the retrieve. So, instead of wasting time fishing out every cast, he drew the fly only a couple of yards before casting again. On that occasion, the rules required you to fish all morning from one small area, then switch for the whole afternoon to a different position on the opposite bank. The two Johns also appreciated that, in these circumstances, it paid to change to different coloured flies at frequent intervals in order to present new patterns to the fish in that area, even though 'cruisers' might still be caught on the initial flies.

By 1984, this event had formalised into the first official French Open, which I was fortunate enough to win with John also finishing in the top ten again. Until handing over to Mike Childs and a committee at the end of 1991 I arranged the English entry of up to ten teams of three at the request of the French organiser, Bertrand Kron. In 1985, the Belgians started their official Open at Lake Weiswampach near Clervaux in the Ardennes. The Belgian Fly Fishing Committee, too, asked me to organise entry there. That was, for me and for our fly fishing, a special privilege. For that was the year of the Heysel disaster, and most English sportsmen were unwelcome in Belgium. For us, however, there was a special letter of thanks after our team, with John finishing fourth and Brian Leadbetter and Peter Cockwill close behind, had made an impression in another respect as well. This is the letter I treasure from the BFFC:

Brussels, 5 November 1985

Dear Mr Pawson,

The Belgian Fly Fishing Committee was very honoured with the participation of an English team at our Grand Prix of reservoir fly fishing from 20 October. We appreciate your kindness, your sporting spirit, your dexterity and your good experience. Fly fishermen are usually gentlemen, and we can confirm that you are the perfect gentlemen that we suppose before your visit.

1. *Tony, aged four, with mother Helen, brother Philip and a bag of Tullich burn trout.*

2. *Total concentration as Tony, still aged four, worm-fishes a promising Coulags burn pool.*

3. *Father Guy with one of the salmon from 'Pawson's Pool' on Scotland's Carron river.*

4. *John, aged seven,*
casts his fly into a Brora pool . . .

5. *. . . and catches his first salmon.*

6. *John, aged four, nets a trout from the Shropshire Onny for Sarah, aged three.*

7. *John and Sarah are masked by Tony's salmon as his elder son Anthony continues to fish the Spey's Craigellachie bridge pool.*

8. *Tony's first salmon, caught in Ireland's Erriff river.*

9. *Anthony nets a large sea-trout for his father from the Cothi river in Wales.*

10. *Mother Helen's 25lb salmon from the Welsh Wye with other contributions from father.*

11. *A bag of sea-trout caught from a tributary of the Erriff river with help from gillie James Meehan.*

12. *August 1939 and Tony nets a grayling from the Teme near Ludlow. But on the eve of war the media favoured a fishing picture of the Prime Minister mosquito-netted on the Laxford river.*

We hope sincerely that an English team shall be come next year at our third Grand Prix, may be with more competitors. We hope also that an English team shall be participate at the sixth World Championship, who is organised in Belgium next year, from 16 to 19 September.

We thank you beforehand for your coming.

Best wishes for the BFFC.

J. C. Fouvez

With these European events providing many friendships, it was my policy to take some teams who were going to have fun as well as those with a potential to win. The events were publicised in some of the angling press and, apart from the top-class fishermen I invited, anyone else who asked to come was fitted in for at least one go at one of the two events.

So far as having fun went, the evenings were in some years enlivened by singsongs led by Gary Brooker and Brian Peterson. Gary is also a highly competent angler, Brian an outstanding Scottish competitor whose performances in their national team I had admired so greatly. Altogether, over eighty fisherpeople (since there were several ladies as well) had the chance to enjoy the experience.

To reinforce English stillwater reputation John, with Brian Leadbetter and Brian Thomas (that quintessential team man), formed a winning partnership on no less than five occasions against over thirty other teams. Peter Cockwill was also outstanding as an individual winner and several times a team winner as well.

Inevitably, it seems competitions tend to become more structured and formal and correspondingly lose some of the fun element. So it was as these Opens developed at French and Belgian request into a three-leg Grand Slam starting in 1990, and by the following year involving twenty teams of three from five countries.

The six English teams entered were totally dominant both years and, in 1991, filled the first four and sixth places in the team event and ten out of the twelve top individual places, including the first four. Over these two years, Dave Grove, Chris Ogborne, Bob Church and Paul Canning were consistently successful, while Jeanette Taylor struck a blow for the ladies by being a member of a winning team in one of the events at Lac du Chateau, together with Peter Cockwill and Micky Bewick. With the development of a new countrywide small stillwater championship, and my hand-over of responsibility for England's participation, selection methods will change. But these results will be hard to match, let alone beat.

John continued his consistent 1991 performances, making a major contribution to his team. With Clive Perkins and John Pearn, he won the English leg at Ardleigh Reservoir and they finished only two place points behind the overall Slam-winning team of Dave Grove, Alan Hayward and Brian Thomas. John himself had one of those unlucky days at Ardleigh where they fished from drifting row-boats on that delightful little lake. In the morning, he caught the largest number of fish, but in the afternoon he landed only two of the eleven he hooked, many of them coming off close to the net for no apparent reason. You usually get one day like that every season, and it is nice to be still a winner when you do.

The final leg at a new Belgian lake near Gent was also frustrating for him, but there he made his own bad luck through concentrating too hard on the fishing. In October, that lake is very difficult and with the results related to adding your morning and afternoon placings, you expect to be near the top if you catch two fish in each session. That he did to finish seventh overall in the Slam. But, at one of the half-hour changeovers, Charles Jardine kindly donated him a small dry Sedge which he prophesied would do well with these very shy trout, which were apt to turn away at the last minute even from a natural fly! With the hooter for the start of the next half-hour session, John forgot to check the hook. Immediately, he was in to a good fish but, because he had forgotten to press down the barb, it was disqualified. That lost him several places and stopped his team winning the Slam overall and himself from finishing in the top three in the individual. It was a painful

lesson to end a highly successful season of remarkable consistency in top-class competition.

My own final competition was the Wilcon Small Fisheries
Championship, at Dever Springs near Andover with its good
stock of large rainbows. In the three years of that event I had
finished third behind son John and Peter Cockwill in the
inaugural year, and second behind Brian Leadbetter in the next
with Peter unable to fish that year. Cockwill is the real specialist
in these stillwaters, and his expertise is quite remarkable as he
seems able to conjure up fish where no one else can. That first
year of this catch-and-release event, he caught nearly double
the runner-up's total, and this year he caught more than double.

The rules are that you move up two places each half-hour.
That first year, he was two places behind me and, moving
always where I had just fished, he nearly doubled my catch.
This year two places behind him, I might otherwise have
claimed that, as I followed him round, he had cleaned out each
position before I got there. There was nothing for it but to
accept that Peter was twice as good, whether going in front or
behind! This time Bob Church was following me round, and I
did appreciate that caused him a problem. There was one
position where it was impossible to cast except from one spot.
Just as the hooter went, I hooked a lively eight-pounder and,
by the time I landed it, Bob had lost half a session's fishing. He
kindly made no sarcastic comment, and I was also indebted to
Jeanette. She was one place ahead of me and started much
better. She then gave me one of her Olive Tinheads with which
she was being so successful, and that completely reversed the
luck.

Some over-careful playing at the end, which lost me three
fish and a lot of time, prevented me being runner-up again.
Still, by finishing fourth my season at least ended by again
getting ahead of the World Cup team members involved,
including Brian Leadbetter who was soon to win his second
championship in New Zealand. So perhaps age had not entirely
dimmed the eye and enfeebled the hand!

For me, the qualification to fish in the first ever home river international, and be appointed captain, provided a splendid finale to my international fishing. To make an England team on proven merit aged 70 and lead it to a comfortable win was an exhilarating climax and the obvious moment to retire from such competition. The Welsh Dee was also a delightful setting and a genuinely testing trout and grayling river. The organisers from the Maelor and Llangollen clubs ensured a happy time for all in a town whose motto is 'Blessed is the world that sings'. Certainly, they sent us away singing without having to wait for the Eisteddfod staged there the following week.

Despite driving wind and drenching rain, the river fished well. For what is primarily a team event, the arrangements were as fair as humanly possible with each of the twenty beats fished once by a member of each of the four countries over the four one-and-a-half-hour sessions. As always in river competitions, for individuals there was much luck involved in the draw, fair as it was for teams with all the beats fishing as well, if not better, in the last session as in the first.

With age making eyesight less keen, fingers less nimble, tying dropper knots during an event takes me more time than can be spared. So, in advance, I tied up a whole reel of Drennan double strength 4lb with droppers at the appropriate intervals. On competition morning, hurrying past a departing group of twenty American tourists, a small trailing piece of the cast caught one of the bags and all twenty were soon entangled. That wasted all my good preparatory work, but the difficulty they had in breaking free gave added confidence in using that type of nylon and appeared a good omen for Drennan team England.

It was my good fortune to be drawn on a good first beat which produced six grayling evenly divided between the black-bodied Goldhead on the point and the size 14 Snipe and Purple and Snipe and Black as the two droppers. A trout of nearly 2lb (39cm in this catch-and-release event) from my next beat and a grayling of around 1½lb in the third were my largest fish, while rounding off with three good trout in the final session took me into second place individually. By coincidence, or skill in some cases, England filled the first three places in exactly the same order as in the qualifying national final of 1991. Martyn Adams was first, myself second, and John Lindsey third.

Ian Greenwood, whose knowledge of the Dee and expertise in fishing it was invaluable in practice, came fifth just behind the experienced Welsh captain, Vince Gwilym. Sadly, a major business problem at just the wrong time forced John's withdrawal. The replacement reserve, Bob Preston, had the worst draws to finish eighteenth, and still leave us a long way ahead of Wales in second place with Scotland and Ireland equal third. With nice streamy runs in my first and last sessions, but my two middle beats on still, dead-looking water of long quiet pools, my own luck of the draw evened out. My controller's greeting as I approached my third beat of 'There's plenty of water on this beat, but no fish,' was far from encouraging. Happily, I was able to prove him wrong – just.

Later in 1992, John's captaincy of the England boat team of fourteen in the September international at Llyn Brenig was similarly successful. His team caught the most fish but finished second, as Wales's forty-seven weighed several pounds more than England's fifty-five. John himself, however, won two major individual trophies: the Grafham, related to the best bag; and the Emyr Lewis for the largest fish of the day, which made it even more surprising that England ended runners-up despite their eight-fish margin.

For a perfectionist in fishing matters, this was not a totally satisfactory result, in the sense that John acknowledged that he was lucky at the start and made a minor error of judgement at the end, which prevented him doing even better for his team. On the practice days, he and his team had assessed the two best methods as either fishing mini-lure-type flies like Vivas or Appetisers, using neutral density or intermediate lines and retrieving only at the pace of the boat so that the flies stayed static in the water; or fishing with small dry flies. On the second day, many did well with dry flies at a corner of the dam, and the agreed tactics were to clean up there early on, as John set himself up to do. However, he was drawn with a

Welshman as partner, lost the toss as to who took charge for the first two hours, and had to accept being motored well down to the wood area. That was his good fortune. On Brenig more than any other lake, fish are disturbed by a cluster of boats, and if you hammer an area one day with great success you are not likely to catch much there the next day. Indeed, that much was confirmed when the dam area subsequently failed to live up to expectation.

On his way down John changed tackle to fish the other style and soon had a small rainbow, which was followed by a better-sized one. Then, despite his Viva being almost motionless in the water it was seized with such ferocity that the rod was almost wrenched from his hands and he was relieved that the 5lb Drennan double-strength tippet survived from the take. Soon, a 3½lb rainbow was somersaulting in the air, then running him down to the backing before the net slipped under it.

By now, there was only a gentle ripple on the water compared to the earlier good wave, so John changed to dries, taking two on a Black Hopper. When it then went completely calm, some fish began to be seen moving through the water and sipping tiny midge. By going down and down in size John finally hooked three, though only one came to the net. With the breeze getting up again, it was back to a Viva, and another trout was soon taken. But John had always had in the back of his mind that there might be a bonanza at the dam at some time and went back there for the last hour, only to find the water dead. Had he drifted on instead he would have joined some others who had their best results in that final hour, and he would have been certain to catch some more. Such decisions on where to fish are crucial, and you can't always guess right!

As a final flourish to his season, John had to dash off, elated but jaded, to put in two practice days at Rutland before the two-day final of the Benson & Hedges UK Championship. For some, eliminators for this countrywide event had started more than a year earlier, with 529 clubs involved. A questionnaire sent out to clubs by Benson & Hedges had indicated that, including competitions within those clubs to decide team selections, over 40,000 individuals were involved in all. By the final, just fifteen teams and ninety individuals remained in contention. Of the six English teams to battle through the eliminators, no less than five were based in the south-west. Joining friends such as Jeremy Clarke, John was fishing with the Bath team. However, it was two others, Blagdon and Bristol Reservoirs, who beat the first-day leaders, Ireland's Iveagh and the Llanilar club from Wales, in an event well staged, as ever, by Benson & Hedges. John Ketley, my first England captain, was an excellent organiser, ably assisted by Brian Leadbetter; the master of administration was Jeremy Cullimore, and the Gallaher's man who has made it all reality is Mike Perry.

Iveagh and Llanilar held on to third and fourth places, with Bath finishing close behind. John produced another consistent performance, with six fish each day on a water unstocked for five weeks – a real test of skill. The daily average was just over three, so that put him tenth of the ninety outstanding fly fishermen in the final.

That was a happy end to my last season in international competition, especially since John's Brenig performance had ensured that he would be fishing for England again in 1993. It was a genuinely unique result for both of us: for this was the only time that a father and son have captained an England international team in the same sport in the same year, a shared pleasure and a great satisfaction that we had both made an effective contribution. For John there was the bonus of selection again for the England World Cup team for Canada in 1993, and for me a final flourish as I was top rod in a team with Mike Childs and Gareth Headland, which finished second out of twenty-eight in the Flanders Cup, fished on Heusden Lake near Ghent.

PART 2

Accidents and Anecdotes

Caught Young

For Charles Darwin, instinct was as much an essential element for man as for the rest of the animal kingdom. A million years of evolution has only slightly diminished its value to the human race. But a thousand years of 'civilisation' has finally distorted and debased it before the worship of reason, sound or unsound, and emotion, so often unreliable and misleading.

For the very young, instinct happily reigns supreme. As when, aged four, I peered over the bridge after a three-mile walk to the Tullich burn, it was instinct which made me thrill to the whispering waters below as the current now mysteriously clouded the surface, now left a clear window to the pebbles and stones on the bottom. It was instinct which ensured that the first slight tug on the line was answered by a much fiercer tug at my own heart. It was instinct which reacted to the sight of a small trout sailing over my head into the heather with the certainty that fishing would be a main and wholesome strand of my life without which I could never be whole.

Despite the veneer of civilisation, that instinct remains dominant in millions, if dormant in others. It is that instinct which ensures the steady growth of the sport despite the vocal antis, many of whom are not even responding to false emotion, but to the 'scapegoat' syndrome which centres their natural aggression on some randomly chosen group in order to bring colour to their colourless lives. That unquenchable instinct has ensured millions in over fifty countries find healthy relief in fishing. With little to help, much to hinder, independent surveys show continual growth of sport fishing year by year in

Britain until the four million mark is passed. No other sport has a literature near the wealth and richness, the quality and quantity; precious few a tradition which goes back over two thousand years. We are the fortunate ones who respond to that instinct and are rewarded with a lifetime of pleasure. That fine writer and dedicated, if self-confessed incompetent, angler, Andrew Lang, summed up for all time that 'hereditary passion, or instinct':

> I would as soon lay down a love of books as a love of fishing. Success with pen or rod may be beyond one, but there is the pleasure of the pursuit, the rapture of endeavour, the delight of an impossible chase, the joys of nature – sky, trees, brooks and birds. Happiness in these things is the legacy to us of the barbarian. Man in the future will enjoy bricks, asphalt, fog, machinery, 'society', even picture galleries as many men and women do already. We are fortunate who inherit the older, not 'the new spirit' – we who, skilled or unskilled, follow in the steps of our father Izaak, by streams less clear, indeed, and in meadows less fragrant, than his. Still, they are meadows and streams, not wholly dispeopled yet of birds and trout; nor can any defect of art, nor certainty of laborious disappointment, keep us from the waterside when April comes. The gleaming untravelled waters allure us from day to day, from pool to pool, till like the veteran on Coquet side, we 'try a farewell throw'.

In that passage, and in his *Confessions of a Duffer*, Lang emphasised that there can be equal enjoyment for the skilled and unskilled, the successful or the unsuccessful. My own instinct, as I suspect that of the majority of anglers, went a step further. It was old Izaak with whom I was instinctively in tune as later I read, 'I envy him, and him only, who catches more fish than I do.'

My instinct has always been to be more active than in Walton's emphasis on patience and quiet, and more in tune with his desire to be successful than in Lang's blissful state of incompetence. Any football manager will tell you that later success depends on acquiring good habits young. That in turn depends on good instruction. In my own case, there was little precept but much practice, and one without the other can never make you perfect. Father gave my elder brother, Philip, and myself some useful early instruction but, for much of the time, we roamed the burns supervised by mother, whose many outstanding attributes did not include skill in fishing. So it was usually a case of relying on mother to put the worm on the hook, trying to learn from a three-years-older brother (or one then almost double my age, to put it in correct perspective) and working things out for myself. While we stalked the burns, father was busy with the salmon on the Carron river into which they flowed. For us, there was the special thrill from time to time as the odd sea trout came up from the Carron to provide an unexpectedly large catch. My botanist grandfather also made a distant but not wholly successful attempt to ensure we were not so absorbed in our fishing that we ignored the flora and fauna around. Lists of plants to find were given us, but only the offer of reward had me making quick searches for sundew or butterwort, or other plants equally prolific beside the tumbling stream.

The results of self-education remain in the virtue of heightened instinct in the practicalities of locating and catching fish, but also in the vice of faulty casting and over-eager striking, soon so ingrained as to be ineradicable. Indeed, my casting action used to worry John so much that, whenever I was photographed, he was likely to be saying, 'Dad, you *can't* let yourself be photographed like that. Your rod isn't anywhere near 1 o'clock on the back cast,' or some such technical nicety.

As I never taught myself to tie flies to any standard, being too impatient to spare the time for it, that brought further problems. When TV were interviewing me after winning the World Championship, the first question asked was inevitably, 'And, of course, you had yourself tied the flies you caught them on?' Well aware that the interviewer would have a fishing knowledge of nil I replied, as if asked a stupid question, 'When I went out at Lord's for MCC against South Africa I didn't have a bat which I had just carved myself. And at Wembley I didn't go out before a 100,000 crowd for an Amateur Cup final wearing boots I had just cobbled together myself. So, in a World Fly Fishing Championship, I made sure I had acquired the best flies available.' That floored TV, but any reader of this book would instantly appreciate the fallacy. Fly dressing is in part a separate art and a separate interest. Yet to be a genuine champion, like John, you need that skill highly developed since you may in practice need to innovate and evolve variants of standard patterns, as he and his team did in Tasmania. Nor can you expect to take with you all the patterns and sizes likely to be needed on strange waters. Fly tying can also be a splendid psychological gambit against rival boat partners. In the early days of competing, when my boat companion started to catch and I anxiously enquired about the fly, the answer was usually, 'Oh, it's a little something I tied up last night. Of course, those strands of specially dyed silk make it quite irresistible.' That left me mentally beaten with only half an hour of the eight hours gone! It was infallible one-upmanship.

Not being a technically correct caster also seemed something of a handicap, if only a limited one. After my son's strictures on my technique, I felt that as a world champion I ought to try to look the part so I went to that outstanding instructor, the late Jack Sheppard. My first lessons in casting were as a 63-year-old so set in his ways that they had no chance of success. Jack watched me in amazement for some time then gave a final verdict: 'You get the fly where you want it, but with three times the effort you require. If I start to try to get you to change to a proper style, your ingrained bad habits will ensure you end worse than you are now. So let's just go fishing together and forget the lessons.' Very sound advice, as usual, from Jack.

It is true, of course, that the most expert fly dressers, and the casters who win competitions and tournaments, are very rarely the best practical fishermen. There are some exceptions. Guido Vinck of Belgium won more world and European casting championships than anyone else but, as those of us who have fished against him in European Opens know very well, he is also an exceptionally good practical fly fisherman. So, too, was that trick caster extraordinary, the late Lionel Sweet, who in his shop near Usk would not only sell you the flies of the moment, but demonstrate how the fish would rise to them, almost transforming himself into the look as well as the motion of a trout. Casting of itself will not make you a good angler any more than clever tricks when kicking into goal will make you a footballer. But it certainly helps to be able to cast as long or accurately or delicately as you need, and that is always easier if you start right.

For those of us who have muddled along working it out for ourselves, there is a crumb of comfort from another sporting experience of mine. The three West Indian Ws, Walcott, Weekes, and Worrall, were once a dominant force in cricket. Clyde Walcott came to stay and work with me for a week to learn about personnel management, and my elder son, Anthony, then only six, was agog to meet the great man. As I came through the door with Clyde, he was waiting with his small bat. With parental pride, I saw him demonstrate the forward defensive stroke, impeccably correct as I had taught him from the MCC coaching book. Clyde burst out laughing and said, 'Only six years old, and they all play the bloody Bailey prod. In the West Indies, we just tell them to hit the ball and enjoy themselves at that age.' In fishing, too, the first essential is that the novice catches something early as a start to enjoying himself.

My own fishing career almost began with one of the strangest catches of all. Aged four, I was in the Sudan where my father was governor of the White Nile province. One day, he arranged a fishing party at one of the dams on the Nile, a massive river which has appropriately huge fish, including Aigle (Nile perch), which run up to 300lb or more. One of the anglers asked me to hold his tackle while he went to get something out of his car. Hardly had he gone twenty yards than one of these great fish seized the bait and, despite holding on grimly, I was pulled over the rocks, only letting go as I tumbled into the water to be hauled out by one of the natives with the party. So

I have never had need to exaggerate, since I can justly claim that the first fish I hooked was so large it caught me.

My mother was a very occasional fisherperson but, out there on Lake No, she too had a long battle with what appeared to be a very heavy Aigle. This one merely bore down heavily without going on the usual initial surging run. After a long struggle, and with some help from my father, she finally brought the catch to the surface – to find she was hooked into the decaying leg of a dead hippopotamus.

When she fished for salmon it was always with a prawn, to the derision of my elder brother and I who had been confirmed fly fishermen from the age of seven. One evening, on a pool on the Tyrcelyn Water of the Upper Wye, my father was rowing her round when a lively salmon took her prawn. Clearly, it was a heavy one from the way it played. Eventually, in the eerie dusk, with the mist beginning to rise from the water and chill the spirits, it was not the nose of a salmon which finally lifted into view, but something which looked like a horn. In shock and surprise, mother let it fall back while father took over the rod, wondering what unknown species of fish this could be, or what tricks the light was playing. What he finally landed was a 7lb salmon which had swum through a rusted bottomless bucket. The bucket had added the weight, and its broken handle had been the 'horn' which was first to surface and startle.

On another day, mother was to do far better than that with her prawn. In the morning, a guest of my parents, a somewhat apoplectic colonel, had caught a salmon weighing 25½lb. My father then took mother out with her prawn, and she caught a salmon which weighed a fraction over 25lb. So father stuffed a few stones down its throat before taking it back to the fishing hut and showing it to the colonel with a satisfied smile – 25¾lb. Unfortunately, the colonel, his suspicions aroused, insisted on weighing it himself, hung it up by the tail, and one of the stones fell out! But it was still the biggest salmon that any member of the Pawson family had caught.

If, for the instinctive angler, the first fish remains a lifetime memory, then even more so is the first salmon, and more deeply felt and remembered again are the special ones which get away and the heartbreak of the loss. I was fourteen before I caught my first salmon, but I was so close to it several years before. Working in the wet heat of the Sudan was a draining experience, and father always spent the long seven weeks' holiday, granted in recognition of this, on the inevitable fishing trip. After Loch Carron he settled for some years on the Leenane Hotel some forty miles from Galway on the west coast of Eire. By seven, I had graduated to boat fishing for sea trout on the Kylemore Castle loughs and was even allowed the occasional cast when father's turn came round for 'The Pool' where the Dawrus river flowed into a small subsidiary lake through a narrow, reeded channel where, in August, the salmon could be clearly seen neatly lined in two rows like a school crocodile. They were also noted for being, while there, as uninterested in flies as crocodiles may be. Came the day when I was eight, and father was allowed a day on the river. While he and Philip fished on unsupervised, I was left with the kindly one-armed gillie, James Meehan. The Dawrus was running down from a spate and in fine condition, but a broad, fast river for a novice.

Father and Philip walked past a small pool with racing foam-flecked current and an eddying backwater close to the bank. 'Could I catch anything here, James?' I asked. 'Well, you might, but then again you mightn't. And if you did, sure it would be a sea trout.'

A sea trout was prize enough for me, and I kept working the fly deep and fast. Perhaps the eddy slowed it down for, while sea trout like it fast, salmon don't. But, suddenly, there was that heavy, immovable resistance, the slow, stately movement, then the wild surge. The trout rod and the limited line on the trout reel were strained to their limit. Finally, there was the salmon, beaten, floating on its side towards the waiting net. Then that snapping out of the small fly as the hold gave way, and my heart broke. How could it be so near and not be landed? How cruel to win that hard battle in that unlikely spot and then lose the prize. 'That's fishing,' I can say with a shrug if it happens now. But then the day, almost the whole holiday, was ruined, and I was inconsolable.

James Meehan had only one arm, but was an expert angler and a generous man with a wealth of stories to fill the dead periods, and constant encouragement for us. In the dining-room of the hotel in which we stayed was a glass case with four beautiful wild browns from 3lb to 9lb. These James had caught in the Finney river one morning, stopping only because with his one arm he could not carry more and balance properly on his bicycle.

James used to put everything bad down to Ireland's past 'Troubles', including any failure of the fish to get themselves caught. We presumed he must have lost his arm in 'The Troubles', but his story about that was more macabre and horrific: 'Me mother left me alone in the cottage when I was a baby, and the old sow ate if off.' Only once did James err, and then he was trying too hard to be helpful. Father realised he had left his net behind when setting off for this same Finney river. As we were passing James's house, he offered to bring his own which turned out to be an antique more suitable for a collector such as Ray Cannon than for practical use. Father duly hooked the largest brown of his life, James duly netted it, the handle duly broke off, and James duly made an unwise grab to recover the huge fish and broke the cast. In a pregnant silence, they watched the played-out fish and the net head float away down the current.

My first salmon finally came on the upper reaches of the Erriff river where sea trout then abounded. At least we called it the Erriff, but I believe it was there more properly a tributary called the Drummin. My father and brother were fishing down from the top, while James Meehan and I concentrated on one large pool near the bottom. This started with a rapid run-in which soon smoothed down to a quiet run in a narrow channel between high banks before broadening into a wide pool, then contracting again to a narrow final glide. The runs were good for sea trout, but even more the still pools whenever the wind stirred them. Size 10 Black Pennells and Connemara Blacks, retrieved fast, with a bushy size 8 Black Pennell on the top dropper to be bobbed on the ripple, were best for the sea trout.

The river was on the low side, the wind not strong enough for the sort of waves which might have stirred salmon. Half a dozen sea trout had been caught already, typical small late-summer 'harvesters'. The pool was so long that, by the time you had fished carefully down to the bottom, the top was rested. So, like painting the Forth Bridge, you could never say you had finished the job, or that the pool was fished out. Fifth time down, I was still hoping for another small sea trout as I approached the glide at the bottom. As I cast under the far bank, there was a huge swirl almost as the fly alighted, and it was at once apparent that this was the longed-for, but unex-pected, salmon. The most anxious fight of my life ensued. When it was finally netted, the joy was so intense that I fished no more, but sat on the damp bank waiting to show off my prize when the others arrived having had much sport with the sea trout.

Nearly fifty years later, I took John back to fish the Erriff based on Aasleagh House and run now by the Eire State Fishery. The river was in flood when we arrived and, while there was no beat free on the main river, we were told we could spend the couple of hours before dinner on this upper water. So we made straight for this pool of happy memory, and John at once had what appeared to be a large sea trout, but turned out to be a salmon. The change in the river was dramatic. When I had last fished it, thirty sea trout in a day was nothing unusual, and a day on Lough Tawnyard, from which it flowed, was a sea trout fisherman's dream. Now the salmon count had improved, the sea trout drastically declined to the point where only two are caught for every salmon. The salmon fishing can be outstanding, particularly during the June and July grilse runs but, in an extraordinarily wet summer, the river had been continually in spate and most of the salmon ran through. So, on some twenty beats, only eight were caught that week, but John had four of them, while I lost four. That time, his luck as

well as his skill was much superior to mine. That was high-
lighted when one of the four surged away just as he was about
to net, and the loose fly caught in the mesh. Inevitably, the cast
broke, at the dropper knot. But it was the tail fly and tippet
which pulled out, and the salmon remained hooked on the
dropper, which now became the point to make landing it a
relatively simple matter.

Lord Grey of Fallodon correctly defined the passion for
fishing: 'Fly fishing is an earthly paradise, and there is but one
quality that is necessary to make us fit to enter into and enjoy
it. We must be born with an intense desire to catch fish with a
rod and line.'

There was never any doubt that John was also born with
that instinct, with one incident proving it beyond argument. I
was fishing the Spey while Hilarie looked after John and Sarah
aged six and five. They were at the edge of a field where a bank
went down to the riverside. On that hot summer day, flies
began to plague a herd of young bullocks, who suddenly
stampeded at the three of them. Hilarie seized Sarah and pulled
her under the bank for protection, shouting for John to run for
cover. He also dashed down the bank, but only to throw
himself on the salmon I had just caught, and left on the shingle,
in order to save it from the bullocks; an instinctive angler from
his earliest days and with a proper sense of priorities.

John started fishing aged four, helped by his three-year-old
sister. Worm fishing for trout was an ideal beginning as it was
for me, but John was an instinctive artificial fly fisher from the
start and averse to the act of putting a worm on a hook. Not
so Sarah, who dutifully threaded them on for him. For both of
them, the float had a magnetic attraction, keeping concentration
intense, making the excitement tangible as it dipped suddenly
under the surface. One of John's first fish, on the Onny river
in Shropshire, just above its junction with the Teme, was a
chub of near 2lb, and joy was unconfined.

John was only seven when he hooked his first salmon in an
equally unlikely pool. It was my first day on Sutherland's
Brora river, and while I never like having a gillie myself I had

hired one for the day to look after John, so that I could try out the river without having to devote time to helping him. We walked up past the coal-mine at the bottom, which had been going to close until the miners bought and worked it themselves. We fished on up for pool after pool, then fished back again towards the car. In mid-afternoon, I had a lively salmon and by then was far ahead of John and the gillie. Walking back to find them I was immediately aware of an excited hubbub. Set to fish a small pool where the casting was easier, but the salmon rarely if ever caught, John had done just that. His fly, forcefully cast double-handed into the gentle run, had been just as forcefully seized. Only at the end of the fight did the gillie give some assistance and he, and I, were nearly as excited as John. But no one and nothing can match the excitement of a first fly-caught salmon at that age.

Next day, I found how close he too had come to disaster, and how surprising it was that he landed the salmon. With no expectation of his hooking anything that size (though surely I should have known how perversely and unexpectedly salmon react) I had given him an old trout reel for his trout rod without testing the line. Testing now, it snapped like a 4lb cast and was fit only for chucking! John ought to have learnt then not to trust his father over tackle.

Rather than continue to inculcate in him my own bad habits once he graduated to fly fishing at the age of six, I ensured he had a week's proper instruction at the Abu Centre at Aviemore. Having myself been brought up to concentrate solely on fly fishing, it was my belief that you should also learn to spin. That, too, he was correctly taught there. It so happened that that week provided the best salmon fishing I have ever had, and John missed most of it. That has proved small loss compared to the vast advantage of learning good habits and correct method right at the start of a fly fishing career.

Feeling that I would be hard put to survive a week of watching the children get angling instruction or disport themselves on Aviemore's trampolines or crazy golf course, I had booked to fish the Avon river, which joined the Spey some thirty miles away. As the charge was £6 for a whole week, I presumed the chance of a salmon was remote. When I enquired I was told that the river could in fact be productive, but only when there was plenty of water. There was a near drought at the time, but having paid my money I thought that I must at least pay it a flying visit. On the way, I took a ticket on the public water below Grantown-on-Spey and was pleased with myself for extracting a sizeable sea trout. The beat on the Avon was controlled by the Delsnahaugh Hotel, and when I enquired there I was given complicated instructions about driving back to the far side, parking in a farmyard, and walking down to the river.

With only two hours to spare, that seemed too time-consuming, and I merely drove on up the road, pulled into the side and slithered down a bank to a nice-looking pool. The water was indeed low, and I fished for an hour with no real hope and no result. Just time for one more pool, I thought. The one below was deeper at the head with an attractive current veering to the far bank. Instinct said it looked distinctly fishy. The pulse began to beat, and it was no longer a surprise when the fly fished down and across on a standard slant was seized by a big sea trout. That was safely landed, and I continued to work down towards the bottom where the water shallowed into a maze of small runs between jagged rocks. Three casts and then down a step was my practice. Eight steps down, the first salmon came, and fifteen steps down the second. Both were landed, both around 8lb. There was just time for a dozen more steps (well, by now I was only an hour past the promised time to return to Aviemore), and on the last a salmon took. This one allowed itself to be walked away from the dangerous tail of the pool with its outcrop of rocks before erupting into a series of violent runs. At last, it came exhausted to a net designed only to cope with a smaller fish. Twice it was balanced across the net only to flop back. Once its head was manoeuvred in, but the rest of the body declined to follow. So it was tailing time. But, just as I was reaching down to take hold, the fly came out.

That one brief visit inevitably turned into five more full days of fishing. By the end of the week, my six quid beat had yielded twenty salmon, sixteen from that pool alone, and several good sea trout as well. For the last day, John was released from his course and helped me catch a final brace from those small runs around the rocks at the tail. That pool also allowed Sarah a taste of salmon fishing viewed from the bank but, for her, there were greater fascinations at hand in the crazy jumble of rocks along the shoreline. Her imagination gave each of the largest and most oddly shaped a personality of its own: two she imagined as lions, while one in particular became her guardian dragon to be festooned with wet fontinalis moss garlands and to give her rides on its back. There is indeed much more to fishing than catching fish, and Sarah has always been the sensible one, enjoying the whole ambience and fishing only as long as the mood takes her. But for six- and seven-year-olds, as for the ardent fisherman father, this was a magic pool even without Puff the Dragon to guard it.

The Avon never fished quite so well for me again but, the following year, it had a thrill in store for John. Again the river was low, but John decided to try a spinner to practise what the Aviemore course had taught him. Fourth cast, a 10lb salmon loomed up and seized hold. He had only a light rod, though a powerful cast, but held the salmon steady. Never having spun myself I was under the impression that spinning tackle must also have magic powers of strength, since the salmon stayed immobile close to the shingle. So I stepped forward and netted it thirty seconds after it was hooked. Only when John caught his next did I realise that, in fact, the strain had been so light that the fish was probably still wondering if it was hooked, and had not even begun to play! That is indeed a helpful peculiarity of salmon. They often seem to take a couple of minutes or so digesting what has happened and can then be walked gently away from danger, provided you don't put too heavy a strain or wind the reel and vibrate the line.

England has always had a puritan streak, and there are still too many whose ideas seem to have been shaped by the old-fashioned nanny with her cry of 'Go and see if Jeremy Fisher is enjoying himself and stop him if he is'. Particularly important is it to encourage the young and the novice at all times.

That was borne in on me with my eldest son, Anthony. He was a keen fisherman when young, but was knocked back by two unthinking and unfeeling reactions. He had just caught his first ever salmon on the Spey, a small one of 5lb. With Hilarie, he went proudly back to the hotel to record the most important catch of his life. 'That's only a sea trout,' said the unknowledgeable manageress. 'We don't record sea trout.' Even had she been right she might have appreciated the letdown this would be and recorded it anyway. As she was wrong, it was inexcusable, unfairly deflating a young angler at a crucial moment in his consideration of the sport. That same year, he was again deflated on the Cothi by an unfeeling and inaccurate colonel. There were hardly any brown trout in that stretch of the Cothi and, when Anthony caught one of 1½lb, I congratulated him in catching the largest brown in the records. But, as soon as it was put in the book, the testy colonel commented to him, 'Ridiculous recording that as a brown. Must have been a small sea trout.' A put-down again, and the colonel had not even seen the fish.

Happily, despite such setbacks, Anthony retained an interest though never the consuming passion of his younger brother. This may have been to the world's good, since too much fishing might have diverted him from his research into cancer and other diseases which has proved so beneficial. To have retained some interest, however, was also to his own good. He telephoned me one day in low spirits to say he had been addressing a seminar of leading scientists in Colorado, and some of the best known had called him a heretic, because a hypothesis he had been working on, if correct, undermined their work. I told him that if he was right about the SH2 Domain and its effects (as he was) then he should be pleased, as it showed he was years ahead of the others. Meanwhile, he had my book on fly fishing around the world, which included an excellent piece by Charles Jardine on where to fish in Colorado, and a day on those delightful rivers would take his mind off his problems. So it did and, once a kindly American had suggested a Black Woolly Worm as the fly of the day, he flew home happy and with some rainbows for supper in Toronto.

While Anthony's discoveries affecting cancer, diabetes and heart disease are infinitely more important, I was amused to notice certain similarities of reaction when he was interviewed recently on his finding. The article included the comment, 'Talking about his work, the words "obsession" and "passion" keep recurring.' Well, so they do in our talk of fishing. When he had the final confirmation that his hypothesis was correct and a major step forward in cancer research, his reaction was described in his own words: 'When one of my staff handed me the results of a cell protein experiment, it was final proof of the correctness of a hunch on which I had worked for five years . . . I felt like rising gently off my chair and elevating like some mystic of the Middle Ages.'

That was a more analytical comment on the indescribable feeling which John and I shared when winning the World Championship. After his Tasmanian win, John was quizzed about it by David Bobin in a TVS interview. Answering to 'How does it feel?' he commented, 'You hear people say after winning a major event that they are "over the moon" or some trite cliché like that. But that was all I could think of when the Australian press and television asked me the same question. It is difficult to appreciate just what you have achieved, and the joy and satisfaction are out of this world and too deep to put into words.' Over the moon, or elevating like a mystic, we are a fortunate three to have had that experience and, despite the very different fields and importance, to know the feeling which words are inadequate to communicate.

My elder brother and I were more sympathetically treated when we might have been heavily put down by my embarrassed father. I was seven when we went for a fishing holiday in Ireland at the Leenane fishing hotel. In the custom of the time, the day's catches were set out each night on a table in the hall and admired by the other fishermen. While father was off on the first day to fish the Kylemore Castle lough for sea trout and salmon, a gillie was hired to take us to a trout stream nearby. While the gillie slept in the heather, we set about catching what we thought would be a trayful of trout to win the respect of other fishermen. Dashing home early we watched eagerly for reactions which were far from what was expected. Not only were the trout small, many of them were salmon parr. An embarrassed father recognised that he ought to have ensured we could pick out salmon parr by the tell-tale 'thumb' marks down its side, and hired a better gillie for the future!

There comes a time when any angler has to make up his mind whether this is a suitable sport in which to indulge, or whether the antis have a point. For myself, it has always been a case of remember Darwin and trust your instinct. Instinct tells you whether to believe in fishing as a sport, but logic supports it also. Christ was a fisherman and took his disciples from humble fishermen, rather than the hypocrites and Pharisees, or other self-righteous, self-important groups. So Christians have some guidance on the subject. For humanists, or all those who believe it is important for man to be true to his nature, there is the encouraging fact that the sport has been part of man's natural actions and reactions for two thousand years or more. For those concerned with society, there is the fact that such fishing has been a significant part of Britain's social history during that time. Dame Veronica Wedgwood, that outstanding historian, wrote of Izaak Walton as 'perhaps the most sympathetic character in English history'.

Conservationists, too, must be in tune with fishing's achievement and outlook in this regard, even if it is selfishly inspired. The conservation of many fish species and many water environments, beneficial to birds and other living creatures, has depended and still depends on concerned anglers. They fought battles long before the 'Greens' latched on and, with the assistance of Parliamentarians, who cherish the sport, anglers continue to take the lead. Fishing has been endemic to man and wholly beneficial to his health and happiness. Those who would abolish it are unfeeling vandals, happy to harm their own species. But each individual should follow his instinct as to whether it attracts him or not. If instinct says 'fish', then go and enjoy it.

If you want to look at it from the fish's viewpoint, remember that man is the only animal whom nature made conservator as well as predator. Many countries have trout only because of that instinct. A vast number of rivers in this country would soon be fishless from poaching and pollution if anglers ceased to protect them, or to support the fisheries which restock them. From time immemorial, man has been a fisherman. It is part of his nature, and interference with nature, particularly by the ignorant, is a dangerous game. Chairman Mao's Chinese government once thought they could revive the togetherness of a nation's wartime spirit, and improve their agriculture, by declaring war on sparrows and crop-eating birds. Villagers everywhere had to beat drums, fire guns, keep the birds flying until they dropped exhausted and were gathered in. Warlike communiqués were issued on the numbers eliminated, rewards given for outstanding kills. The results? Without sufficient birds to cull them, the insects multiplied so fast that disease and disaster affected the crops.

Some other well-meaning lobbies now face complex problems of this kind, often pushing their single-minded concern at the expense of the fish. A few years ago, programmes on seals were aimed solely at seal protection. Now TV programmes have begun to appear pointing to the over-populous seals causing problems themselves, not least in the elimination of fish. Protection for cormorants and other fish predators has caused a similar imbalance against the fish. There are no such complex problems for fishermen. Their efforts may not be altruistic, but they are the main protection fish have. That is provided all anglers keep to the proper disciplines, codes and treatment of their fish, and give full consideration to helpful developments such as catch-and-release.

Whether fish feel any pain has been a debatable point. The detailed independent scientific study which ended in the

Medway report concluded that there was no hard evidence that they did, but no certainty that they did not. That genial and experienced angler, Tom Saville, who studied zoology at Manchester University, put it more succinctly and intelligibly in his recent book on reservoir fishing:

> I studied their brains and nervous systems, eyes, blood vessels, musculature, everything. Any thoughts I had about fishing being cruel to fish were quickly corrected as a result of this knowledge. It was obvious that fish did not have the ability to feel pain as we humans do. Their nervous system is very primitive – one step ahead of that of a worm, but not as advanced as that of a reptile. This was illustrated some years later when a python I kept as a pet hadn't the sense or feeling to unwrap itself from a heater, around which it had coiled, and cooked itself to death overnight! If a snake cannot feel any pain of intense burning, there is no way a fish can feel any pain from being hooked. I fished, and still do, with a clear conscience.

The final argument comes from an unexpected source, the League Against Cruel Sports. Not so long ago they were publishing advertisements in all angling magazines emphasising, 'The League is *not* opposed to angling. Angling for consumable fish is more humane than trawling, and responsible coarse anglers put their fish back.' A copy of that advertisement is printed in Appendix III on page 258, so that anglers don't forget it, should emotive attacks by the ignorant intensify.

To me, it also puts two points much more clearly than anglers and angling bodies usually do. So often we are told we ought, as anglers and angling bodies, to ally ourselves with every other form of country sport. Why? Angling is quite capable of standing on its own and, as the League rightly defines, is quite different in kind and character. The advertisement's heading is, 'The truth is, we oppose bloodsports, not angling'. There are many anglers who may themselves make that distinction and be rightly annoyed at being linked to something which they may dislike and which may drag them down into its own problems. I am not myself interested in shooting or hunting, and not particularly enamoured of either but, as long as they are legal, I totally accept others' right to pursue them. But I believe a close link with them is the one major danger angling in Britain faces. The trite old saying is often trotted out: 'Hang together or you will hang separately.' The truism in this case is the reverse: 'Hang together and you may indeed hang together, though innocent yourselves'. There was a warning of that in McNamara's Parliamentary bill aimed at hunting and shooting and coursing, which was so nearly passed. That was drafted *specifically* to exempt angling, the Labour Party having had a late, but hopefully permanent, conversion from its once expressed desire to abolish the sport. On the practicalities, that conversion is another clear pointer. Obviously, they have given careful consideration to where four million angling votes might go!

So in relation to bloodsports it is, in my view, a case of hang loose if you want to survive; but, within angling itself, it is a different story. There it is indeed a case of hang together and you have the power to fight your corner against anyone. That includes the EC, which is likely to be much more of a threat than a British Parliament. In the run-up to the elections in April 1992, we had weeks of politicians accusing each other of being idiots, until some of us might almost have believed them, had we been less charitable. Not all our own politicians have shown good sense in being aware of the problems of trying to form a vast European state, when the world around is splitting, or trying to split, into small units, as indeed is the mood within Britain itself. Recently, I found myself watching helplessly as a row erupted in the Belgian Fly Fishing Committee between Walloons and Flemings, who promptly split asunder. If you cannot even get a Belgian fishing committee submerging its nationalism, what price lasting political unity in Europe? While Europe dominates, however, other countries' ability to impose their will, particularly countries like Germany, must be a source of concern.

Co-operation with European-based bodies like the Confédération Internationale de la Pêche Sportive is one of the musts to be able to give massive response should another bureaucratic Lord of the Rings, such as Jacques Delors, with his Tolkien-esque ring of personal power, take it into his head to attack fishing. Happily, that is a very remote possibility so far as our own politicians are concerned. They appear to have accepted the strength of the arguments as well as the strength of popular support for angling (contrary to widespread belief, some politicians *do* concern themselves with right, with morality, and with popular interest as well as with votes!). Indeed, it was a politician who put the best case for angling to the recent Angling Review Body, set up by the Sports Council and on which I served. Labour MP Llin Golding is secretary to the Lords and Commons Fly Fishing Society, and part of her submission in praise of angling is also printed in Appendix II on page 255.

Provided anglers do not fall out amongst themselves, and the millions who are understandably averse to being organised are none the less prepared to be organised at short notice in such a cause, angling need have no fears. Amusingly, it seems to be some of the more privileged anglers, with their private waters, who are apt to express fears that others will put *them* in jeopardy. It is fine that they defend their rights and publicise the methods they are fortunate enough to enjoy. Yet when some of them denigrate coarse fishermen, or competition fishermen, and complain that they are jeopardising the sport, they are in fact attacking those whose numbers ensure the protection of their own privileges. Without them, they would soon attract the same kind of class-based attack as intensifies the opposition to hunting, which is perceived as a sport of the wealthy and privileged.

If fishermen hang together, then, they can indeed see off any opposition to what Wordsworth characterised as 'the blameless sport'. If further defence were needed, it might come from the therapeutic qualities of fishing in human terms. As one example, Foster an Angler, the charity for children with special needs, has discovered a calming influence which is of special value for difficult youngsters. Over nearly ten years of working in this field, its director has noted the change fishing can bring even in those regarded as unmanageable. 'They are used to human conflicts and human confrontations. Suddenly, however, they find that you cannot confront nature. The fish don't mind if you throw a tantrum, and the river rolls on regardless if you throw something at it. Soon they become absorbed in their sport and are always well-disciplined and easy to control when fishing, as it keeps them eager and relaxed.'

This is a charity which has been mainly the concern of coarse fishing, but is one with which I was very pleased to help when Roy Mason picked it out as a main recipient from a Lords and Commons fly fishing charity event at Church Hill Farm Fishery, sponsored by Gallaher's.

As another example, while game fishing has its hazards it also has, directly and indirectly, greater health benefits than other sport. That was well described in the *Observer* magazine by Dr John Collee:

I've written about my grandfather before in this column, but it has struck me only recently that a lot of his health and vigour and happiness was attributable to fish. My grandfather lived for fish. He spent most of his retirement wading up to his chest in the river Spey. He'd bring the salmon he'd caught round to our house in Edinburgh – great silver leviathans which, while I was still at prep school, were usually bigger than me.

He'd lay them out in the kitchen with their heads on the sink and their bodies on the draining board and their stiffening tails reaching almost as far as the wall. Then he'd proceed to gut them with his sleeves rolled up like a mortician, conjuring out, for the benefit of us children, interesting things which he found inside, like a liver or a pair of kidneys.

He would talk the while about how he'd fought this fish for almost two hours, how it had tugged him up and down the river, how it had hid below the banks, and how, after a superhuman effort, grandfather had tricked and teased and cajoled it into shallow water where he could bonk it on the head with the handle of his gaff.

This was the stuff of legends, and grandfather, his forearms grown so big from wrestling these monsters that a small child couldn't put both hands around them, was a legendary figure – a short, bald, apple-cheeked man who loved telling stories, particularly stories about fish. Until his eyesight began to fail, he would sit in his study assembling trout flies from thread and silver foil and chicken feathers. Even the flies had magic in their names – the Greenwell's Glory, the Black Spider and the Bloody Butcher.

He taught me how to guddle for fish, wading up and down the little burn near our cottage in the Borders. I remember the thrill of reaching into the bearded darkness under the river bank, shivering with cold and fear in case an otter should be hiding there and encountering, every so often, a writhing trout which, with practice, you could grab behind the gills and fling on to the bank. I tried this again recently but I've lost the knack.

Grandfather dined on the fish that he caught and gave huge slabs of salmon to his friends. He kept live fish in his garden ponds – sleek, piebald goldfish which, in the summer, would kiss the undersurface of the water with their big, soft, circular mouths. In the winter, when the pond froze over, we would feed ants' eggs to the miniature goldfish in the indoor tank.

My grandfather died on the day of his 80th birthday, lying on the couch in the room with the fish tank in it. His problem was high blood pressure which the pills he took never seemed to affect. It was the fish, I realise now, which allowed him to live as long as he did.

Fish, you see, are extremely good for you. In a study reported in 1989 by Mr M. I. Burr and his colleagues, more than 1000 men who had survived their first heart attack were monitored to see how diet might influence their survival. It was found, surprisingly, that merely cutting down on animal fat had relatively little effect on subsequent life expectancy, but the group who were encouraged to replace their red meat consumption with fish outperformed all others – a saving of 17.5 lives per year per 1000 men.

Less scientific, but just as tantalising, is the observation that the Japanese, who eat a lot of fish, have a longer average life expectancy than any other developed nation. A Japanese woman now lives about five years longer than her British counterpart. She tends to waste these five years going on expensive European bus-tours and buying Gucci handbags in the Champs-Élysées. But it makes you think.

What also makes you think, if you enjoy nibbling at the undersurface of medical research, is that you don't even have to eat fish to derive benefit from them. Erika Friedman of the University of New York has measured the blood pressure of volunteers who were asked to look at either a poster of fish, an empty fish tank or a tank full of fish. The greatest drop in blood pressure was shown by the group looking at real fish. In fact, the drop was equivalent to that sustained by people doing transcendental meditation.

Its calming influence may explain why the goldfish is now the most popular pet in the world. One in eight British homes has a fish tank, which I always thought was just something to keep the grandchildren happy, but adults are obviously benefiting from it in subtle ways.

In another of Ms Friedman's experiments, fish tanks were placed in dentists' waiting rooms: it was found that patients who'd been looking at fish were more tolerant of pain. This was a scientific 'double blind' test, in which the dentists who reported the results didn't know which patients had been looking at the fish and the patients didn't know what they were being evaluated for. The only ones who knew what was going on were the fish, and no doubt they still have a lot more to teach us.

Well might Confucius say that time spent fishing does not count against a man's life and Dr Collee that much health and happiness can be traced to fish and fishing. Measurably with fish, immeasurably with fishing, a lot of what you fancy clearly does you good.

Chapter of Accidents

A magazine once contacted me because it was doing a series on what was involved in winning a World Championship. As regards fly fishing, they quizzed me in detail under their various listed headings such as concentration, mental application, agility, physical effort, etc. When the article appeared, I found there was one heading on which they had never asked questions, believing they knew the answer. Under the heading 'Safety/Danger' they had included: 'Might get wet, ha! ha!'

As I was recovering in hospital at the time from being seconds away from drowning beyond recall, that was no laughing matter for me. It also betrayed a startling ignorance of the fact that fishing, and particularly fly or sea fishing, is a sport with many fatalities and many injuries and dangers. Good instruction and sensible precautions are essential to safe fishing, and this needs to be taken seriously by all new anglers.

Industrially, those most at risk are not only such newcomers, but those who have done potentially dangerous jobs for so long that they have come to scorn the risks, or take short cuts. Certainly, in my case, it was the old problem of familiarity breeding contempt after sixty years without a serious problem. That was one lesson to pass on, but there were plenty of others.

My worst accident occurred when I was in a punt-type boat on a medium-sized stillwater on a bitterly cold and very windy opening day. Appropriately, that was 1 April, for I was indeed a fool that day. My partner was John Golding MP and, with the confidence that we would have no difficulty catching well on opening day, we arrived late. We were then directed to the only remaining boat, one more appropriate for a single angler. One drift down in this, racing along on the waves, convinced us that it was more comfortable on land. At the downwind end of the lake we spent a profitable morning casting into the fierce wind, with the fish congregated there as is so often the case.

By the time we saw other invitees driving past to lunch down the road only a few yards from our bank, it seemed time to row back. First mistake was to let John sit in the bow as he found it more comfortable (some would say my first and major mistake was to be in a boat at all with someone with so little watermanship!). The second was to concentrate on the heavy rowing without realising that the high waves at the bottom of the 'gather' were bound to shoot over at times. The third was not to check with John that there was no problem of this nature, so that the first comment from him when we had gone three hundred yards or so was: 'We are sinking.' 'We are what?' I said before looking round to see the flat nose of the boat angled towards the bottom and John already thigh deep in water. He could not swim, so I told him to abandon ship and cling to me. Not a strong swimmer myself, I held on to the upturned boat with one hand and made some progress mainly by kicking my legs. That was hard work as I was wearing wellingtons and much heavy clothing for the cold day, including a very heavy padded raincoat. Fourth mistake was to think I had reached shallow enough water and try to stand up. In fact, the water went over my head. Unexpectedly, I lost all impulsion, and the swallowing of water aided my passing out with hypothermia so that I floated face down.

Happily, a passing car saw the problem, with Bob Morey wading in to help us ashore and then spending ten minutes trying to pump me out with some welcome medical assistance at the end. When I came to in the ambulance, my main concern was that I might have been part cause of a by-election. However, John had been the sensible one and was wearing a flotation jacket, so that he drifted out untroubled clinging to me. During my two days in hospital, by strange coincidence I was sent a sea angling book to review which underlined what I now knew well, that it is often the swimmers who drown, the non-swimmers who survive. By swimming you can drain all your body heat, as I had. By clinging to something or someone and keeping absolutely still you preserve it for the maximum time. In those two days, I also read of no less than six other fishermen drowning, so it is something to be taken very seriously and it makes good sense to wear a flotation jacket, in boats particularly.

In retrospect, but only in retrospect, this near-tragedy did have its humorous moments. When I finally came to I also had a large bump on my head and, as the ambulance drove away, I noticed the boat upside-down. The last I remembered, it had been floating on its side. I presumed therefore that it must have fallen over and hit me on the head, but several others have told differing and ever more improbable stories of what they saw happen.

The one thing for sure was the bump, and presumably the doctors were concerned that I was also concussed. One arrived and asked me to tell him exactly what happened, which I did. Five minutes later, another appeared and asked me again. When I had finished the second recital, a shadowy figure in the corner commented, 'I don't agree with a single word of it.' That turned out to be John Golding, so I told him it was my story and, anyway, no one was likely to believe a single word a politician spoke, so he had better leave it to me!

By now I was feeling very rough, particularly when a third doctor appeared a few minutes later and put me through the same routine. As I lay back exhausted, a large man rose from a chair in another corner, clumped over, licked his pencil in the time-honoured way and said, 'I am a police constable. Can you tell me exactly what happened?' Fed up by now I responded, 'Yes, officer. I made a complimentary remark about Maggie Thatcher, and this Labour MP then hit me on the head with his priest and pushed me overboard. Could you arrest him for aggravated assault?'

'I think only a Chief Constable can deal with this,' said the policeman, beating a hasty retreat.

John was delighted when the *Daily Telegraph* next day gave a long description of him with a final sentence that he had been saved from drowning by an 'unknown angler'. He was less amused when someone told me in his hearing that, as a police car arrived on the scene and approached the group trying to revive me, the following conversation occurred:

'What's happened here?'

'Two men nearly drowned, officer.'

'Who are they?'

'One is the world fly fishing champion.'

'Who is the other?'

'Oh, he's just an MP.'

He was not best pleased, either, by a radio broadcast that the hospital had sent him home. He was in fact due to speak in Kettering that evening and was released in good shape which, so far as the hospital was concerned, meant he had been 'sent home'. So far as the listeners were concerned, he had been sent back to Newcastle under Lyme. That was his explanation of a very poor attendance at his meeting, anyway.

I could at least claim to be prophetic because I had written earlier in an article that, as a non-swimmer, John should not be let loose in a boat, but for the fact that as a politician he probably believed himself able to walk on water. Certainly, he did just that with his flotation jacket and later claimed that he had saved me, rather than vice versa. In fact, that was probably true but, as an example of whether a politician gets believed or not, I was the one awarded the Royal Humane Society's certificate as was Bob Morey, more deservedly, for his prompt action in pumping me out. Regrettably, it was only the local paper which believed my story that the boat only sank because of the weight of fish we'd caught! (Well, I did have an eight-pounder in my catch.)

It is possible to laugh at misfortune when it has not proved fatal but, as in all water sports, there are major risks which have to be taken seriously by the experienced as well as the inexperienced. As example of that, in the Hampshire branch of the Salmon and Trout Association, one of the most experienced members drowned a few years ago when river wading in Scotland, as had his father before him. Wading and boat fishing are never to be taken lightly.

There are other dangers not to be ignored. When Yorkshire Electricity sponsored the national river final they took the opportunity of further publicity about the danger of touching carbon-fibre and similar-type rods against live wires. That has been a cause of many serious accidents. I also had a reminder of how good a conductor such rods can be, or more accurately an awakening to the danger, since I was not aware of it.

The 1983 World Championship was in Italy on the Sesia river, which has some wild browns and, on this occasion, some stocked rainbows as well as the Marmorata or marbled trout, which run up to 30lb or so. These Marmorata rarely take the fly but, during the championship, we were shown two samples of around 20lb each, caught by local anglers by 'other means'. In our practice area, there were no stocked rainbows and catching anything proved difficult. Even though we were high up in the mountains above Borgo-Sesia in Piedemonte, the heat was stifling, the temperature near to 100°, the atmosphere heavy and close despite the high altitude. With startling suddenness and much 'son et lumière', a thunderstorm broke on us with dramatic stage effects.

Keen as ever I fished on while, to my surprise, the twenty anglers either side of me made rapidly for the bank. 'They are afraid of a bit of rain,' I thought to myself, as it was now drenching down. Then came a bright flash of lightning after a monstrous thunderclap, echoing and reverberating round the mountainsides. From a pylon only three hundred yards away came an even brighter flash and a fire as the lightning struck home. There were plenty of people to tell me I was fortunate that something other than my rod had conducted the lightning and, since then, I stop fishing when a thunderstorm is so close. That can, however, be a difficult discipline on occasions, since such atmospheric effects can stir fish to unusual activity. Once, on the Cothi river, I had fished for a week catching sea trout by night, but never by day, and never moving a salmon. Came a thunderstorm and, within an hour, I had two salmon and three sea trout with action nearly every cast. Once the storm passed, the fish returned to their somnolent daytime indifference.

In that Italy championship, there was a minor mishap of a fishing kind two days later. For my second session, I was on a pool which had been fished by one of our team before. During the interval between sessions, Peter Thomas had warned me that the controller there, who was meant only to monitor our fishing, might proffer ridiculous flies or unacceptable advice. The pool was indeed a delightful one, wide and with the fast run-in breaking into little eddies and separate streams and glides before smoothing down at the tail. For over an hour, I fished like a novice, missing several rises before catching a couple of fish, then being broken by the first large one I hooked. To compound the fault, I had failed to tie up a spare cast and had now to waste time doing so. In such a situation, you tend to be all thumbs and nerves anyway, and my controller took that moment to offer his special flies. These were well hackled, but tied directly on to the cast without eyes. The two fly cast itself was a yard-long piece of nylon thick enough to be some 10lb breaking strain. However, it has always been my rule to assume the locals know best and to give their advice a try.

So I tied this particular concoction to my 4lb leader and gave it a go. After ten minutes . . . nothing. So I turned round and had started to say, 'Thanks, but I am going back to doing it my way,' when the line tightened. That proved to be a nice rainbow and, in the next hour, nine more rises meant nine more fish. The slightly off-set hooks struck home firmly each time, and the local patterns did indeed appeal. Looking at my watch I saw there were only a couple of minutes to go when a trout of some 2 to 3lb seized hold. Compared to the pounders or less I had been catching this was a vital prize, and I played it with due care until it was ready to net. Unfortunately, I had left my net on the bank and, wading out, had to look round to find it. By now, my controller was hardly an impartial judge, but very much on the side of the man who was using his flies. With his type of cast, no doubt landing nets were a superfluity, and now with an excited exclamation he grabbed the line and tried to heave the fish ashore. The 4lb nylon promptly snapped, and fish and flies disappeared while he stood thunderstruck. I burst out laughing, slapped him on the back and thanked him for being responsible for my catching five more fish or so than I really deserved. Compared to that, the 'accident' he had caused was of no significance. After the weigh-in we enjoyed a drink together.

Carbon rods carry a risk apart from acting as electricity conductors. Should they break, beware of any little slivers penetrating the skin. They are difficult to extract and liable to cause unpleasant infection, not to mention real pain. Two expert and experienced anglers of my acquaintance suffered months of agony and inconvenience in this way. One of them was Trevor Housby, fine all-round angler and inventor of that most successful and abused of flies, the Dog Nobbler.

Another danger for fly fishermen are the flies themselves. That is why it is essential for novices to wear glasses when learning. I was teaching wife Hilarie to fish on a windy day; as she tried to lengthen her cast, the fly was blown into her face and she clapped her hand to her eye. It was a dreadful moment for me because a barbed hook in the eye can cause loss of sight. Happily, the fly was only in her eyebrow. The hospital at Builth Wells was used to anglers in such condition, and the doctor who saw her was himself a keen fisherman. She was not amused when he said, 'The way I am going to get it out will be a bit more painful, but it will save the fly.' He was given forcible instructions to forget about the fly!

The same hospital also had to treat my father. Very competent salmon fisherman though he was, a Spey cast in a high wind whipped the hook of a large, highly-coloured salmon fly through his chin. The pain of it was as nothing compared to the shame of it as he sat in casualty cupping his hands round the fly to try to conceal his embarrassment from the other sniggering patients.

Glasses are often desirable for the expert, too, since out of the scores of thousands of casts you will make it needs only one to go wrong to lose the sight of an eye. Lewis Douglas, the American ambassador to England after the war and the only foreigner ever to have been a member of that most prestigious group of Test fly fishers, the Houghton Club, lost an eye when a salmon fly flicked into it.

I have to admit that I am sometimes lax about using polaroids. Fortunately, I was wearing them when I particularly needed their protection. I feel some affinity with Andrew Lang, writing in his *Confessions of a Duffer*: 'Nature that made me enthusiastically fond of fishing, gave me thumbs for fingers, short-sighted eyes, carelessness and a temper which (usually sweet and angelic) is goaded to madness by the laws of matter and gravitation. For example: when another man is caught up in a branch he disengages his fly; I jerk at it till something breaks.' I too tended to pull impatiently on flies stuck in trees, rather than reel in until the rod tip is touching the fly, to try to poke it loose as sensible anglers do. On this occasion, a weighted fly, stuck in a tree far above me, was fiercely pulled until it pinged back at vast speed cracking my glasses, but not damaging the eye.

The spread of barbless hooks and catch-and-release is overall a desirable development *provided* it is done properly. The best advice and rules on this come from Canada, where the British Columbian Wildlife Service set out these principles:

There is a growing trend among anglers to release, unharmed, a portion of their allowable catch. The Fish and Wildlife Branch heartily endorses this philosophy of voluntary catch-and-release. The release of certain species is also mandatory in some waters where fish stocks are depleted. By following a few simple rules you can be certain that released fish will live to spawn and/or be caught again. Remember that a fish that appears unharmed when released may not survive if not carefully handled:

1   Time is of the essence. Play and release fish as rapidly as

possible. A fish played gently for too long may be too
exhausted to recover.

2   Keep the fish in the water as much as possible. A fish out
of water is suffocating and, in addition, is twice as heavy. He
may pound himself fatally if allowed to flop on beach or rocks.
Even a few inches of water under a threshing fish acts as a
protective cushion.

3   Gentleness in handling is essential. Keep your fingers out
of the gills. Do not squeeze small fish . . . they can be held
easily by holding them by the lower lip. Nets may be helpful,
provided the mesh does not become entangled in the gills.
Hooks and lines catching in nets may delay release, so keep the
net in the water.

4   Unhooking: remove the hook as rapidly as possible with
long-nose pliers. If the fish is deeply hooked, cut the leader
and leave the hook in. Be quick but gentle – do not roughly
tear out hooks. Small fish are particularly susceptible to the
shock of a torn-out hook.

5   Reviving: some fish, especially after a long struggle, may
lose consciousness and float belly up. Always hold the fish in
the water, heading upstream. Propel it back and forth,
pumping water through its gills. When it revives, begins to
struggle and can swim normally, let it go to survive and
challenge another fisherman.

Whether you practise catch-and-release or not, barbless hooks
may be desirable as a safety precaution. From everywhere
except the eyes, barbed hooks can be extracted from anyone
with little additional pain, in many cases by looping strong cast
round the hook, squeezing the flesh on either side, and giving
a sharp pull. There is also a warning from one fishery manager
who now permits no one other than anglers near his lakes.
Before that rule, he heard one day a great commotion around
his lake. Unaware that his son had wandered down with his
dog, an angler using two flies had made a back cast which
caught the dog in the eye with one fly, the boy in the cheek
with the other. The maddened dog then ripped the hooked fly
through the boy's flesh, scarring him for life before it was cut
free; the dog had to be immediately put down, such was its

agony. Barbless hooks, of course, slip out much more easily, with no real damage to flesh, and are much less likely to cause serious damage to an eye. So a wider use of them may well reduce accidental injury as well as damage to fish.

Wading is also a cause of fatalities to fly fishermen with the urge to get that step further to cover the promising lie. I am certainly not one to advise on this except perhaps for one credential, which appealed to my father. In the Sudan in the 1930s, he had to rely on a plane to take him to the remote parts of his region. In those early days of flying, my mother was worried that the pilot had already had a dozen crashes. 'Don't worry,' said father, 'by the law of averages he can't have many more, and if he does he certainly ought to know what to do about it by now.' In the same way, I have fallen in so often I *ought* to know what to do.

On wading, I can only comment as one who has not been as careful as he ought. It is, in fact, very rare for me *not* to go over the top of my waders. One such experience typifies my own too casual approach and many near-disasters. John and I were fishing Loch Shin in September on a bitterly cold day with a fierce wind driving sleet and snowflakes before it. John was catching well wading near the shore ahead of me, so I thought it time to leapfrog him when we came to a wide shallow bay. I knew it was safe to wade diagonally across except for the occasional peat trench dug deep into the loch. These could normally be spotted with ease, even when wading well out, because of the dark scars they left on the shoreline. One, however, was concealed there behind a bank of blown sand and, intent on my fishing, I blundered straight into it with the icy water going over my head.

Common sense told me I had only to let myself drift a few yards to be past the deep channel. Yet the survival instinct said, 'There is a shallow only a yard away if you swim back.' But, in those clothes, against those high wind-blown waves, that yard took an age. And, when I did kneel on firm ground, it crumbled away, and I was back in the trench before climbing out at the second attempt. With hindsight, I now know I was fortunate not to pass out from the cold, compounded by exertion, for John had no reason to know what I was doing behind him.

Somewhat shaken and exhausted, I made it back to the shoreline and walked back to the hotel. After a hot bath and a change of clothes, the fishing urge struck again and, with many promises to be careful, I set off to try higher up. Watched by John and Hilarie I waded in – and third cast, slipped on a rock to go over my waders again. John thought it very funny, Hilarie did not.

It was in the Loch Shin area, too, that John had a scary experience. Sunday in the Highlands is not quite as strict as it was, and no offence is taken if you fish far from the public gaze. One such Sunday dawned bright and clear. At the Overscaig Hotel I had decided on a day of rest and writing letters, which also suited my daughter, Sarah. John was restless for more fishing and decided to explore the chain of Gorm lochs in the hills above Shin, so I drove him to the area, pointed out the way I thought they lay and returned to Overscaig. By midday, I was myself restless for fishing and became aware from another look at the map that I had launched him at the wrong angle.

That was good enough excuse to suggest to Sarah that we went in search . . . taking our rods, of course. After a long climb, we hit the Gorm chain at one of the middle lochs. By happy coincidence, out of the many miles of these lochs we had come to the exact spot where John could be seen below fishing on a promontory. While I followed with the rods at more stately pace, Sarah went dashing down to greet her brother. When she was in hailing distance, he turned round and stared at her before saying, 'Are you real?'

'Of course I'm real.'

'Not an illusion?'

'Don't be silly.'

But John was not being silly. He had just had such a shaking experience that he was still disorientated and, with no expectation of seeing myself or Sarah up there, thought he was indeed hallucinating. After fishing in this highly productive loch he had tried to take a short cut to the promontory by wading across a narrow bay which looked muddy, but shallow. In the middle of it, he found himself sinking as if in a quagmire. The more he tried to pull one foot out, the more the other was driven down. Advice that you should lie down to spread the weight is anyway hard to follow in such circumstances, and useless now as it would have left his face below water. At best, he expected to be stuck there until the following day, for he would not even be missed until it was dark; at worst, he might go on sinking until he drowned. In a final frenzy, however, he had somehow hauled himself out, though it was an hour before he was composed enough to fish again. Hardly had he made ten casts than Sarah's voice so startled him.

When John recovered he was lyrical about his earlier experience, despite the frustrating start. Having climbed for an hour past one false crest after another he reached the summit, expecting to look down on the Gorm chain. But, after my pointing him in the wrong direction, the lochs were only far distant blobs of silver glinting in the sun. Hurrying there he sprang into one gully, only to find himself face to antlers with a magnificent stag, which looked him over then quietly stalked away. Surprises like this added to the exhilarating feeling of being on his own far from human care or human interference amid wild scenery and heading towards exciting new water, which he alone would explore.

This special type of fishing experience has been memorably described by Francis Francis:

> I know nothing more pleasant than wandering dreamily away
> up amongst the hills by the side of some tiny beck, new to the
> angler, with no sound but the pipe of the plover, or the curlew,
> or the distant tinkle of the drowsy bell-wether; no encumbrance
> but a light rod; no bother about what flies will or will not suit;
> no tackle beyond a yard of gut and two or three hooks in a piece
> of brown paper; a small bag of moss with well-scoured worms
> within; a sandwich or a cold mutton chop – the latter for
> preference – in one pocket, and a flask of the dew that 'shines in
> the starlight when kings dinna ken' in the other. Far, far beyond

all care; away from rates, taxes, and telegrams; proofs, publishers and printers'-devils; where there are neither division lists, nor law lists, nor share lists, nor price lists, nor betting lists, nor any list whatever; where no newspaper can come to worry or unsettle you, and where you don't care a straw how the world wags; where your clients are trouts, your patients worms, your congregation mountain black-faces, water-ousels, and dabchicks; your court, hospital or church the pre-Adamite hills with the eternal sky above them; your inspiration the pure breeze of heaven, far, far above all earthly corruption. Here, in delightful solitude, sauntering or scrambling on, and on, and on, upwards and upwards, from wee poolie to fern-clad cascade; casting or dropping the worm into either, or guiding it deftly under each hollow bank and past each ragged stone, pulling out a trout here and a trout there in the fair summer weather, with now a whiff of wild thyme or fragrant gorse, and now a shaugh of the pipe, and an amazed and charmed gaze at the mountain crags above, and the ever-changing scenery of the hills as the clouds flit over them, with just sport enough to give amusement without enchaining the attention so much as to prevent us drinking in all the delights that nature spreads for us – this is, to my mind, the true delight of angling.

There is a special charm about such wilderness fishing, but there are dangers to be guarded against. It pays to be prepared. My brother, Philip, and his wife, Peggy, had cause to be grateful for such preparations. Setting out from the delightful Scourie Hotel in Sutherland, to which they go annually, they parked the car and walked three miles across rough and boggy country to Sandwood, a sea trout loch close to the sea. There Peggy sprained an ankle and could not walk back. Leaving her with their dog and the midges for company, Philip set off back to the car for help. It was then 4 p.m. From the car an eight-mile drive to the nearest police post. On arrival, the local bobby immediately asked for the exact map-reference of the casualty and phoned it through to the RAF at distant Lossie-mouth. At 7 p.m., a helicopter landed beside her, and she and the dog were brought safely back to the police station at Rhiconich, where a doctor from Durness was already waiting.

Chapter of Anecdotes

The nigh-on 100 years of fishing experience that John and I have notched up between us has inevitably produced a whole array of stories, some amusing, some exciting, and some downright strange. The following are a few samples.

Anglers are, of course, the most helpful of people, but they do tend to get absorbed in their fishing. The first time I qualified to fish in a national final at Grafham I thought it desirable to fish there in practice. Never having been before, I tried confidently to book a boat, only to be told that it was not permitted to go out alone. It was suggested instead that I fish off the dam, where a good evening rise was shortly to be expected. That was not the right type of practice, but better than nothing. Grafham was fishing well, and the dam was already so crowded that I had difficulty finding a space to squeeze into. Soon the rise began, and to right and left of me intent anglers were long-hauling towards the distant rings of rising fish.

To my relief, I was soon stepping forward in my gumboots to net a nice rainbow. I failed to notice the wet slime at the water's edge and as I put my foot on it I found myself sliding down the face of the dam on my back. With a proper sense of priority I threw the net and fish out first, then my rod, then thought about stopping myself plunging into unknown depths. Finally, I was left clinging by my fingernails to crevices in the wall, while the water lapped my armpits. With sodden clothes and boots filled with water, it was nearly as much of a long haul to pull myself out as that of those absorbed anglers on either side casting to those rings which riveted their attention. Only when I lay dripping and exhausted, recovering my breath, was there any reaction. 'Nice fish you had there, son,' was my neighbour's only comment. He, too, had a proper sense of priority.

My father and I both gave convincing demonstration of our priorities, with fishing taking precedence over cricket. He is for certain the only man to play in a Varsity cricket match at Lord's and not know he was on the winning side until a month later. Having been out early on the last day father thought, like most others, that the game was over when a downpour drenched the pitch with Oxford needing 38 to win with three wickets left. So he got permission to leave the ground early to catch the sleeper up to the north of Scotland where he spent a month incommunicado camped by the Dionard river near Cape Wrath. Only on return did he find that the pitch had been mopped up, and in atrocious conditions an injured Oxford batsman, batting one-handed, had seen his side home. My uncle also used to tell me that, earlier that year, when my father was awarded his Blue as a freshman, he had to persuade him not to decline it because it was going to cost him three days' fishing in Scotland!

In my own case, having played four games with Kent immediately after my demob from the Army in 1946 I was awarded my county cap after tactfully participating in a big partnership with my captain against Championship leaders Glamorgan. 'It goes without saying you will be playing in all the rest of our games this season,' said Bryan Valentine.

'Sorry, skipper, I am just off for three weeks' fishing holiday,' was not an answer which went down well. It was probably lucky I didn't mention it before the award of the cap. Father and I also share a disreputable cricket record in that he turned down the captaincy of Yorkshire and I declined an offer to captain Kent. But both of those were for business, rather than fishing reasons as, sadly, earning a living has to take the ultimate priority, even over fishing.

It is all very well for Confucius to say that time spent fishing does not count against a man's life, with the inference that you are so absorbed in your sport that you don't notice the passing of time, but you can get too wrapped up in it for your own good. One night in Austria on the Gmundener Traun, John and I were lined up with Reinhard Resch and Gerard Tegelaar waiting for the sedge rise to start. We were in an area known to be full of rainbow trout, though there was no sign of them at present despite the myriad olives floating down. At last, a desultory rise began to sedge pupa. Then, prompt at 7:30 p.m., the water erupted in a whirl of rising rainbows and grayling all round us. That would last exactly thirty minutes until dark fell and the sedge disappeared.

John's girlfriend, who had come down to watch, chose that moment to paddle barefoot a little upstream. There was a sudden cry as she cut her foot on broken glass. The Dutchman and the Austrian rushed to her assistance . . . well, they *were* nearest. As she was helped away up the path in the still of the night, and with voices carrying so clearly over water, she heard very distinctly the brief exchange between father and son.

'Lynn's cut her foot, and Gerard and Reinhard have gone to help.'

'I *am* sorry. The trout are really on tonight, and that was a good one I've just released. What's it like in front of you, Dad?'

It was nearly the end of a beautiful friendship for John.

On rare occasions, such absorption can be turned to your advantage. The Cothi river in Wales had a marvellous run of large sea trout which, in low water, can often give great sport late at night or early in the morning. One year, I had had to curtail my usual visit because Sir Stanley Rous had invited me to play in his team of mixed county cricketers and the Indian tourists in a charity match at Esher. Keen not to miss the end of the evening rise or the start of the dawn patrol, I had made sure by fishing through the whole night and leaving it late before racing off to the match in my car. As I got near I was delighted to see there had been heavy rain in the night which would now delay the start, but not so delighted when I was told I would be opening the innings instead of having the nap for which I craved.

Half an hour later, the umpires went out to inspect a pitch far too damp for play in a first-class match but, in a charity game, it is usually a case of anything goes. There was one small puddle still on the edge of the square, and I was hopeful as the umpires peered at it for some time with much muttering and shaking of heads. They then walked solemnly back to the pavilion with that portentous tread in which umpires specialise and announced that play would not start for ninety minutes as the night's flood had been so bad that water from the nearby stream must have swamped the ground. So I got my nap; but first I sneaked out to recover the sea trout I had slipped into the puddle just before the inspection.

Since sea trout like a fly moved swiftly, there is always the possibility of hooking another as you play one fish. That can be unfortunate if that fish is a salmon. Twice I have had a well-hooked salmon on the tail fly, only for a sea trout to seize the dropper and tug and dart and wriggle to such effect that the salmon is shaken off. It's little consolation then to land the 1lb sea trout!

John and I fished together on the Ballynahinch Water on Ireland's west coast, a favourite of that immortal cricketer K. S. Ranjitsinhji who had developed it. In later life he became a real heavyweight, and the river has many stone piers built out into it to make the best spots easy for him to fish. Father had kept wicket behind him when the Oxford University team demolished the Gentlemen of England, and Ranji had invited him over for a memorable few days there, so in a sense it was a nostalgic visit for me. The river was not in its best salmon form. With his usual combination of luck and skill, John had a large salmon in the first pool he fished and, between us, we had the only two sizeable salmon caught that week by the hotel guests. The sea trout fishing was excellent, however, particularly in the evening. There John's luck for a time deserted him in regard to hooking two at once. Four times he had two good sea trout on and four times, as he was about to net one, the other managed to shake both off. Finally, he did land two together, only for the top one to give him a nip and an unpleasant unhooking problem. It was a bat which had swooped on the dropper just as a sea trout seized the point!

That reminded me of an experience Welsh rugby folk hero Gareth Edwards recounted to me of a night fishing on the Towy. He was fishing with some friends, including Norman Jenkins, known more familiarly as Jenks. 'There was no moon, the darkness was stifling, the night so still you could hear animals scuffling in the bushes, and the hoot of an owl was clearly audible above the murmur of the water. One hour's eerie silence was suddenly broken as Jenks's reel gave a welcome screech.' It was then *Jenks* who began to screech. 'At once we went rushing down to find out what had happened. So anxious were we that one of us broke the basic rule of night fishing and shone his torch towards the river bank. The flickering beam finally seized on Jenks, looking mad but unhurt. His story flooded out: "I was casting well across the river and, almost before the fly could have landed, I had a take. For a moment the line was pulled out, but then the fish seemed to lose all power, and I reeled it in fast. In the dark I thought I must have a small sewin or a half-pound brown trout, so I ran my hand down the cast to release it. But it bit me – and then began flapping as well. It was a bloody bat and, when I threw the cast away to get rid of it, it simply clung on and bit me again – and then again!"'

Only once have I assisted in catching three sea trout at once. That was on the Lower Oykel, and Hilarie, whose fishing is usually confined to dapping, decided to have a brief try. The two-piece rod was a bit loose at the ferrule joint and, in trying a forceful cast, she sent the top section hurtling into the river. I took over to recover it and, presumably because the rod piece had taken the flies deeper than usual, I found not one, not two, but three small sea trout firmly hooked to the three-fly cast. Novice's luck is indeed a byword in salmon and sea trout fishing.

Before England's first impromptu entry into the embryonic

World Championship in 1982, I organised a get-together of our team with some fishing at Avington in its lakes and stream. Some pressmen arrived and, talking to one of them, I noticed Alan Pearson hook a double-figure fish. The reporter remained oblivious of this interesting occurrence and ploughed on manfully with his questions: 'Do you really take a fishing competition seriously?' he asked. At that moment, Alan's large fish parted company with his fly. Alan's response was to hurl abuse and his rod after the departing monster. 'You can see some of us do even when not competing,' was the answer I managed amid the laughter.

It was also there that Alan had greater success by immersing himself rather than his rod. For the Izaak Walton tercentenary in 1983 I had arranged a special event at Patshull Park. French television had sent a crew over and were prompt on the scene as Alan fished Avington, one of the five venues. Alan was equally prompt to hook a 12-pounder, but his reputation seemed at stake when it took him down to the backing and broke him. Determined that no such loss should be recorded on TV he stripped off, duck-dived down to the bottom, recovered his line, tied it back on and landed the fish to the delight of the camera crew. His neighbour on the lake was not so pleased when first BBC, then ITV rolled up later, and Alan acceded to their pressing demands for an action replay.

Something similar was later to happen to me with my largest salmon. The Brora river was in flood, and while I had a 10lb breaking-strain cast I had two droppers also for the sea trout. As the flies came round behind a boulder near the far bank, there was a swirl and the brief glimpse of a broad silver flank. In the fast water a long hard fight ensued with the autumn salmon playing deep and heavy. After three-quarters of an hour, I felt I was on terms as the second dropper was well out, and the fish close to the surface though still invisible in the muddy water. Next moment it had charged off in an unstoppable run down this long pool and, with two droppers weakening the cast, I feared to put too much strain until it neared the outflow into a long rapid. Had it reached the rapid I would surely have been broken, but it stopped at last almost on its lip. Hastening down the bank, reeling in as I went, I waded out close to it and walked it thirty yards upriver before getting back on the bank.

It must be tired out now, I thought, but not even the top dropper could I get above the surface. Then I became aware of the local bailiff at my elbow, and he offered to net it for me. Mistakenly assuming all Scottish bailiffs would be experienced in netting fish, I passed him my large net which, however, had a thin wooden shaft. Straining hard, I was now surprised to see the salmon's tail emerge. In its dash downstream, the top dropper had caught there and I was now playing a 27lb fish as if foul-hooked. When it did come within range, the bailiff would frighten it off again by plunging the net in above the tail when the rest of the fish was, of course, facing downstream. After many imprecations and much advice he did finally net it and, ignoring my request to pull it out gently, raised the net high with a yell of triumph.

At that, the shaft shattered into five pieces with salmon and net head falling back into the river. Not to be denied I plunged in after it, emerging dripping and exhausted but with the salmon as prize.

'What's this pool called?' I asked the bailiff.

'The Madman's,' he replied, 'and that was even before we had *you* fishing here.'

My next largest salmon also gave unusual problems. The Laxa in the north of Iceland was a river to which I had been invited by someone who said, 'It's a splendid river if you don't mind a bit of weed.' Confident in my own ability to keep a fish out of a bit of weed, I booked to go. What I had not appreciated was that in the middle reaches of the river was a small lake entirely overgrown with weed, tendrils of which broke off to float in a steady stream down the river.

The moving mass of small weed fragments soon wrapped themselves round the fly and the knot joining cast and line (I was unaware then of the invaluable needle knot). So having got out a long line every few casts I had to reel it in to clear the fly (no good pulling it in by hand when wading, since the coils of line were soon covered with weed). So far I had hooked five salmon and lost them all, as the weed collecting round the knot steadily expanded into a football of weed which gravely interfered with playing the fish.

So far, too, the visit had not proved a happy one, as my companions were all Iceland air pilots who had persuaded their pilot friend to land our aircraft on the lava-rutted surface of a road near the fishing hut. The hut itself was provisioned only with dried fish and dried horsemeat, into which they tucked with relish but which I found revolting. Only by catching and cooking sea trout and picking the wild bilberries was I able to feed myself. So it was a somewhat dispirited, but still determined, angler who realised he was into a 20lb-plus salmon of lively disposition. Again the weed built up in a vast ball and, after nearly an hour, we seemed to have reached stalemate. Just playing the weed was bending the rod tip down close to the water, while the strain exerted had no effect on the tired fish which lay a cast-length away, waggling gently just out of wading reach. Finally, the fish drifted closer in, and by dint of going well over my chest waders I was able to grasp its tail at last and heave it on to the bank. By then it was a question as to which of us was the most exhausted.

Fishing for, or in front of, TV can be hazardous. Gareth Edwards and BBC Wales were making a series entitled *Going Fishing*, in which Gareth fished and talked with celebrity friends such as Max Boyce, Geraint Evans or Frankie Vaughan. I was asked to fish with him on the Itchen, and my instructions were brief and precise. 'So far we have a lot of talking and one quarter-pound fish. We are relying on the world champion to remedy that.' Fine, except that it was early April and cold, and there was unlikely to be a rise. However, looking up from the Itchen Stoke Mill I could see several encouraging dimples on the surface and expressed rash confidence in my ability to give them plenty of action. Crouched behind a bush I was poised to cast to the risers under the opposite high bank along which the footpath ran. 'Wait for us. We aren't ready,' came the shout.

Camera crew, sound recordists, lighting assistants (despite the sun), clapperboard lady and all, they trudged noisily and very visibly along the far bank past the rising fish, turned round thirty yards up, carefully set up the cameras. 'Ready to roll,' they called. 'Now catch us some.' The surface of the water was now undisturbed, the trout long gone. Later, compromises were organised and enough were caught to satisfy them.

After my winning of the World Championship, local TV announced that they wanted to film myself and John at Avington, but could spare only an hour and could not arrive until the afternoon. On arrival, they announced there was only one place from which they could film and issued the usual demand for me to catch one quickly. Avington can be hard in the afternoon, and the spot they had chosen was hardly promising. So it was with great relief that, after a few minutes, I felt a hard take. 'Fish on,' I cried, and the camera rolled. A good splashing fight it was, and the net was ready when the cameraman said, 'Blast. I didn't put a film in. Hold on while I go to the car and get one.' He did finally get his picture, but of a very unsprightly fish being netted.

On another occasion, BBC Wales were filming with Gareth around Winchester and wanted to end with suitable footage of a mock Izaak Walton catching a fish. The excellent fishing writer and taxidermist, Peter Stone, was dressed up as Walton with a long rod of the time and a horsehair line attached direct to the top. Only then did I appreciate some of TV's difficulties. Apart from catching a small trout for them in the stream Peter had to make a brief speech sitting on a log. The recording of this scene would have made a good entry for *It will be All Right on the Night*. Peter was word perfect, but for the first time I realised just how unquiet our quiet countryside is. First take was ruined by a plane flying over, then it was a tractor starting up, then another angler began screeching a reel – and anyway reels did not exist in Walton's day. It was only on take twenty that an exhausted Peter Stone was let off the hook like his little trout.

As we went back to talk to fishery manager Roy Ward, the

pretty clapper girl said, 'I was interested watching him catching that fish. Could I feel what it is like to play a trout?' Kind Roy promptly said, 'That stock pond has only small fish in it. Let her hook one there, Gareth, and put it back.' Just as the fly was dangled in, Roy had a sudden thought. 'Watch out, Gareth. There's a 4-pounder in there. Don't hook that.' Too late. Inevitably, it had headed the rush and hooked itself and, with no reel, Gareth and the girl were running dementedly along the side to avoid a break. 'Do a Walton,' I called to them, 'throw the rod in and let the fish pull it round until he tires.' That was too late, too, for fly and a length of horsehair had long gone.

As a world champion you get some odd requests. Returning one Thursday from distant fishing I telephoned home to say I would be late . . . as usual. I was told the *Observer* news desk was desperate to get in touch. Somewhat surprised that it was not the sports desk about my Saturday cricket reporting, I dutifully made contact, and the following one-sided conversation ensued: 'We've had a bright idea. A large prize is being offered for the first person to catch a salmon on the Thames, so we've laid on a camera crew and we want you to go and do it on Saturday. Be sure you catch a salmon before 6 o'clock, which would be our deadline . . . Why are you laughing? You are the world champion, aren't you? Surely that means you can catch a salmon without any trouble?'

Ah well, you cannot expect a *news* desk to know anything about fishing, when none of the nationals' sports desks do. There was, in fact, a slight hitch for the person who claimed that award. When he proudly sent his salmon to be mounted, Peter Stone had to report it was actually a dark-coloured 7lb trout; as it was killed out of season, the angler was in danger of a fine rather than an award.

On another occasion, I was fishing at Dever Springs when an able lady angler came round from the other side to speak to me. I had seen her catch a couple of fish already, so it could hardly be for advice. 'I've managed to catch this Damsel fly nymph in my arm. Can you get it out, please?' The barbed hook was sunk deep into the flesh and, unlike the actor,

Bernard Cribbins, who specialises in whipping the hook out in such circumstances, I expressed myself as incompetent to do it without much tearing of the flesh.

'But I thought you were a world champion. You *must* be able to do it properly.'

The best I could manage was that, as a world champion, I wasn't in the habit of implanting flies in myself, which was a pretty lame excuse.

The new single National Fishing Licence is something that anglers have craved for years as they became ever more fed up with having to buy a series of different licences if they travelled a few miles from home. The National Rivers Authority is to be congratulated on so promptly and successfully addressing this problem. As in many fishing matters, considerable assistance was given to them in coming to this solution by Lord Mason of Barnsley. In recognition of that he was issued with National Licence No. 2, Prince Charles having received No. 1.

Among the reasons why Lord Mason gave the NRA initiative such effective support may have been a memory of the type of embarrassing situation the previous complex system was apt to create. On one occasion, the Lords and Commons team was fishing a friendly match against a team of eminent lawyers. The venue was the Duke of Wellington's water at Stratfield Saye. In the middle of an enjoyable day, a Thames water bailiff arrived, and his inspection of licences showed that only two of the Parliament team and one lawyer had the correct licence. As they say, one law for the lawgivers and enforcers, another for the rest of us! But Roy Mason and the NRA have now given us a very reasonable licence law and licence charge, for which they deserve our thanks.

The Lords and Commons fly fishers have done sterling work in raising money for various fishing causes with Roy Mason, and originally John Golding, taking a leading role. Having had to organise many of the events I have found the Parliamentarians tough opponents. That, of course, relates not so much to their fishing as to their Parliamentary skills. Having been beaten out of sight, you could still rely on John Golding to give the

television cameras, by devious comment and thumbs-up sig-
nals, the *impression* his team was victorious. No terminological
inexactitudes, you understand. No being economical with the
truth. Just an ability by misleading word and gesture to stand
truth on its head.

It was nice to be asked to organise the events because clearly
my value as a participant had earlier been somewhat dubious.
Amoco were sponsoring one such event, and I was pleased to
be invited by David Swatland to take part. A few days later
came an embarrassed telephone call: 'I'm sorry, but the sponsor
says you aren't well enough known to be among those invited.'
That was in Kent, too, the county for whom I played cricket
and football! As they say, fishing is a great leveller.

From the entertainment world, Bernard Cribbins and Chris
Tarrant are two excellent anglers who give great support to
such charity events, as in the past has Frankie Vaughan and the
late Eric Morecambe. Both Frankie and Eric were participating
when I won my first ever fishing trophy in an event at Patshull
Park. The inscription goes twice round the cup, but I can gaze
proudly on the 'Porky Scratchings Charity Trout Match
Winner' trophy on my mantelpiece.

Among several hilarious moments in those Lords and Commons charity matches was one at Bayham Abbey Trout Fishery. Conservative MP Sir Geoffrey Johnson Smith was taking
a long time to land a not very large fish with adverse comments
on his performance from the likes of John Golding. In explanation, Sir Geoffrey made the unfortunate comment that he
was playing it so lightly because he 'distrusted his old weak
leader'. There were roars of support for this remark from the
anti-Thatcherites. So that I don't appear politically biased I
should say that the two leading Labour anglers, the usually
skilful Golding and Mason, had just been giving an equally
entertaining performance as a hooked fish entwined itself and
the cast round their anchor rope, leading to counter-comments
about their party being anchored to the bottom again.

On the more serious side, apart from the great contribution
to such good fishing causes as the Handicapped Anglers Trust or

Youth Fishing which such matches raise, many of those taking part have done sterling work on angling's behalf in Parliament. That includes, among others, Lord Mason, John and Llin Golding, Sir Geoffrey Johnson Smith and Cranley Onslow, with the first three no doubt having helped convert their party from anti- to pro-fishing.

When pop star Roger Daltrey opened his Lakedown Fishery, which has since proved successful enough to expand to a fourth lake, his agent phoned to ask me to attend the press day. John answered, and when the agent realised he was speaking to my son he became anxious. The conversation continued, 'How old is your father?'

'Oh, very elderly.'

'Would he appreciate Roger Daltrey's musical eminence?'

'I doubt it. He's as square as they come. Do you want me to go along too and ensure proper respect for Daltrey?'

'How kind of you.'

So John had ensured himself a good day's free fishing – though I was the one to recognise Roger on his arrival.

Roger's three lakes consisted of one for floating line only, one for floater or sinker, and one for dry fly only, all with a fly size limit. He told us we could catch and return fish, but could only keep two. I had no intention of keeping any until I stopped to chat with a friend fishing the dry fly lake. Not aware in advance of this limitation I had not brought any dry flies with me and soon got bored watching him. So I took out my bushiest Black Pennell, blew on it, rubbed it on my scalp to add a touch of grease, and cast out. At once a large brown swirled at it, and the surprise was such that my involuntary strike was much too early. Next cast it took again, and this time I was ready. Soon a 6½lb brown in beautiful condition was landed and kept as it was the largest brown I had ever caught.

The photographers present centred on that as the fish of the day, and it was certainly good publicity for the fishery. In the middle of the photographic session, however, a wrathful Daltrey descended on me: 'You were not meant to keep one as large as that. You will have to pay a pound a pound for that.' I was delighted to do so, but cannot contain a wry smile whenever I see that American Express advertisement with Daltrey watching a fish caught on that lake and saying, 'I suppose I will have to put the other one in now.' He's only joking, of course, because Lakedown is always a well-stocked and entertaining fishery.

Non-anglers talk about the patience you need. They have no understanding that the only patience an instinctive fisherman requires is that needed to survive the time when you are not fishing; once on the water you are totally absorbed and, even on a blank day, you are always *expecting* to catch a fish, no matter how many fruitless casts you have made. It was not patience which was required in those small burns of my childhood like the Tullich and the neighbouring Coulags, but stillness, for their wild trout were eager for the worm. Surprisingly for a four-year-old, I was so mesmerised that I was prepared to sit absolutely still in the heather, letting the worm swim down some small pool until, at last, the line and my nerves vibrated to the pull of a small trout which would sail over my head with the force of the strike.

As the Tullich burn tumbled down a steep mountainside, there was one high waterfall which had worn out a deep inviting pool below it. But above there were no trout, and father decided to try to stock it anew. So he set me to fish the pool while he waited with a bucket. Soon a small trout came flying out for him to unhook, put in the filled bucket and then scramble up the rocky, cliff-like side of the fall to release it in another pool some fifty yards above. As I crouched unseen in the heather, and fish after fish took the worm, he soon complained he was having to work like Sisyphus, condemned forever to roll a boulder up a hill only for it to roll down to the bottom again. After the nineteenth trip, I was firmly told enough was enough!

While we children fished the burns, father was usually down on the Carron river which, in spate, was a good salmon and sea trout river. Some forty years later, I went back there with

John and Sarah, and we were surprised to see one of the pools with a white marker proclaiming it 'Pawson's Pool'. The owner had no knowledge why it was called that, but I was able to suggest the reason. It was a small pool in which my father had hooked two large salmon. Below it was a rapid overhung with tree branches, where it would be impossible to follow and a break would be certain. Inevitably, the twenty-pounders headed that way, whereupon mother in tweed skirt was ordered into the water to throw stones in front of the bolting salmon. Her aim was good enough to turn both of them, and both were landed.

While John caught a salmon lower down, I did later hook one in that same pool. It swirled at the fly when I was not expecting a fish, so low was the river. But, when I changed to a much smaller size, it took hard and made off upstream. That left me momentarily very happy as the run-in was shallow and gentle, the pool above long and quiet. Then, with dismay, I saw it headed straight for a small piece of hooped wire stranded in the middle of the broad stream. Straight through it went and, by the time I had threaded my rod through it too, the strain was so great on the fine cast I had been using in low water that the salmon was running free. So it wasn't third time lucky for the Pawsons.

When we fished the Carron river near Pawson's Pool, John caught a salmon spinning with a Devon Minnow. A few days later, we fished Loch Merkland in Sutherland. We had always caught a lot of trout there, but a two-pounder was the largest either of us had landed, though I had once hooked one much bigger. That was on a windy day, and when it swirled close to the boat its tail caught the dropper with the point fly firmly in its mouth. It then played as if foul-hooked, and I could not bring it close enough for John to net before it plunged down unexpectedly, the reel jammed, and the cast broke. The trout had at times lain quiescent on the surface, and I estimated its weight at 5lb or more. That caused merriment and scepticism back at the Overscaig Hotel, where the records showed nothing above 3lb in the previous twenty-five years. A year later, I went into the Bridge Hotel at Huntingdon and saw cases of large trout on the bar wall. Assuming these must be specimens from nearby Grafham, I was surprised to notice on one the legend '9lb, Loch Merkland 1925'. So now I suggested to John that there must still be big trout in Merkland, but probably cannibals that would only take a fly on the rarest occasion. So why not try his Devon Minnow? For three hours he did so without catching anything except for a couple of small trout, while I was enjoying good sport on the fly rod at the other end of the boat. 'Give up the spinner and join in the fly fishing,' I advised him. But once he tries something John always persists. An hour later, as I was telling him it was a waste of time to go on, his rod bent, the line raced out, and a wild trout, dark as an autumn salmon, leaped high. That was 6½lb. We landed to celebrate and, only ten minutes after relaunching, his line was racing out even faster. That was 7¼lb, with a 3½lb trout to round off. The hotel was goggle-eyed at that bag, and there was a reversal of normal form as the two local gillies plied John with whisky to get him to tell them all.

When we returned to Overscaig the next year, John decided to try just once more with the spinner as he had reverted to his favourite fly fishing after that sensational day. 'I'll give it a few hours on the off-chance,' he said, 'but I can hardly expect to catch a monster again.' Once more, nothing happened for several hours. Then as I was gillieing him close in to a rocky bay and anxiously considering what damage rowing might be doing to the tennis elbow from which I was suffering, John suddenly exclaimed, 'Bother, I've caught the bottom. Stop rowing, Dad.' This was followed by, 'Heavens, the bottom's moving.' A rare fight followed, and the tennis elbow was forgotten as I was instructed to row hither and thither to avoid snags or follow the bolting fish. Finally, I was asked to row for sheltered water close to shore where the fight to the finish was conducted. For some reason, a piece of pink fluff had caught near the end of the line and, for the last few minutes, it resembled a tug-of-war as the fluff emerged from the water only to be pulled back again. Daughter Sarah found herself in the middle of an unscheduled panic as the trout came near to the surface, only to disappear again with my instructions to her to keep the net out rapidly followed by orders to put it back in the boat again. For once, she forbore to tell me to do it myself, and a trout over 8lb was safely netted, the largest wild brown any of us have caught.

Sarah is a highly competent and very sensible fisherperson despite, as the youngest, getting the dirty end of the oar on many days out. As she was apt to say, 'Whenever the fishing is good I have to row and, as soon as everything goes dead, I am invited to fish.' That was only a slight exaggeration. Her other objection was that, when she hooked a fish, we were both so anxious for her to catch it that the stream of contradictory advice unnerved her. She became very skilful at fishing a small spinner, as well as flies, on the weeded Altnacealgach lochs, particularly Urigill. When she hooked a trout on a spinner, that was not so obvious as on a fly rod, and she became adept at playing them so quietly the first we knew was when she would say, 'Could you please net this fish for me?'

The only time I recall a very justified rebellion was when the three of us were fishing Loch Brora for sea trout and a possible salmon on a very windy day, and Sarah was having a turn on the oars. As we drifted close in to a rocky shore to which the wind was driving us, my fly was suddenly seized by a salmon which made off at high speed. 'Row back fast,' I commanded.

'I am not going to be blamed for you losing your salmon,' said Sarah flinging down the oars and telling John to take over. The salmon did come off, but at least I blamed no one but myself.

Sarah had her own back recently when she teamed up with Jeanette Taylor in a ladies' team of three for the French Open on Lac du Château in 1988. 'I am just going to enjoy myself and not take this seriously,' she said beforehand. When I passed her hurrying off the island over the narrow walk-way after catching two in the first half-hour session, she looked pretty intent and competitive to me. She didn't catch quite as many as John, but on the placing system she beat her world champion brother and father in her only formal competition. After that she has retired on her laurels, though Jeanette Taylor is keen to persuade her back into competitive action. Fine, as long as it is not against John and myself! Jeanette herself is a most consistent competitor who has done exceptionally well in international competition. She was a member of one winning team in 1990 at Lac du Château, well supported by Peter Cockwill and Micky Bewick, and made a full contribution to the England team doing so well in the Commonwealth event in New Zealand.

Sarah particularly enjoyed the trout fishing on the Altnacealgach Lochs, mainly short lining her flies and bobbing the dropper back to the boat which is a very effective method there. She also used her small Mepps on occasion, working it with skill between the prolific weedbeds. These lochs were developed by the great P. D. Malloch of Perth, outstanding in his day as angler, tackle dealer, and expert on pisciculture. Malloch's main trout fishing was on Loch Leven, then regarded as the premier trout lake in the world. When the Scots held their first national competition there more than a century ago, Malloch was favourite for this greatly over-subscribed event to which Francis Francis, as fishing editor of *The Field*, donated a special prize. Malloch did indeed catch the largest fish, but ended as runner-up. While those yellow-bellied Leven fish were a good size, what Malloch later called 'the famous Altnacealgach Lochs' were teeming with small trout six and seven to the pound. Malloch quickly appreciated the spawning areas were too good there, with the vast head of trout becoming larger than lochs like Urigill could support without their becoming stunted or diseased. So he arranged for these lochs to be hard fished, reducing the population to a sensible size, where the trout could grow on and the diseases common in crowded waters be avoided. As a result, Urigill, Cama, Borolan and Veyatie still provide some remarkable trout fishing with a profusion of half-pounders and the occasional trout of two or three pounds as well as some Arctic char. Much larger trout are also taken, but mainly by trolling large flies or spinners.

1. *Dawn on Tasmania's Lake Samuel as John battles with his first big wild brown in the 1988 World Championship.*

2. *Dusk two days later as John and his Australian competitor friend, John Rumpf, walk back through the Bronte lagoon's tussocky margins, wondering how they have finished.*

3. *Tony casts for a difficult trout in Avington's stream.*

4. *John plays a rainbow in Avington's first lake.*

5. *Tony fishing Rutland's north arm with Andrew Hargreaves MP.*

6. *John* (left) *paired with James Melville in the first session of the 1992 Benson & Hedges final at Rutland.*

7. John strikes into a big
Gmundener Traun grayling in Austria
while Tony plays a rainbow.

8. John about to release a standard
Traun grayling of around 3lb.

9. John fishes the Traun dead-drift method
for grayling using a weighted nymph.

When we first fished there we stayed at the Altnacealgach Hotel, then splendidly run by a Mrs Attwood who certainly satisfied my father's five requirements for a fishing hotel: good food, good fishing, good drying facilities, good beds, and a constant supply of very hot water to ensure all returning anglers could have a reviving soak after a long cold or wet day on the water. When she left, the hotel steadily deteriorated with the fishing becoming the sole attraction, great though that was for us. The next landlord was more concerned with building a pop group, and we were startled one evening as we sat in the small lounge when he marched in an accordian player he was trying to promote. The unfortunate lad had a hard time of it, as his only audience was ourselves and a couple of stranded German tourists whose car had broken down. Each new song was introduced in a stilted way as 'Your favourite and mine', followed by some lengthy Scottish title which remained as incomprehensible to us as to the Germans. The only variant was when he announced his 'special favourite' . . . then forgot its title! Perhaps he was put off by Sarah, sitting a yard away in front of him and determinedly reading her book without once being distracted. To cover the general embarrassment I called loudly for an encore of 'These are my mountains and this is my glen', while John and Sarah glared at me.

The next tenant was a good sheep-dog trialist, but hardly the man to keep a fishing hotel. It was something of a shock to go into the rod room to find five tethered sheep-dogs barring access to your rods. There was also the sad occasion on which a visiting party decided to arrive in style and land by seaplane on Borolan, just across the road from the hotel. John and I were fishing on Urigill. It was one of those typically unpredictable north Scottish days. From praying for a wind as we idled along in a flat calm, we were soon contemplating running for shelter as a gale hit the loch and such driving rain that I could hardly see John at the other end of the boat. This storm meant great difficulty for the plane in finding the right loch, only achieved after much frantic searching. The loch itself was also a nightmare place for such a landing, small, shallow, and with outcrops of rock just below the surface in unexpected areas. It was a shaken pilot who left, and a shaken party who staggered into the hotel. As John and I left early for Urigill next morning we were told they would follow in more leisurely style. To get to Urigill you had to row across Borolan, then face a three-quarter hour walk over boggy moorland. From where we were fishing we saw them arrive near lunchtime, but then stay fishing close to where they launched in one of the deadest parts of the loch. We finally decided to row over and advise them where to go but, halfway across, we saw them disappear the way they had come. The boat had been left drifting away down the wind, and when we recovered it we found the problem. McLeod, the owner, had forgotten to give them any rowlocks, and crude attempts to make a rope rowlock had not proved very efficient. That party didn't stay long.

Not long after that, the hotel burnt down with arson and insurance claims involving the police. So, for future years, we transferred to the nearby Oykel Bridge Hotel, where the five requirements of my father really are met. Indeed, the food is so good on a help-yourself basis that some energetic fishing is almost a necessity to work it off. By then, we knew the Altnacealgach lochs so well, and John's command of both reservoir and lochstyle method was so effective, that there was some surprise at the numbers caught. There was even more surprise on the face of the gillies who enquired of him what flies he used. 'I was catching them today on a Peach Doll on the point, a Punk Rocker, which has Mayfly similarities, as middle dropper, and my variant of a Pennell as top dropper.' Not quite the standard flies expected in Scotland, but the Peach Doll soon became popular on these lochs though, interestingly, while highly effective on Urigill, it was not much use on Cama. The other interesting aspect was the best size of flies for these lochs. The trout may only average half a pound or less, but so many Mayflies and other large terrestrials drift on in quantity that size 8 hooks, at least on the point, are best. Most of the traditional flies do in fact work well, particularly Silver Invictas,

Wickhams, Soldier Palmers, Mallard and Claret and Black
Pennells.

The Blue Zulu is also much favoured and used to be the key
fly for Urigill. We once rowed across Borolan and walked over
to Urigill in company of two newly-weds. The man was telling
his bride of his great catches on the Blue Zulu and of the good
fishing in the sandy bay at the top of the loch. The breeze was
strong but pleasant as we launched away. A couple of hours
later, it was blowing a gale and it had become almost impossible
to row against the white-topped waves. As the wind rose, we
had landed on a sandy spit where a burn came in. We had some
splendid fishing there, with the stormy weather seeming to
bring up larger than average trout. The spit was almost opposite
the boat anchorage, so we were able to struggle back across the
waves, getting further drenched in the process. As we moored
the boat we saw the disconsolate pair squelching up the
lochside. They had caught nothing and had to abandon the
boat. It did not seem the ideal honeymoon for the non-fishing
bride, and I recalled my mother's comments on father's view
of an ideal honeymoon. That was to take her on a three-day
hike in the Lake District to visit the stream on which he caught
his first trout, spending the night in a shepherd's cottage when
they could find one. The comments were not complimentary.

For me, a slashing rise to the dropper bobbed on the surface
is the most electrifying of all, far more exciting and satisfying
than the slow, observed rise to a dry fly. Even when salmon
fishing I have a dropper for preference, often of sea trout size
when both are about. That can add to the entertainment, particularly on a river like the Erriff in Ireland where size 8 Black
Pennells are as likely to catch salmon as sea trout. In support
of my view that you rarely disturb fish if you wade quietly
along as if part of their environment, the most remarkable rise
I ever experienced was on that river. As I bobbed the fly back
close to me, hoping to attract a sea trout, suddenly a salmon
swam up between my legs to seize the Pennell! It escaped
eventually by the sort of leap common to Erriff salmon. Instead
of soaring up into the air it set out to break the long-jump

record, and there was no way of stopping the sudden jerk that broke the cast. On another occasion, I thought I had a salmon under control when it leapt half-way up the opposite bank, tangling and snapping the cast as it slid back through the bracken and heather.

On the Craigellachie beat of the Spey some splendid sea trout used to show in the evenings. As dusk is also a good time for salmon, I had a sea trout fly on the dropper and a salmon pattern on the point in my usual belt-and-braces fashion. There was a heavy take of the well-sunk flies, and the fish's powerful run convinced me I was into a 20lb-plus salmon. Suddenly, the line came slanting up at racing speed. It was obvious that a spectacular leap would follow, so I prepared to lower the point of the rod. That proved useless as the water erupted with a 10lb salmon hurling itself one way, a 4lb sea trout the other. The inevitable break freed the salmon, but the sea trout came to net.

There were, of course, many salmon caught on the dropper, but tying them on probably cost me the largest one I ever hooked. That was on one of the bottom pools of Norway's famous Laerdal river. The best fishing was on the far side of the river, and you had to row across to a fishing hut there where I had left most of my tackle and waders. The time was late August, when the salmon were meant to have passed through and only the big sea trout were running. As I walked up in my shoes and casual clothes and carrying my rod with a three fly 7lb cast I spotted some moving sea trout. Stepping gingerly out on the nearest croix I cast over them, and at once hooked a four-pounder which came off at the net. Casting again I saw the fly enveloped in a great swirl and a huge humped back lifting out of the current.

The salmon went porpoising up the far bank as I struggled to follow. Then it sulked deep down in the current while I strained to move it. My host and other members of the party converged to watch this most static and dull spectacular. Each offered to try to shift it as they got bored watching, but none could make an impression, and all except my host began to drift back to their own fishing. Only after three hours did I begin to get on terms and manoeuvre the fish out of the stream into the quieter water below the rock wall on which I stood. Mentally, I had already decided I would lose the fish and so was not agonising about whether I could catch it or not. I was prepared to play it all day if necessary but, unfortunately, my host had a business engagement and kept looking anxiously at his watch. Typical Norwegian kindness and hospitality prevented him leaving me at such a time, and his tenseness made me aware how acutely anxious he was to leave. By now, I had the top dropper out of the water, but still could not see the fish clearly. To relieve my host, it was now 'do or die' time, and I began to increase the strain despite fears that, with dropper knots weakening it, the cast must break. For a few moments I seemed to be winning but then, with a shake of its head, the salmon set off on a stately run back to the fjord and, as I held fast, the inevitable break followed. My host was then free to race away to his waiting seaplane.

Those sea trout at night provided some of the most thrilling fishing I have known. In winter, that valley enclosed by steep mountains is never touched by the sun but, in summer, there was still soft, glowing light throughout the hours of dusky night. Fishing with streamer flies, you waited in taut expectation for the sudden fierce pull and then the scream of the reel as a sea trout of 5lb or more tore away down the fast current. The largest I had was 13lb, and it took me down two pools with following never easy in the half-light. By day you could catch also, but with more difficulty on black dry flies, and again it was heart-stopping to see these large trout come slanting up through the clear water. When did we sleep? Not often.

Myths often have greater power and are more fervently believed than the truth, and in no sport is that more widespread than in fishing. There is, for instance, the very obvious fact that on bright moonlit nights fishing for sea trout can be no more profitable than on a bright sunny day. But, on the Cothi, two of the regular fishermen were a couple of colonels, who developed the fixed idea that leaving the weak porch light on in the house would ruin the fishing on the Black Pool, several hundred yards away and screened by trees. The absurdity of this belief was for long unexposed as the light was always turned off by the last to leave.

One night, however, one of the colonels, normally so meticulous, forgot to switch it off. As I came back after midnight, a furious row was in progress with the other accusing him of deliberately ruining his fishing. As I was blank myself I tried to calm the aggrieved one down by saying, 'I am very sorry you had a blank, but it's been a very difficult night, and perhaps that was why you didn't catch.'

'Had a blank?' shouted the irate colonel, getting even angrier. 'How dare you suggest such a thing. I have had five fine sea trout, the largest 7lb, but just think how many I would have caught if this idiot hadn't deliberately left the light on.' It is typical of fishing myths that, even when they are exposed, their believers remain blind to reality.

Brother Philip experienced the end of another Cothi myth, though this time its demise was acknowledged. This is his account of it:

'One of the colonels – let us call him the senior colonel, as he was the one who found, rented and organised the Cothi fishing – had two more firmly-held beliefs which his guests could ignore at their peril. The first was that no self-respecting sea trout ever took after midnight; the second was that night fishing was useless if the river was high. The latter theory, although generally true, was finally disproved by himself! The river one night was so high that spinning was permissible – although strongly disapproved of by the senior colonel, who settled down for a post-prandial whisky when it got dark. Meanwhile, the junior colonel had gone out with his spinning rod and soon returned with a 5lb sea trout. This galvanised the senior colonel to action. "H. and his bloody ironmongery!" he muttered in a loud voice, "I'll show him!," and stomped off to get his trout rod. He put on a salmon fly and, within the hour, was back with a 6½lb sea trout. In the course of time, we were allowed to fish after midnight with impunity, and my records show that most of my best sea trout – say, 4lb upwards – were caught between 1 and 2 a.m., although the best of all, 8½lb, came very soon after dark.

'It was on the Cothi, too, that my wife caught her first salmon. I had spent many unrewarded hours helping her to fish for salmon that never came but, on this occasion, she had gone on her own with Sandy the dog to Corner, a very long pool with a flat sandy beach at the top end. When I got back for a late lunch, only our friends, Pam and Alec Maurice, were there. Thinking the dog must have run off, I seized a sandwich and set off to help find him. I crossed the bridge and hurried through a short bit of wood on the far side. As I emerged, there in front of me was my wife, dog at heel – and a 10lb salmon in her hand. She had hooked it nearly two hours earlier. Not knowing what to do next and fearful that more than minimum strain would break the cast, for the next hour and a half she followed it up and down the pool. Eventually, with fisher and fish both equally exhausted, the salmon gave up, turned on its back and was gently hand-lined on to the sandy beach.

'Once over the hurdle of her first salmon, her fortunes steadily improved. One of her favourite stories is how we fished another long pool together, this time on the Oykel river. She started at the top, I in the middle. Later we changed over. She caught four salmon, all around 10lb. I caught none (although, if given the chance, I like to point out that I had little time to get my line out before being summoned back to net the next fish!). That year, the two of us were fishing a three-rod beat on our own. Last year, there were six of us. I shared with Julia, our younger daughter; Peggy with William, younger son; and our other guests (he an expert, she less experienced) shared the third rod. Conditions were good, and we expected a great week. Between us we caught only three salmon. The other guests at Oykel Bridge that week fared no better, most of them worse. I and William caught nothing, nor did the expert. His wife should have had one, but the fly she had tied on herself came loose at the end. Peggy caught one; and Julia, who had seldom fished for, and never caught, a salmon in her life, got her first two – and would have had a third if I had been quicker with the net. Was that beginner's luck or the modern theory of female pheromones attracting salmon?'

Philip's garden borders on a Devonshire river which can be a target for poachers when salmon are running.

'The Walkham is a small river. When it is low, salmon – like the proverbial ostrich with its head in the sand – seek shelter with their heads in the roots of trees, leaving their tails sticking out. A short stick, a wire noose, and they fall easy prey. Once, when the river was full, a guest of ours was fishing a pool downstream with a spinner. He saw a stick poking up on the far side of the current, and weaving round in a strange way. He hooked it and coaxed it to the bank, where his wife caught hold of it and started to pull a salmon tail-first up the bank. But the noose broke, the salmon slithered back and swam off. Next day, the river was still high and our guest was spinning in the same pool when he hooked – fairly – and landed a 7lb salmon. Round its tail was a broken wire noose!

'The poachers also come at night, with powerful lamps. One night, about 2 a.m., I saw lamps on the bridge at the end of our garden. Below the bridge is one of the main salmon pools. I rang the bailiff, who said he would get two policemen and be down in half an hour. I waited in the rhododendrons at the end of our drive, watching the lamps still on the nearby bridge. Three shadowy figures crept down the road, so I climbed out and followed. Shouts from the bridge. When I caught up with them, the bailiff had one man on the ground and the police were chasing the other two who had run off on the moor across the bridge. They soon returned with their two captives, but no sign of any salmon or poaching gear, essential evidence for a conviction. The police car was summoned by radio. Waiting for it, the police asked the poachers, who had a dog with them, what they had been doing. 'Looking for rabbits,' was the reply. 'Funny place to look for rabbits, on a bridge,' said the policeman. When the car arrived and the poachers were safely in it, we all went searching for the evidence which we were sure had been jettisoned. It was an hour before a triumphant call from one of the policemen announced that he had found a fresh salmon in a clump of bracken. He took it back to the car and held it up in front of the poachers. 'Funny sort of rabbit,' he said.

'The temptation to poach, if that is the right word, can affect us all. One Sunday, at the Oykel Bridge Hotel, when the river was dead low and the fishing had been virtually useless, our son William was walking past the Oykel Falls when a lady called to him. She had been watching salmon trying to jump the falls. One had missed and stranded itself in a cleft of rock half-way down. She could not retrieve it and asked William if he could manage it, which he did. Together they decided to keep the salmon, cut it in half and share it. Appropriately, the lady's name was Lady Salmon, wife of the eminent judge, Lord Salmon of Sandwich.'

While my parents were abroad when I was very young I spent a lot of time with an aunt in a London flat, which I would have found exceptionally boring were it not for book-cases full of bound *Punch* magazines, the cartoons in which kept me fascinated for hours on end. One particular cartoon has always stuck in my memory and comes to mind whenever I hear distorted versions of the meaning of 'limititis'. It showed a Chadlike figure peering over the wall of a lunatic asylum at an angler below: 'Caught anything?' 'No.' 'How long have you been fishing?' 'Eight hours.' 'Come inside.'

The man who coined the word 'limititis' was, of course, a professional game angling instructor as well as a fishery man-ager. As a manager he might naturally have been urging people to enjoy themselves without catching anything, which would be greatly to the economic benefit of ASGFM members. But as an instructor in the art of fishing he could hardly be urging people to fish so badly that they caught nothing.

The sensible meaning of limititis is that, while it is natural to try to catch your limit, you should not approach a day in the mood that it is a disaster if you don't. You should accept fishing as a challenge and remain happy on the days when the fish win rather than you. You can then take greater pleasure in the days when you do well than if you caught regularly so well that it becomes monotonous.

Stocked fish 'limits' are economic limits, and the fishery manager will anyway ensure by his stocking that the average catch is 2.8 or whatever over the season to keep a nice balance between attracting customers and keeping stocking costs within bounds. It is the oft-quoted misuse of limititis as meaning that it is wrong to *try* to catch your limit of four fish or so, which reminds me of that cartoon.

Every fisherman, and particularly every competitive fisher-man, knows you can happily while away eight hours trying, hoping, expecting to catch with every cast even though you come in 'clean'. But to deliberately fish badly in order not to catch your quota of fish, that *does* qualify for immediate removal to a suitable asylum.

Indeed, those mawkish and whimsical 'only here for the scenery and the beer' writers, who might just as well go walking as fishing, are also perceived by the majority of normal, keen anglers as being hypocrites, or asylum candidates. There is more to fishing than catching fish, with the ambience and companionship high on that list. But to deny that the main aim of fishing is to catch fish is to deny the obvious and to discredit and discount the skills and arts involved in the sport.

The only anglers with whom I feel out of sympathy are those who try to put down or spoil the fun of other legitimate fishermen. Usually, that is done in the attempt to show themselves as 'superior' in some way, with that 'superiority' often based on misconception or myths.

Fishing myths like this, as we have seen, grow so easily. An 'expert' has only to write that nymph fishing, once itself so abused, is a purer way of fishing than ordinary wet fly, and there are bound to be plenty of sheep-like characters to accept that as some fishing absolute. I had an example of the worst of such nonsense when fishing with John at Allens Farm (now Rockbourne Lakes). That April, one of the smallest of the delightful little lakes was very coloured and opaque, and when John came to it he took time to consider the likely way to catch fish there. He decided sensibly enough that a size 10 olive mini-lure fished deep would be as good a chance as any. So it proved, as he had two good fish within half an hour. Two other anglers had been fishing there for a couple of hours and, as they had caught nothing, one came to ask John, who was about to move on, what fly he was using. John not only told him, but showed him. Without any thanks, the angler went back to his friend calling out in a deliberately loud voice to ensure we heard, 'Would you believe, he was using a *lure* fly rather than fishing properly with a nymph like us.'

Their 'nymph' was, in fact, a Mayfly Nymph on a size 8 long shank hook which they were dragging close to the bottom. Mayflies are rare there at any time, but there were certainly none on a cold day in early April! So they were as much lure fishing as if they had been using a Baby Doll, or an Appetiser. They were not 'pure' fishermen, merely a couple of rude and stupid ones far removed from the Waltonian tradition.

As for fishing 'absolutes', a visit to New Zealand might be valuable for some. In the 18th century, there were absolutists whose 'absolute' statements were progressively disproved as new worlds opened up. Their remaining dictum was that a typical 'absolute truth' was that all swans are white. New Zealand's black swans finally torpedoed that last prop of the sect that died.

There is a special excitement in catching fish where or when you have been told it is particularly difficult to do so. How much greater is the smug satisfaction when you catch one where you have been told it is impossible! My first such experience was with the admirable James Meehan. I was ten at the time and fishing the Glenloss, which joined Joyce's river, before running down into Lough Corrib. When it was in flood, the big Corrib brown trout would run up this tributary and the higher reaches of Joyce's. But now the river was low and clear, and my father, brother and I were still fishless as James launched me on the last pool. Again nothing came in the deep run at the head, but ever hopeful I fished on into the clear shallow tail of the pool. For the third time James had said, 'Reel in now – you'll never catch a fish there,' when my first such big Corrib trout seized hold, and joy was unconfined when a three-pounder was finally beached, with James as delighted as I was.

Two fish caught in the most unlikely ways were also memorable, though subjects of amusement rather than congratulations. One of New Zealand's noted guides, Tony Hayes, had taken me out on the famous Tongariro river. This is a wide, fast river where the rainbows run low, and it is essential to get down quickly to them. With a pair of heavily weighted nymphs I was casting upstream to Tony's directions and had already released three up to around 7lb. But, with a light fly rod and light line, I was not casting far enough against a fierce wind to satisfy Tony. He then showed me a way of improving this by letting the line float down behind you until the current stretched it taut, and then flinging it forward in a single action with no false casting. Experimenting successfully with this, the occasion soon came when a particularly fierce squall made it prudent for me to leave the line behind me hanging in the shallow rapid below. Suddenly, the rod was nearly wrenched out of my hand as another 5lb rainbow seized hold. Hardly classic nymph fishing, but fun!

On the Beauly river near Inverness I had once fished with, in my own view, good technique without moving a fish for a day and a half. Then I found myself approaching a pool, the head of which was virtually unfishable because, on the far bank, the current was too fast and below my bank was a deep whirlpool of a backwater impossible to work a fly in. To get to the start of the very fishable part it was necessary to cross a stile several yards inland. In a lazy frame of mind, rather than reel in I left my line trailing in the whirlpool. When I started to retrieve it as soon as I was in a position to cast I found a fifteen-pounder had hooked itself. Yes, fishing is a splendid mixture of luck and skill and, in salmon fishing in particular, nothing is ever for certain.

It was on the Beauly, too, that I had another moment of satisfaction. The beat had an old and a young gillie, neither of whom were much concerned about guests enjoying themselves. They waged their own private war about who could put most salmon in the record book. This was a marvellous sea trout river, but it was only possible for me to fish for sea trout in their lunch break. Sea trout did not count in the record book, and it was made clear that, on pain of dire disapproval, you were not allowed to waste time fishing for them when you might be concentrating on catching a salmon to boost their quota.

Willie, the elder and more dictatorial of the two, was looking after my hostess on the Cruives when I decided to fish the pool opposite. By Willie's tradition, this was only fished from a moored boat when the river was high, and was useless when low as now. It was March when there were many kelts about, but I was sure I had seen fresh-run fish moving in this pool and was giving it a try. Willie, the tyrant, promptly dispatched my hostess on an errand I felt he might have run himself. Erskine Barratt, widow of my godfather and many times a casting champion in the glory days of the Usk casting championship, was clearly irked at having to deliver Willie's message. Without looking closely she called out, 'Willie says you are to stop wasting your time and go and fish elsewhere.'

'Certainly,' I replied happily, 'but I'll just land this fish first.' For I was playing a salmon and a good one it was too, and all the sweeter for being one in the eye for Willie.

In the first two national finals for which I qualified, the fishing at Grafham proved hard, and along with several others I ended blank. Appropriately, the luck changed for my third final at Chew Valley, with being drawn in 'lucky' boat 7 another good omen. My partner was another world champion-to-be, Brian Leadbetter, although at the start it looked like being anything but a good day for us. With some thirty boats huddled fairly close, you always get the impression that everyone else is catching if you are not. After an hour and a half, neither of us had moved a fish and we were beginning to fret.

One of the anglers in the next boat then landed a fish, and Brian called across to ask what he had caught it on. 'Ace of Spades,' came the reply. It was probably a helpful one, but at that time neither of us had heard of that good black rainbow trout fly. 'He's pulling my leg, isn't he?' said an aggrieved Brian.

'He's entitled not to tell you if he doesn't want to and perhaps he's just having a joke,' I replied.

At that moment, Brian hooked and soon landed his first fish of the day on a Grenadier, that most popular of Chew flies. 'What did you catch that on?' enquired the Ace of Spades man. 'Jack of Diamonds,' Brian called back.

We both qualified and have fished together in many international matches in Britain and Europe since then. So I am well aware that Brian's cheeky answer was only on the assumption that he himself had been misled, though that may well have been a misapprehension. Usually, he is more than ready to tell anyone what he is catching on, though that is not always a great help to them. As the comedians say, it is not the jokes but the way you tell them that matters, and so with Brian it is not so much the fly as the way you fish it that matters. Anyway, as an inventive fly tier, if Brian tells you he is fishing with a Viva, the pattern he has tied may be very different from the standard variety!

John qualified for that same final at the youngest permitted age of eighteen. But he was still at Lancing College and had to seek permission from the headmaster to participate. This was given, but a few days before the event the head telephoned me to say he had a dilemma. 'We have a very important football match against Eton College and we want John to play and, as a good team man, I know he would not wish to let his side down.'

'What are you suggesting?' I asked.

'The Dean of one of the Oxford colleges was dining with me last night, and we discussed this and agreed John would have only one chance to play against Eton, but many more opportunities to fish for England. So do you agree he should play with his team?'

'That's your decision to take, Headmaster. But my view is, first if you undertake to do something on a particular day you should always stick by it, even if something more inviting comes up; and second, I think that a national final is more important than playing against Eton. But you may have other views.'

Predictably, he did and, to John's disgust, he was substituted after twenty minutes and Lancing lost anyway. No doubt the fact that I qualified for the international made him feel he could have done it also as he had caught better than me in the qualifier at Chew. He qualified again the next year, whereas I did not. However, I was at Grafham as the *Observer* had not only agreed to my writing something on the final, but had also given a small sponsorship towards its running. I was therefore invited to fish with the competitors though keeping out of their way and acting as gillie to the Confederation president, Adrian Ashness. When I drifted within hailing distance of John in the afternoon, he was doing quite well and, as I passed, he hooked a big fish virtually certain to qualify him. Trying to watch him as he was about to net it I managed to run the president aground. After apologies and relaunching the boat, I was about to give John the thumbs-up when I saw him sitting head in hands. The four-pounder had come off just as he was netting it. With unintentional tactlessness I then caught two at once within sight of him and ended having fished for two hours less than the competitors and caught more than any of them, whereas I had always blanked at Grafham when in the final myself! For John, there was a last flick in the eye from fate since he ended just a few ounces short of making it into the international team. That's competition fishing. When it matters crucially to you, things go awry; when it doesn't, it may all be plain sailing.

Happily, John was qualified again the next year and, for him, it was third time lucky too. But, like me, he was made to sweat. He was partnered by Mike Childs on Rutland, which has been such a happy hunting water for John over the years. In September that year, it was fishing hard, but some big fish were coming out. The choice was to search for a few stock-sized fish or go for one of the big browns chasing fry round the weeds. It was Mike's choice, with which John happily agreed, to go up the less fancied North Arm and try for a large one which in itself might put you in the frame. Before midday, John was again into a beauty, and again it came off as he was poised to net it. No doubt he felt like jumping in the lake after it, but this time there was instant relief. Within a few casts the rod bent again, the reel screamed, and this time a brown of close on 4lb came to the net. John eventually finished in the top ten.

John landed that big brown in a more orthodox way than his cousin William dealt with a couple of similar size as recounted by my brother. 'From the bank at Loch Merkland I watched William out in the boat as he leant over until his rod, arm, and most of his head were under water. As the distant boat chugged back a similar commotion occurred with William again hanging over the side, head in water. When he landed, he had two wild browns of 4lb and 5lb respectively.

William's reel had jammed each time in the middle of the fight and by following down into the water with the rod he had avoided a break. That was twenty years ago, both beautiful golden fish still remembered at the Scourie Hotel. Last year I hooked a salmon on Loch Stack. When it first came near the net it dashed off again on a run which took out all my line. There was a new top ring on my trout rod and the cast-connector now stuck in it. By imitating William I was able to land a fresh-run 9lb salmon. Perhaps there is a lesson here, but if you make a habit of it a buoyancy aid may be desirable for safety's sake!'

PART 3

Tackle, Tactics and Thymallus

Grayling: A Really Game Fish

The grayling may be one of the salmonidae but, in Britain, they have never achieved the mystical fascination of trout or salmon, nor has the catching of them been promoted to the same status-symbol fishing. On the Continent it is very different. There the French reverence the Ombre, and the Teutons the Esche, as much or more than trout, both as game fish and for eating. The Umber, as it was once called in England, has had a much less respectful time over here. True, Walton and Cotton fished with equal enthusiasm for trout and grayling, but did the grayling no favours by referring to it as the 'deadest-hearted' fish. That was no doubt because of the contrast to the wild antics of the trout when hooked, as opposed to the grayling's more sedate tactics. The Dove, where Cotton fished for them around the celebrated Temple, and on down below the Pike Pool, so called not because of a predatory fish but from the pinnacle of rock in its depths, is a gentle stream without much current. In such water the grayling fight sluggishly, relying on their weight and the resistance from their outsize dorsal fin, rather than aqua-batics. In fast water it can be a very different matter.

Happily, that was my own first experience of fishing for them as a schoolboy. My father came home from the Sudan for the summer, and we progressed from rented accommodation in a fisherman's cottage in Scotland to hotels in Ireland, to a rented house in Wales, all as bases for good fishing. In Wales, the house at Tyrcelyn also had rights over a mile or so of the Upper Wye, which provided a totally absorbing playground for the month of August. Only if the river was high was there much chance of a salmon and, in the long, hot, lazy days of the departing summer, we had other quarry to delight us. Stretched out on a big bough above the Boat Pool I could see chub and trout circling below and try to dabble for them from the tree, with all manner of interesting problems if one was hooked. Then there were the shoals of dace on rock ledges, their small mouths so incredibly swift to eject the dry fly that they schooled me to an instinctive fast strike. Sadly, this was much faster than was usually desirable except for the quick-rising Irish trout, where boatmen are apt to advise striking 'five seconds before you see the rise'.

In the evening, the trout would feed greedily in the shallow runs. We could fish on prolifically into the dark, with a Wormfly as point, and anything well-hackled to bob as dropper, until the incipient moon began to glint on the rippling water. But, above all, there was Gravel Pool and its sizeable grayling. Gravel had its name from the bottom over which the broad river flowed in a shallow run for some 100 yards, as a change from deep rocky pools. This was no holding pool for salmon, but fishing upstream dry fly in the hope of trout we came on grayling instead. How well they played in that fast water and how intriguing were their rises as they soared up from the bottom to snatch at the fly. It was another fifty years before I found that the way they rise makes it much easier to hook them if you drift the fly down on them.

Their denigrators also call grayling foolish because, on some occasions, they will keep rising even if you fail to hook them, partly I suspect because they do often miss the fly, which is poor reward for all that effort. But these were pound-plus fish which soared up unexpectedly and excitingly, usually to give you only one chance. For me, they were instantly attractive enough for wholehearted agreement with Francis Francis's comment that, 'If the trout be the gentleman of the stream, grayling is certainly the lady.'

Grayling, too, have the special attraction that, when both are in season, they are often active when the trout are quiescent and, of course, they are in prime condition when you cannot fish at all for trout in rivers. That authoritative writer on grayling, W. Carter Platts, writing in 1939, quoted two different verses to underline those points:

> Sirs, would you ask me on a day
> When speckled beauties shun the fray,
> Why fortune seems so far away
> And skill so unavailing
>
> Advice I'll give – it's merely this
> (When ignorance begets no bliss)
> Far better give the trout a miss,
> And try your luck with grayling.

Platts himself put into rhyme their value when you cannot even try for trout, with apologies for bowdlerising Kipling:

> It's Thymy! here, and Thymy! there,
> And 'Kick the beggar out!'
> But it's 'Good old sub for fario!'
> When the fence months shield the trout.

Thymallus thymallus was already the grayling's name when Claudius Aelianus wrote of it in the 2nd century with the comment: 'The river Ticinus, in Italy, produces the fish called Thymallus; it is about a cubit in length; in appearance it partly resembles the Sea Perch and partly the Grey Mullet. When captured it has a remarkable odour, so that you would say you had in your hands a freshly gathered piece of thyme. It is taken easily in a net, but not with bait or hook. It is taken only by a small gnat, the troublesome little beast which, day and night, is a nuisance on account of its buzzing and biting; with this, which is the only food of which Thymallus is fond, is it captured.' Fishing is full of myths and, unless the smell of the grayling, or of thyme, has changed, its pungent odour is not at all like thyme. It will also take a range of baits from worms to grasshoppers, though nymphs and small dry flies are very effective, especially those small black gnats. How did the

ancients tie one small enough? Or did the grayling elude them
as they are still so apt to do when rising furiously to the small
black fly known best as 'fisherman's curse'? John and I have
both benefited from the desire in the south to 'kick the beggar
out' from prestigious trout streams.

In Hampshire, grayling are regarded as vermin to be caught
anyhow any time. That has given us some splendid winter
sport when we were invited to fish for them on one of the best
beats of the Test below Stockbridge. Not surprisingly, however, our most exciting experience of them was in Europe,
where grayling are so highly prized. In Austria, John and I
were introduced to the large grayling of the Gmundener Traun
and an effective technique for catching them.

Our mentor was Reinhard Resch, whom I had first met in
the World Championship in Italy. 'Come late in September,'
he wrote. 'The fishing then is harder and therefore more
interesting. It also means there are fewer anglers, and you can
fish undisturbed.'

The Traun is one of those rivers where the water is so clear
you imagine it to be shallow only to find it is deep if you jump
in incautiously. There is a fast current, too, as it flows down
from the Traunsee between steep wooded banks. By day,
grayling are the principal target with an especially good stretch
for them from the first dam to the road bridges, and a very
productive weir pool just above Steyermuhl. One feature of the
Traun is a profusion of wild rainbows, whose surging power is
as great as a steelhead's. Even a 2lb fish may strip you down to
the backing, and one he rated as 'just average' went off with
Reinhard's new line to leave it tangled among downstream
branches. Yet the grayling are still regarded there as the more
important. The fishing is limited to barbless hooks and is catch-
and-release only, except that you may keep and pay for up to
seven rainbows in a week. But no grayling may be retained, so
highly are they rated.

By the riverside, Reinhard was soon demonstrating the
technique which brings daytime success. It is a peculiar mixture
of traditional nymph fishing and coarse fishing skills. 'Most of

the fish lie in the darker, deeper water. You must go as close as your trouser waders will allow, then use these full-function, fast-join leaders to work your leaded nymph right down to the bottom. If you let it drag or rise a few inches too high you won't catch.' The casts were braided and had thin slivers of copper wire inserted to ensure fast sinking. The fast join aided rapid change of the final tippet, which needed to be as fine as 0.16mm or less. A tiny red wooden bead at join of cast and line acted as a necessary strike indicator, and could be slid up or down according to depth required. Reinhard then demonstrated the casting method – a roll cast, checked above the water as in the parachute cast, so that the line and leader fell coiled close to the indicator. This allowed the nymph to sink down deep before the current dragged it off course. At once, the line had to be mended and paid out, and it was necessary to go on mending and paying out so that the nymph swam down thirty yards or so without any tautness in the line pulling it off course. It looked easy as Reinhard demonstrated with the fluent casting and easy control born of much practice, but two hours were enough to convince us that plenty of such practice was needed to acquire even reasonable competence.

John was the first to strike. It was a 21in fish and must have weighed around the then UK record of 3½lb. Reinhard's only comment was: 'That was a nice start, even if it is a little small.' He was not joking. John was later to catch three in succession between 22 and 25in. The largest any of the party caught was a 26-incher which must have weighed 7lb or more.

The spectacular evening rise also involved grayling, but it was the witching hour for the rainbows. At 7 p.m., the river would be flowing quiet, its surface undisturbed despite a hatch of olives. Then an occasional trout began to show, and there was a good chance of catching on a sedge pupa, particularly if fished with a little drag. At 7:30 precisely, the sedges rose in clouds, the bats wheeled in, and the river erupted wherever there were shoals of rainbows. Fishing with a very short cast, a white line, and a dark sedge you could catch four or five in the next forty minutes. So hard did they play that it was impossible to take more in the time, however rapidly they took. As it grew dark, the white line was a useful pointer. That, and the short cast, allowed you to have a good idea where your fly was long after it was impossible to pick it out on the dark water. Then you struck at any rise in its vicinity.

By day, dry fly with a Buck Caddis was also an effective method, and not only if you saw rising fish. You could float it down in the known grayling areas and, every so often, one would glide up from the bottom to take. In the fast current the large grayling used their big dorsal fin to great effect, running powerfully like autumn salmon and often hurdling out of the water to fall back in a shower of spray. When finally played out they lay quiet as you unhooked them, unlike the rainbows which never gave up and might well leap away, again breaking the cast as you tried to unhook them.

The Reinhard method would have been very useful to me the previous year, when the World Championship was on Poland's San river. The grayling there are very plentiful though they do not run quite so large. The San has its level controlled by a dam and, when we fished it, the river was wide, but shallow, so that in chest waders you could reach most parts. Inevitably, there were many more white-water areas and swift runs than on the deeper Traun.

The favoured method of the very expert Poles I christened the 'rolled nymph'. This looked ridiculously simple, merely involving two weighted nymphs, a leader of the length needed to reach the bottom close to your feet, and a short line of three or four yards which was roll cast, worked down past your waders, and roll cast again. The skills, of course, were first in locating your shoals of grayling, with the larger ones in that faster water; then in timing the strike when, in the fast water, it was so hard to detect a take at all. The nymphs also needed to imitate the naturals and be so weighted that they sank at once, as they would only catch near the bottom and they were only going to be worked over a few yards before being recast.

On the San river bottom the grey-flag nymph proliferates

and, after the event, my friend Jozef Jelenski, then the Polish team manager, wrote to explain the method and express some surprise that we were not well versed in it, or in the best nymphs to use:

'The rolled nymph is the same method Frank Sawyer and other earlier river-keepers used in order to extract large numbers of grayling from your trout streams. I have found in Dr Heinz's book, *Sportfisherie*, published in 1905, almost the same green caddis larva, Hydropsyche, grey-flag. The most important part of the technique is timing the strike. You must strike immediately after seeing the end of your line move. Some anglers do not even bother to watch the line. They are counting to four or so, then they strike and cast again. This method is called the "stupid Johnny method", yet it gives good results in strong currents.'

I had indeed wondered why some of the Poles looked so awkward in making a short roll cast, almost as if they had to false cast to get the nymphs near the surface before flicking them back upstream. That was, of course, just the action of striking, then immediately recasting if there was no contact. This particular stupid Johnny did not master the technique or find it entertaining. The more intelligent Johnny in the family can fish it well, but emphasises that, with so much which is instinctive involved in the method, he has no hope of becoming as expert as some Poles and Czechs with their lifetime experience of it.

The rolled nymph in fast white water and the long drift on slower deeps are two techniques highly developed in Poland. The studious Jozef Jelenski, who has written a detailed book on their grayling fishing methods, also summarised for me their approach to early summer fishing on a river like the San, which has many trout but a multitude of grayling: 'We use small dry flies imitating pale olives, olives, and midges such as Blue Upright, Blue Winged Olive, and Black Curse. We tie them on extremely small hooks, e.g. No. 16 and 18 extra short shank, rather than 20 or 22. We also use very fine leaders 0.14 to 0.12mm diameter. These we use on the quiet shallows and deeps but, in strong currents, we are always prepared to fish with weighted nymphs. These are mainly grey and green imitations of a grey-flag larva, black imitations of a leach and greyish freshwater shrimps. Dry sedge (Cinnamon, Black, Brown, Grey) can also be of use, especially if warm spring lasts long enough. The mayfly hatch starts in such conditions as well, and so be prepared to add No. 8 wet or dry Greendrake, especially for trout in slow-running currents. Take with you strong and reliable hooks. I am using Mustad Sproat 3904A No. 8 to 12 for nymphs and 14 to 18 for dry flies.'

With the rolled nymph, the strike is the key to success, and Jozef pays great attention to it in all his fishing. 'What we call "aggressive" wet fly fishing resembles your method of retrieving in a way which gives the impression of life and movement to the fly. It is, however, worth noting our method of striking, which is by striking with the line, not the rod, while vacuum-retrieving. So the jerks in the retrieve must be energetic, though the length of each retrieve and the pauses can be varied. They must be very short pulls with longer pauses when fishing with freshwater Louse or wet Sedge. In Streamer fishing, however, each pull must be at least a foot with almost no pause before the next. For trout and grayling in Northern Poland, the best method is the "induced take" using a Sawyer Killer Bug.'

For different people, fishing gives different pleasures. Jozef's satisfaction is that of the explorer and researcher forever looking for a new experience.

I cannot recall to mind my best day. Is it the one on which I first caught a Danube salmon on fly or a good bag of trout on Mayfly ending with a three-pounder? Or one of those classic days so often described in books, when the fish were not taking, so I sat and pondered then shouted loudly, 'Now I see,' changed my fly and at once caught a big trout? It is none of these, for no single day ever satisfies me. The best is in a three-day cycle. The first is for experiment with what I guess to be good. The second is for assessing how the technique works and making all necessary adjustment. The third is for the best of the fishing, having made the precise amendments to tactics and flies. Thereafter I find it becomes a trifle boring. For me, the search and research are everything. In Poland, the fishing background and references are poor, and fishermen apt to keep what they have learned to themselves. So, for me, it is the fishing research, and the publication of my findings, which is the most thrilling process.

Take, then, one example of what has really excited me in my fishing. On the Dunajec, Bohr, Poprad or Kwisa rivers at the end of July or in August after sunset come swarms of Oligoneuriella Rhenana, a big Mayfly not found in Britain. The females as one-inch-long pale grey duns have abdomens almost orange in colour. In flight they change into spinners, sometimes trailing loose whitish skin. The hatching of duns, the change into spinners, the mating, and the laying of eggs last altogether only half an hour or so near night. That period has been awaited with keen anticipation by dry fly fishermen, but is something of a disappointment when it comes. The fish are gorging themselves on the myriads of flies and, in the darkening light and with so many naturals, they only pick out your artificial at intervals. So not many are taken in this short hatch which resembles a snowstorm. I used to wait with others then use a Heather Moth on a really big hook, which is the best imitation of these insects mating. Even so, I could never catch more than a brace in this frantic burst of activity.

In the evening light the fly looks white, but is grey. I tried without success to find its nymph. Finally, I abandoned the search believing it must live in deep currents over which the Mayflies had flown. Then one day I found in a grayling's stomach a dense jelly of big purple eggs mixed with some segments of black case, resembling fragments of sedge cases. Later, I realised these eggs were the same as in the dun and spinner of Oligoneuriella Rhenana. But how did the grayling come to eat these tiny eggs? Then I saw some anglers fishing with black nymphs having good results in the middle of the day. So I searched for a natural resembling their black nymphs and finally found some next August in shallows close to currents. They were shiny, black as dark chocolate, and looking like armoured knights. Inside were matured eggs. These eggs were yellow in July, orange in August, but almost purple by the beginning of September. Nymphs look sturdy but are fragile with only their ability to crawl or swim fast saving them from destruction in floods. This fragility means they are crushed in a fish's stomach and not found whole in shape there.

So there it was. All you find in trout or grayling stomachs are masses of yellow, orange, or purple eggs; all you see is the evening hatch looking like a white snowstorm; but to do well you need to fish in the middle of the day with a black nymph!

That still left me two absorbing tasks. Experimenting with a variety of methods I found the best was to fish a long line, somewhere between the rolled nymph and the Austrian Traun method you described to me. Next, how to make an exact imitation, since no such artificial had been tied. For this method you need a lighter nymph. I use therefore thin copper wire to weight the hook, a No. 10 Mustad 3904 A, which shapes the underbody like a cigar. Then I flatten it with pliers and cover it with yellow or orange floss. Then I prepare a sturdy quill from the dark skin of the stem of a cock pheasant tail feather. The shape of the quill ends as a long triangle, coloured shiny black chocolate, of decreasing intensity. Tying the narrower end of the quill to the end of the underbody, the end half of the body can be wound in segments of increasing width as on the natural. Then the wide part of the quill must be tied on and divided with a razor into three separate parts of a sturdy wing case. Tying silk, dubbed with hare's wool, is wound round as underside of thorax, like the natural, then the wing case is made by tying at the head the separated parts of the quill, one after the other. The fly is then complete and is sturdy enough to fish, provided the silk covering of the copper underbody is smoothly tied and well soaked with clear varnish.

After such research and the implementing of my findings by working out the tools and techniques, I have total satisfaction and look forward only to finding a new problem to solve. My temperament always forces me to search for new waters, new places, new techniques and new friends, so my best days are always the days to come.

For some, all the excitement is in the fishing; for others, it is in the pursuit of knowledge with the anticipation as important as the achievement. For an expert such as Jozef or a duffer such as Andrew Lang, there is equal enjoyment. Lang, a self-confessed incompetent, could still echo Jelenski's ideal: 'There is the pleasure of the pursuit, the rapture of endeavour, the delight of the impossible chase, the joys of nature. The gleaming untravelled future, the bright untried waters, allure us from day to day, from pool to pool.'

After winning the World Championship in 1984, I handed over the title the following year to a Pole, just as John was to do four years later. On their own water the Poles had been unbeatable, excellent dry fly fishermen and outstanding exponents of nymphing for grayling on the San. I asked Leslaw Frasik, the new champion, how they had devised the 'rolled nymph' technique. 'It was by a close study of your Izaak Walton's *Compleat Angler*,' was the reply which floored me. Well, old Izaak, himself advised by Charles Cotton, did advise getting close to your grayling while fishing fine and far off for trout. And it is a pleasant characteristic of grayling that, if you wade in quietly close to a shoal, they will treat you as another legitimate river creature and not scurry away for shelter.

John has wide experience of grayling fishing and, in one of the sessions in the World Championship in Finland in 1989, caught the only four grayling taken in his section as he fished through a night of chill and rain after a taxing daytime session. When he later met the new Polish champion to congratulate him on taking over, he gave him a Drennan rod. In return, the Poles gave him some of their special nymphs and had a session describing some of their methods. At the end, John commented to their captain, Jerzy Kowalski, 'You are in a different league in grayling fishing.'

I had the same feeling when I practised for that first home river international on the Welsh Dee. The Poles and Czechs had dominated the World Championship there in 1990 with their big hauls of grayling. Whenever I was asked in the tackle shop at Llangollen or by my practice guide how many I had caught, confidence could have been undermined by the shaking of the head and the reiterated statement, 'The Polish team would have sixty or more in an afternoon.' Or: 'I fished with the Czechs, and they caught five times as many as me on tiny dry Cul de Canards and special nymphs.' Happily, as I reminded them,

the Poles and Czechs weren't participating in home internationals, and that was September when the grayling were
really on, while our match was July when they are less
forthcoming.

One matter I was able to clear up for them. My controller
for one session said, 'We were surprised to see the Poles wade
into the water at the start of a session and shuffle around
looking, but not fishing. Were they trying to herd the grayling
into a circle?' Probably not. What they were likely to be doing
was to disturb the bottom and hope some attractive food items
drifted down to whet the grayling's appetites.

All the old experts on grayling concentrated on dry or wet
fly fishing or on techniques such as long trotting with worms.
The 'dead drift' is in fact a very similar technique to long
trotting, but fishing it with weighted nymphs does not seem to
have been considered. Indeed, there is very little, if any,
mention of nymph fishing as a main grayling technique until
that nymph expert, Oliver Kite, wrote about it in his *Nymph
Fishing in Practice* in 1963. As late as 1965, Kite was also
making the point in the *Angler's Annual* that grayling were
underrated. He was writing of the fly fishing philosophy of the
French and included this comment: 'Note, too, that in France
the grayling is held in high esteem as a game fish, a view which
I, alone among English fly-fishing writers, seem to share; and
the grayling rivers of the Jura and elsewhere have an entomol-
ogy very different from the gentle and mostly grayling-free
chalkstreams of La Belle Normandie.' *Almost* alone would have
been a fairer comment had he read wider, but the general sense
was correct.

In that article, Kite also characterises the French as very
active anglers, which is how I have found them and which gives
me a fellow-feeling with French friends such as Bertrand Kron
and Robert Taillandier, though I am always more concerned
with the action, they with the perfection, as Kite noticed: 'The
French are perfectionists in some respects. They cast better
than we do and are altogether more interested in tournament
casting, having a keener appreciation of the advantages

improved casting ability confers on a fly fisher. They are always trying to improve their technique. In a quiet lull before the rise begins, they are less inclined to sit about listening to the birds, and admiring the flowers. I have noticed their best anglers constantly practise difficult casts into awkward places and, when the fish do at last move, they attack them speedily with confidence and finesse. It is a joy to watch.'

John's grayling experience has involved him in experimenting himself with a variety of methods apart from the standard dry fly approach. He has found it necessary to vary them greatly according to the type of river, the British ones he enjoys most being those that lend themselves to the greater variety of methods, as he explains:

'For me, the Traun below Gmunden is a classic grayling river with its clear water, strong flow, broad sweep, relatively even depth, and its grayling of up to 65cm or more. There the fish lie deep, getting some shelter from the powerful current, and are rarely going to expend the energy to battle up to the top unless there is a fly hatch to encourage them. That is why the method of drifting the fly down long distances at the pace of the current and almost bumping the firm bottom is so effective. It is a method we have called the "dead drift", and the main skill is in leaving enough slack as the weighted nymphs drop in so that the line does not immediately start pulling them sideways towards you, as it will if you let it get taut. That will look so unnatural that the grayling will ignore the nymphs. Equally, if you leave too much slack, your strike at distance will be ineffective, even if you spot the take in good time. So it needs much practice to master this technique both as regards "parachute" casting with weighted nymphs and swimming the nymphs down long distances at the pace and direction of the current only an inch or two above the bottom, rather than bumping lifelessly along it.

The Test is a classic trout chalkstream, rather than an ideal grayling river, despite the proliferation of grayling there. It is, of course, a delight to fish, and I have had several enjoyable days there when that was so kindly arranged for us in the winter to have a World Cup practice, or to fish there as part of the selection process. There are a number of sizeable grayling there of 2lb or more, as well as a mass of small ones. But very different techniques are needed in this narrow, relatively shallow, relatively slow-flowing river. In winter, there are occasional hatches still making it profitable to fish dry fly but, for most of that time, it is best to nymph.

The nature of the river makes it unsuited for the dead drift, and normal upstream nymphing pays off well. It is best, however, to have a reasonably weighted nymph on the point and a very lightly weighted Hare's Ear as the dropper and main catching fly. In the very shallow runs, where there are often shoals of small grayling, ordinary down-and-across is very effective, and I once watched Brian Thomas and Geoff Clarkson catching at will in one such run. In the slower, deeper parts, however, you need a variant, the controlled down-and-across. This means casting almost straight across, or even very slightly upstream, and giving the nymphs time to sink with the line still slack before working them across in the standard fashion. If you fish the ordinary down-and-across method in such water, the nymphs will skate round too high to be effective. Using a variety of these three methods you can have marvellous grayling fishing in the water below Stockbridge, where we were so privileged to be invited. Fishing there a couple of times with Chris Howitt, we were able to work a stretch from opposite sides, adapt to use any of the three methods depending on the type of water, enjoy the very special ambience of the Test, and have a bagful of good grayling as well in only a few hours' relaxed fishing.

My two favourite grayling rivers in Britain are the Welsh Dee and the Wharfe because of the variety of challenges they set and the delightful nature of the water and of the setting. There are areas of the Dee where the dead drift works well, and it also has many white-water runs where the big grayling lie and you can use the Polish "rolled nymph" method, fishing short near your own waders. The real trick in this type of fishing is being able to work out where the grayling will be and, even more difficult, to detect the take before it is too late. I can appreciate how years of practice make the best of the Poles and Czechs streets ahead of us in this type of fishing. Their beginners' "stupid Johnny" method of counting to three or four, then striking before recasting, is of some assistance at the start, but is unsatisfactory

10. *John about to release an Alaskan king . . .*

11. *. . . and a chum salmon.*

12. *Peter Cockwill shares the pleasure of another king caught . . .*

13. *. . . and released back into the Chosen river.*

14. *Daughter Sarah with a 5lb rainbow from Rooksbury Mill, near Andover.*

15. *In disguise, Tony uses Waltonian tackle on the bend of the Dove beside the famous Cotton/Walton Fishing Hut.*

16. *Tony plays a trout in Australia's Little Plains river . . .*

17. *. . . and a big rainbow in New Zealand's Rangitaiki river.*

18. *John and Brian Thomas with the top Tasmanian guide Noel Jetson and typical wild browns from Little Pine Lake.*

19. *The joy and freedom of remote Scottish lochs as Sarah and John land for some bank fishing on Sutherland's Urigill.*

20. *Tony with a salmon from the Ballynahinch fishery, developed by the cricketer K. S. Ranjitsinhji in his retirement.*

21. *John with the Champion of Champions cup in 1991.*

22. *The French forecast John's World Championship win after his success in the European Open at Lac du Chateau.*

Le fils du champion anglais qui – ce n'est un secret pour personne – est un futur champion.

23. *A selection of Tony's trophies dominated by the imposing 1984 World Championship cup.*

24. *John's sixth team win in European events, this time at Ardleigh in 1991 with John Pearn and Clive Perkins.*

and as often as not misses the exact timing anyway. If you are prepared to practise long enough you begin to develop a sixth sense so that you strike without knowing why. The slightest hesitation or deviation in the leader's progress may trigger a strike, or it may be just a gut reaction. But the essential is to strike instinctively and without hesitation. No matter if there is nothing there, or if it is a rock snagging you. If you react without thought and without delay you will often find it is one of these splendid large grayling which will give you a good fight in the fast water.

A weighted nymph on the point and a size 14 Snipe and Purple as dropper is a good cast for catching both trout and grayling in the Wharfe. The Wharfe is perhaps the best of all, particularly as grayling become more numerous in the lower reaches below Burnsall. The character of the river changes so frequently that you find pools where the dead drift works well, others where you can fish normal upstream or down-and-across. Indeed, I usually find that when I am fishing upstream I meet most of the other anglers fishing down! There are also pools where you may need to try all four methods before you are satisfied you have fished it out completely. It is a lovely river of delightful variety, with every kind of challenge and with good-sized grayling and trout. What more can an angler want?'

My own enjoyment of grayling fishing has extended to the Derbyshire Wye, one of the rare examples in England of a river where rainbows breed naturally. There I have caught grayling on such dry flies as a White Witch or a Blanchard's Abortion, and even on the Derbyshire Beetle with its two little red eyes. Sadly, however, on the Dove, grayling seemed few and far between on the Izaak Walton Hotel water, prolific though the trout were. So for an account of catching grayling higher up on that famous stretch close to the Temple, that fishing hut the bankrupt Cotton built for Walton and inscribed as sacred to anglers, I rely on an American, Robert Deindorfer. Writing *The Incompleat Angler*, he was guided in the master's footsteps by that formidable lady water-keeper, Dora Oliver, who was equally kind to me in showing me round this private property. We catch up with the pair below the Temple at the Pike Pool.

As I rubbed mucilin on to the fly, Miss Oliver came up the dirt
track along the river, stood watching for a few moments, broke
some bread into scraps to feed the blue tits – lovely birds, tiny,
all soft pastels, which have a hard time of it through the winter.
'Mind you take a grayling here in the Pike Pool,' she said,
moving along, the dog trailing behind.

On my third cast after her departure, I was on to another
fish in a heavy crease of water, a grayling, a good grayling,
given to quicksilver runs, its tell-tale dorsal fin opened like a
fan, using the current, drumming downriver, straining the 5x
leader, running hard, a marvelous fish, fourteen inches by the
tape, slim and perfect.

In *The Compleat Angler*, where seldom is heard a
discouraging word about any particular species, not even the
wretched ruffe, Walton reached an extravagant peak in
cataloguing the virtues of the grayling. 'For he will rise twenty
times at a fly, if you miss him, and yet rise again,' he observed,
which, if true, strikes me as a great virtue indeed, especially in
terms of the angler. 'He has been taken with a fly made of the
red feathers of the paroquet, a strange outlandish bird; and he
will rise at a fly not unlike a gnat, or a small moth, or, indeed,
at most flies that are not too big. He is a fish that lurks close all
winter, but is very pleasant and jolly after mid-April, and in
May, and in the hot months. He is of a very fine shape, his
flesh is white; his teeth, those little ones that he has, are in his
throat, yet he has so tender a mouth that he is oftener lost after
an angler has hooked him than any other fish. Though there be
many of these fishes in the delicate river Dove, and in Trent,
and some other small rivers, as that which runs by Salisbury,
yet he is not so general a fish as the trout, nor to me so good to
eat or to angle for.'

On the basis of my first and only grayling to date, those
were my sentiments exactly. After the stirring experience with
the fish in the Pike Pool I wandered on down the Dove at no
particular profit except for an eerie sense of detachment. All
round me the slack day lay peaceful and still. I lost a grayling
in a swirl of fast water, undoubtedly the fault of that tender
mouth, I gently remind myself, and while I never saw a fish so
avaricious, or fatuous, as to rise twenty times, another actually
did make four passes at a small nymph without ever quite
committing itself.

150

That expert angler and grayling *aficionado*, Reg Righyni, also recorded catching grayling lower down the Dove just above its junction with the Manifold. The Manifold is another remarkable stream which disappears underground for several miles before resurfacing in a beautiful stretch of trout and grayling water close to the Izaak Walton Hotel. In his book, *Grayling*, Righyni records that experience:

Shortly after the war 'Tommy' Tomkin suggested a couple of days on his beloved Dove and the Manifold, and soon I caught my first Derbyshire grayling. It came from the Dove, just a hundred yards or so above the point where it is joined by the Manifold. It was a splendid fish: a little deeper and relatively heavier than I had known before, but otherwise I noticed nothing unusual.

I fished my way down to the junction, and then went a few yards up the Manifold. In no time there was a grayling in the net and I was very impressed by its pinkish hue. As I unhooked it I was struck by what I thought was a most peculiar formation of the mouth and assumed that it was a freak. The upper jaw was very much overshot and protruded well below the lower jaw, giving it a beak-like appearance. An inch or so away, on the underside of the fish, there was a bulge that looked like a little crop. I thought I must make a point of showing this apparently odd creature to my friend.

Within a cast or two, another grayling was giving me a stubborn fight. On landing it, I was surprised to find that it was identical to the former one. In a short, very busy time, I had a nice basket of fish. All those from the Manifold were similar and I realised that this, to me peculiar, appearance must be a common feature in this water.

That evening in the hotel named after the most famous of all anglers, I sat in the room – then very little changed from its original form – where Izaak Walton in person used to relax and take his glass after his days on the Dove. The enchantment of the occasion was very, very real to me. I had the thought that in this present very different age, a quiet winter day on a grayling stream probably retains more of the atmosphere of Izaak Walton's times than any other kind of fishing.

That tender mouth is something of a myth, as is the comment that grayling will foolishly keep on rising. Both probably stem from the peculiar way grayling soar up from the bottom, sometimes missing the fly completely, sometimes lipping it and being lightly hooked. Taking nymphs deep or dry flies floated down on it the grayling is much surer in the take, more certain to be netted. What is not myth is that it gives great sport to the fly fisher.

Grayling can never aspire to trout's charisma, but they do have a charm of their own for those who delight in this type of fishing. The last words on them, summarising their attraction, must come from Righyni:

> I know from experience that no words of mine can make any impression on those who have turned their minds against the grayling. My mention of them is for another purpose. It is to show the younger angler and the novice the need to make their own judgement of grayling fishing from personal trials. To allow themselves to be denied this splendid sport purely on the grounds of the views of the disparagers could be most regrettable.
>
> Once the newcomer can reflect on a few hours of October dry-fly fishing, crammed non-stop with intriguing incidents, or the gyrating fight of a powerful December grayling at the end of a long, fine, float-fishing line, he can make his own inviolate decision. If this is to proceed with grayling fishing, he will find himself in good company, whether it be on North Country rivers or chalk streams.
>
> It is surely significant that some of the finest trout fishers are devotees of grayling fishing. And no matter how the individual enthusiast may make his personal comparison between fishing for grayling and other game fish, he is certain to agree that, on suitable days in autumn and winter, the grayling provides most contenting enjoyment.
>
> What more can be asked of a fish?

What indeed!

Lake Tactics

'Lochstyle' is used now to describe any fishing from drifting boats with small flies. When I started fishing more than sixty-five years ago, it meant a particular type of fishing which was then successful on Scottish lochs. The main features were to fish with sinking line and work the dropper to the surface as soon as practical, then bob it over the ripple using larger, bushier flies if the ripples turned to waves. 'Short lining' was the easiest method of controlling the flies and bobbing the dropper, and the explosive rises to the bobbed fly are, to me, still the most exciting of all. It is that old traditional method which John and I still employ on the prolific Altnacealgach lochs to which we so often return. With his longer casting and better control he is usually the more effective, but we both catch more than enough to keep us happy.

To call all reservoir fishing lochstyle is to underrate its complexity. Certainly, you have to be able to fish that method whether on a reservoir or the wild waters of Ireland or Scotland. But to be really expert on reservoirs you need to be equally good fishing Hi-D on the bottom or small dries on top, nymphs just below the surface, or flies in mid-water. You need also the instinct to guess where the fish will be on a huge expanse of water like Rutland, and at which depth they will be feeding at which times in the day.

In 1981, I watched England finish as runners-up and Dave Thomas win the highly professional World Coarse Fishing Championship at Stratford-on-Avon. When I asked Dave what differentiated the top-class match man from the thousands and thousands of average performers, he said that, apart from impeccable technique, it was the ability to keep making the right choices out of the fifty or so possibilities, and to keep adjusting to what the fish were doing. On reservoirs I have no pretensions to have mastered all those techniques, or be able to make those judgements. Since I rarely fish them now I tend to keep close to the genuine lochstyle method in which I was brought up, and sometimes it works well, often not. John does have the full range of techniques and makes intelligent use of them. For me, Hi-D is the dullest but technically the most difficult technique of any, but I can understand the pride and enjoyment in mastering it as John has done. For lake boat tactics he is the one to speak for us.

'There have been contrasting developments in the last few years in reservoir fishing. The more regular use of dry flies, pioneered at Grafham, has proved very effective, also at waters like Chew, Blagdon and Bewl. Equally, sunk line fishing has been greatly refined and improved, especially in competition, during a period when the hot summers have militated against floating line fishing by day. In my own case I had specialised in top of the water fishing but, in order to justify my place in the 1987 World Cup, I had to become much more expert in sunk line methods. Chris Ogborne also willingly made the change, though by instinct he was even more wedded than me to floating line, in which he was the acknowledged expert.

Apart from the excitement of that event, this has proved an immense benefit since I can now enjoy and practise every type of fishing on the drift. While I still enjoy top of the water most, and find it very entertaining, there is a real fascination in sunk line tactics. When the fish are up and you can see what is happening you know exactly how you ought to fish, and then presentation, control and discipline are vital. With sunk line fishing you start with no obvious pointers and using the clues from your own results and, from what you see happening around you and to your boat partner, you start to build up a picture of what the fish are doing down below. So it is like trying to solve a mystery story, but a "What is happening" rather than a "Whodunit?"

My normal drill, unless weather or water conditions, or fish
showing, or recent results, point to a particular type of fishing,
is to start with a Wetcel 2. You can fish reasonably at any
depth with this line, though it takes much longer to get down
deep than with a fast sink. When you find where the fish are
you may be able to go on using the Wetcel 2, making minor
adjustments of depth as the fish adapt. Alternatively, it may
become clear it is a Hi-D day, or a top of the water day, and a
complete change of line to floater, intermediate or fast sink is
essential for real success.

Bob Church was the first to develop Hi-D tactics and realise
how many could be caught on the lift and the hang. It was
therefore an exceptional experience for me to be in that 1987
team of top-class anglers and to learn so much in our many
months of practice together. Because we acted as a team from
the start all gave freely of their knowledge, and I was inevitably
more of a taker than a giver, since the others were so much
more experienced. All I could then do to return their help and
advice was to ensure I learnt from it and played my part in a
team win. What a relief and pleasure it was that I did make a
full contribution and, indeed, in relation to the river and
stillwater fishing in the individual event, I was able to
contribute helpful ideas of my own.

While I was indebted to all, and to Geoff Clarkson for
making us such a cohesive and hard-working team, especial
thanks had to go to Bob Church, who gave good advice at the
start, and Brian Leadbetter, who taught me so much. From
Bob, I learnt the Hi-D method well enough that it enabled
Brian and myself to run away from all opposition on the first
day on Rutland, outscoring most of the other forty-eight
anglers by an average of ten to one!

If you get among receptive fish with this method you will
catch faster than with any other technique provided you get
flies and technique precisely right. Most fish will be taken on
the initial pulls, or the lift and hang. The essential on that
World Cup day, as on many others, was to adjust as the fish
moved up or down a little in the water. When they came up, I
shortened the length of line I was casting. If I had continued to
throw out thirty yards of heavy fast sink line I would not only
have had the flies too deep for half my retrieve, but they would
also have started below the fish when it came to the vital lift

and hang. Trout are much more likely to follow up and take a
fly which has started from their own depth than if it flashes up
past them.

That day, there were a lot of stock fish about and these
responded well to coloured mini-lures. Such flies are usually
best anyway to *locate* fish as they do attract a lot of follows.
But often the fish follow them without taking, and I prefer a
cast to include a nymph, and a fly like a Hare's Ear, as well as a
mini-lure of the "traffic lights" coloured variety. The flash lure
may well attract fish, but the others will be the ones to catch
most consistently. You have to be aware, too, that there are
days when such mini-lures will actively scare off the trout, and
you are best not having one on your cast at all.

To help you build up the picture of what is happening
below, whatever sunk line you are using, you need always to
know the depth at which the flies are fishing. That is partly by
knowing the sink rate of the line and the flies you have on,
partly by counting it down consistently.

With Hi-D fishing, most of the takes come on the first
retrieve or the lift or the hang. On occasions, the fish will also
take on the drop, though that is very hard to detect if you are
not in contact with the fly at all. You have then the choice of
letting the flies fall absolutely free to your required depth or of
"feeling" them down. Unless you are expecting takes on the
drop, it is best to get the flies down as fast as you can to the
depth where you expect to catch. If you get takes on the drop,
it usually means that you are fishing too deep. Free fall also
makes exact positioning easier, since the pace of the drop will
remain uniform, if you count the line down letting it fall
totally unhindered each time.

There was a good example of that in one qualifier at Bewl.
My boat partner and I were keeping pace with each other, but
not doing particularly well, when we started to drift into a
small shallow bay. At once, I found fish right on the bottom.
Because of the speed of drift over this small area, it was
essential to cast long and get your flies right down as soon as
possible. Short though the drift was, I kept picking up one or
two each time while my partner remained fishless despite my
showing him my flies. He then began to imitate me exactly,
counting the flies down precisely as I was counting them. But,
as with so many, he still felt safest keeping some contact in case

there was a take on the drop. The result, of course, was that his flies were going down slower, and by imitating my count he was fishing several feet higher than me, and over the heads of trout, which continued to ignore his flies. Later, the wind got up too hard to drift such a short area, and we had to move. When he then had a couple of fish, I knew they were higher in the water in the new location, and adjusted accordingly to keep catching well enough to win that qualifier.

Since so many fish can be taken on the hang, in any form of sunk line fishing it is essential to fish that well. When you are confident in its effectiveness, it is surprising how long you can hold the flies there and still get a take. My own method is to lift until I can see the top dropper. For that is often the fly which they will follow up, and you can see the take, varying the strike according to the fish's reaction. Sometimes, they will snatch at the fly in a scary way. You can still catch them, but you need to strike fast. Some will take confidently, and then you hook them best by waiting for them to turn and head down again. The "hang" does not just mean you keep your fly hanging, it is also meant to imply that if the trout take like this they will hang themselves, provided you give them enough time.

Many anglers fish the hang by lifting their rod as high as they can. That is fine, but makes it difficult to strike home quick and hard enough with those nervy snatches at the fly. For that reason, I keep my rod as close to the water as I can and keep as firm contact with my line and cast as possible, so that the strike is quick and firm enough to hook the snatchers.

In those practice days with Brian Leadbetter, he also taught me another technique which he had worked out with his usual intelligence and common sense. Particularly for competition, you have to bear in mind the concept of "waste time". That applies not just to a lot of "false casting" which keeps your flies out of the water. Most days you will find the majority of fish taking in the first few pulls, or on the hang, or when the fly is bobbed or held close to the boat. If any of that is the case, and you cast twenty-five yards or more, you are wasting time each cast on twenty yards of unproductive retrieve. So Brian taught me to fish much shorter in those situations and hold the dropper in the surface film for several seconds at the end. With the hot summers diminishing the good days for top of the water fishing, that technique has not been so much in use by me of late, but a variant of it worked very well in the Bewl qualifier in 1991 as described in an earlier chapter in Part 1.

That method also had another practical lesson to impart to me. Brian had become very expert at it and heavily outscored me while I tried to master it. I was getting closer to him when we both had the national final to fish. Still not totally confident in it, but realising it was a good method, I decided to stick with it all day. My boat partner began to catch better than me with ordinary long casting and quick retrieving, but I kept on. In the end, I did quite well but did not qualify. Brian, as usual, did but even he changed method as the fish reaction changed. So the two lessons were, first, always be flexible and ready to adjust; and, second, learning new methods is for pleasure and practice, not for a day of decision. Then you need to stick to that which you know well and feel confident in doing.

It always pays to try something new if you are not catching, whether it is a different speed of retrieve, different flies, or fishing at different depths. You have to search for fish but, wherever you decide to fish, always believe there *are* fish below you, which *can* be caught if only you are competent enough. But, while you make these adjustments, always stick with a method in which you feel confident. No amount of instruction or reading will provide the little intuitive adjustments, which become instinctive second nature when you have had success with them.

As example of my own approach, I instance one Benson & Hedges match at Bewl. I had a disappointing start, missing several fish until I realised the reason. By then, I could see Jeremy Lucas catching large quantities and I knew the method he was using. Mimicking him might have appeared an obvious option, but he was fishing a method which was not one in which, personally, I had great confidence. So I merely rethought my tactics on the basis that there were clearly a lot of fish there to be caught and they must be responsive to one of my own preferred methods. As a result, I then caught very well on floating line with a team of nymphs in which I had faith. No hope of catching Jeremy, but I helped my team by finishing in the top of the following group. Had I tried to imitate Jeremy I would not have done nearly as well.

The same applies with dry fly fishing becoming more

popular on reservoirs. This is an enjoyable technique and, on some days, a very effective one, particularly for the experts in it like John Horsey. Nothing would seem to be easier than throwing out a cast with two or three dry flies and watching it drift around, provided you can retain intense concentration and good enough discipline to present the flies well and time the strike right. But what makes the real expert is his constant awareness, his peripheral vision, his accurate casting, and his ability to present flies well at distance. You will only be fishing dry, if you are sensible, because there are signs of the fish on top. So, apart from intense concentration on your flies over long periods, you have at the same time to observe moving fish over a wide area. That is not easy, and often for the top-class anglers it is a case of practice and intuition making perfect.

Having spotted a surface fish, those with the skill and the knack will instantly judge its speed and direction and cast accurately just ahead of its expected position when the flies land. On a still, heavy day, it pays to be able to cast a three-fly leader more than twenty-five yards. But, if you cannot do this in these conditions and get a proper turnover of the cast and a proper presentation of the flies, then best to limit yourself to that which you can do perfectly. While reasonably competent in the method I do not fish it often enough to match Horsey and the like. What I *do* know is that I have more success casting a little shorter and presenting the flies properly, rather than trying to emulate them and getting an extra few yards at the expense of the flies landing in an unpalatable jumble unlikely to attract a sensible trout.

Of course, for many, reservoir fishing also involves other techniques like bank fishing, or from anchored boats, or even the Northampton method of setting the rudder to drift bow first downwind while casting fast sink lines thirty yards either side, paying out twenty more yards then letting the flies sweep round in a huge curve like backing up for salmon. Those methods have not appealed to me as much as boat fishing on the drift, so I would not presume to give advice on any of them.

As regards anchoring, however, the Hi-D method remains an effective one and, if you find a shoal of fish and anchor there, it is a real killer. At the start of the 1991 season, Bob Church arranged his usual friendly competitive event for leading anglers on Rutland to raise money for what he then thought was a good cause, the Northampton Town Football Club. After the way it treated him and the other directors, the fund-raising was rapidly changed in the following year to helping the outstanding Czech World Cup team come over here to fish the second leg of the European Grand Slam! On this occasion, the April weather was at its worst with a near gale. That made fishing on the drift difficult and uncomfortable, but I found a bay on the Normanton side where there were fish close to the bank. Starting the drift tight against the shore, after drifting out twenty yards or so it was straight back and start again. Such short drifts might seem to waste a lot of time but, in fact, they were central to the "don't waste time" theory, since this kept us fishing only in the productive area. This worked so well that I was five or six fish ahead of anyone else when, because it was not that serious an event, the decision was taken to allow anchoring despite the weather beginning to ease.

The high wind had made it impossible to fish on the drift the small hole near the church, where it was known there was a concentration of fish. So the obvious move was to motor over there, though it was already crowding up when we arrived and we had to anchor on the outer edge. As this area had remained unfished, this gave an example of how deadly the Hi-D method can be in such circumstances, with others catching so well that my lead soon disappeared. On the edge of the small deep, and with the anchor dragging from time to time, I was lucky to finish in the top three. That taught me that the two first essentials in anchored fishing are first find your fish, then make sure your anchor and anchoring technique are good enough for any water! Fishing skills came a poor third on that occasion. But I have found that in locating fish and their depth, the Wetcel 2 technique is equally effective whether drifting or anchored.'

Jeremy Herrmann is the most consistently successful of the young fly fishermen and is an exceptionally good reservoir bank fisherman. Talking to him after he had taken his usual limit at Blagdon, while others struggled on a bright, calm day, it was obvious how he makes best use of his technical ability and his understanding of trout's behaviour patterns. As he comments, that does not mean going along with the advice to 'think like a trout', since that would put your intelligence rating as about one tenth of a chicken's IQ. It means using your human intelligence and common sense to the full in observing what happens and what methods and flies achieve results. It also means taking the trouble to develop a basic skill to the fullest extent you can. This is Jeremy's sensible concept.

'Long casting is a prime requisite for success from the bank. So, too, is the use of a very long leader (20ft-plus) coupled with being able to present the flies well. If I have not seen a lake before, and there are no obvious signs to guide my choice, I would always start with a Wetcel 2 and with a Taddie as point fly. A fly of that type is as good an attractor as any when you are fishing blind and without experience of a particular water. The Wetcel 2 allows you to search at different depths until you find where fish are feeding.

'Retrieve is the most important aspect of lure fishing yet, curiously, the most frequently ignored. So often, when fishing on the banks of reservoirs, fishermen can be seen mechanically casting as far as possible and stripping back at the same pace. As has been mentioned, trout are not intelligent (thank God), but their instinct warns them off taking flies which are constantly moving at the same speed in the same way, particularly when they have seen a couple of members of their shoal succumb. This is where the thinking angler scores for, by varying the retrieve, otherwise disinterested trout can be teased into taking the lure.

'There is a huge battery of retrieves available to the bank angler, but the most useful are the "figure of eight", the slow strip, the fast strip, and the FTA, which stands for "fool them about" and is a combination of all types of retrieve with the specific intention of annoying a following trout into taking the fly. Last, but certainly not least, comes the continuous hand-over-hand retrieve, which can be a very useful way of taking trout which have seen the stop-start styles. (Think how many times you have caught a fish reeling in.) Perhaps my philosophy concerning retrieve, which is incidentally far more important than fly pattern, could be summed up in one phrase: "Look what others are doing and then show the trout something different."

'Fish location is obviously a crucial factor in bank fishing. No matter how appetising your fly looks, if a trout can't see it he ain't going to take it! Careful observation of the wind's effect on the surface and how this will affect the underwater currents can lead the angler to hot spots. However, failing that, looking to see how other fishermen are faring is as good a way as any of locating fish.

'The other essential, of course, is to show the trout what they want on the day. You have to work that out from your own experience, or by trial and error, until you find the combination that is effective. There are times at Chew or Blagdon when the water is clear and the fish are obviously feeding on buzzers close in, when you can feel totally confident of catching well. In such circumstances, I use a weighted nymph as point and two buzzers as droppers. When the trout are really on the feed in the margins, this method can be lethal. There was one evening when everything looked ideal at Blagdon and my girlfriend Pam came with me. I cast that team of flies as far as I could then handed her the rod to work a slow retrieve. Incredibly, she hooked nine fish in eight casts. Only one got off and, as she was retrieving to cast again, another hooked on!

'If there is an obvious requirement to fish dry fly, I would use Drennan double strength, but my leader is usually the standard Drennan sub-surface green. You cannot better that. Even when you are hoping for big powerful fish, like some at Blagdon, I never go above 5lb and, on difficult days, I may have to come down to 4lb. It can make all the difference to go as fine as you dare.

'On some occasions, particularly on the concrete bowl-type of reservoir like Farmoor, Boobies are often the most effective flies. Obviously, when using them, the leader has to be short enough to let the fly float only just above the bottom (3 or 4ft is about right), but you still need to cast a long line. That is particularly important when there are a lot of bank anglers driving the trout away from the margins.

'It was at Farmoor that Micky Bewick gave me a useful tip about using Boobies. I had realised that the first essential is to ensure the fast sink line has really taken the fly to the bottom before beginning the retrieve. Better to wait a few extra seconds to be sure, as Boobies are effective when hovering above the bottom even before you retrieve. Micky's tip related to the retrieve itself. Trout take Boobies in an unusual way and normally give two or three plucks before taking. The slow retrieve is essential, but it is also desirable to do this in a specific way. If right-handed, angle the rod out to the right and retrieve very slowly, figure-of-eighting gently with the left hand. If you retrieve with the rod pointed straight at the fly, it may be that the trout feel a slight pull as they make their initial inspections. Instinct, not intelligence, then warns them off. With this type of retrieve there is no firm contact to frighten them, and they finally take hard.

'Long casting, long leaders, intelligent thought about fly patterns and the depth at which to fish them, appropriate retrieve, and choosing the right spot are the crucial elements in reservoir bank fishing.'

When fishing the genuine Scottish lochstyle technique with John and Sarah when they were young, we devised a method for rapid exploration of an unknown loch, which worked well. At the Overscaig Hotel on Loch Shin, a boat was provided, but no one could give any guidance about fishing this excellent trout loch. Shin is twenty miles long, quite wide and very deep in the middle. So where to fish it?

Obviously, you needed to keep in the shallower water close to shore. Equally obviously, the top end of the loch where burns came in was likely to be good, particularly close to spawning time, or when the burns were high with their currents going far out into the loch. But that left many miles of bankside areas, some good, some barren. How to discover which of those to fish? What we did was to row round close to shore with Sarah trolling one rod, myself rowing and watching another troll rod, and John side-casting, often a very effective method where true lochstyle tactics work. Once we struck fish we stopped and drifted the area, fishing lochstyle. Soon the pattern of the loch around the hotel came clear. Where the shore was all rocky, the fishing was poor; where it was peaty, it was better; where there were small bays with marshy banks and the occasional rock in the water, it was best of all, with one exception. On the far bank was a power station, the turbines of which sucked in, churned up, and returned to the lake all manner of small fish and other aquatic creatures. So that was a rich feed area for trout, and drifting there brought us some of our biggest fish, but there was one snag. Without warning, the water was sometimes pumped out in a huge cascade straight into the best fishing area. We also got the impression that the operators enjoyed a tempting target, so even on a hot day you needed to take your thickest rainwear to fish round the power station without being drenched to the skin.

In a clever combination of work and pleasure, John took the unique features of Hampshire stillwaters as the subject for his dissertation as part of his geography degree at Southampton University. That included researching whether the large trout Sam Holland and Roy Ward were producing at Avington Lakes were indeed the result of selective breeding and selected environment, rather than overstuffing them with food as detractors incorrectly claimed. But the unique features of most of these fisheries, which particularly appeal to John, are their water clarity and small size, both of which encourage spot fishing.

Indeed, the only type of fishing in these waters which gives him real pleasure is spotting and stalking individual fish. That again is a contrast between us, as I am equally happy to fish 'blind'. I enjoy the thrill of the sudden unexpected take by a heavy fish and tend to keep on the move searching for guessed hot spots, rather than trying to spot before casting. We don't agree either on another aspect. Unless fish are showing on the top, or it is a day for small nymphs near the surface, or fishing a Daddy Longlegs on the top, or just sub-surface, I always use an intermediate to avoid surface wake. John prefers a floating line as standard because of the better control it gives him. But there are always more ways than two of catching fish, and it is both more productive and pleasanter to keep to the method you enjoy and in which you have confidence.

Anyway, the contrast mattered little when we both fished in the first small stillwater championship of Great Britain at Dever Springs. John was runner-up behind the inevitable Peter Cockwill, while I was only one fish behind him in third place. A professional video of the event credited me with an embarrassingly arrogant-sounding remark as my final fish of 70cm (around 14lb) was being measured before release: 'You saw what a skilful piece of fishing that was,' followed by an unintelligible babble of comment in the background, needed putting in context. Happy that I had done well enough to satisfy myself, I had been relaxed enough to turn round and chat with my controller and with Sarah, who had come down to watch. During the conversation, I had left my fly lying on the bottom and when I lifted up to cast again I hooked the large fish. That resulted in much caustic comment from behind, while I was maintaining that I had eyes in the back of my head and had intentionally ambushed the fish. That led to my final remark and a renewed volley from behind! Ambushing is, however, a tactic that often works well for spot fishers, like John. Work out the cruising path of the trout, leave the fly lying on its route, then lift it off in front of its nose. That is often a successful way of catching difficult trout.

Even if you cast blind most of the time you always need to be watching for fish you can see, which may often be almost under your feet, and able quickly to adapt to fishing for them. On big trout lakes like Avington or Dever, that means using weighted flies, or nymphs when the fish are not feeding on top. The seen fish in such clear water will be heavier and deeper than they look, and it is necessary to cast accurately and for the fly to drop quickly to their level.

Fishing blind, it usually pays to start with a sizeable fly or nymph and a quickish retrieve to interest the recently stocked fish. Nor does it matter then if the fly makes a bit of a splash on entering; indeed, it is all the more likely to attract them. But such stocked fisheries are a mixture of relatively easy fish early on and difficult ones later, which have seen it all. It is then that John's small Corixas, skilfully worked, are more likely to succeed. On that same video, John made the point that his success that day was due to fishing relatively large and fast at the start, then rapidly fining down to something very small.

As regards flies for the larger ones, all that is needed is a selection of Cockwill-type Taddies or Jeanette Taylor's Tinheads, or Cat's Whiskers, or Mini Nobblers. For nymphs, Damselfly, Mayfly, Pheasant Tails and Montanas, backed by small Corixas, are adequate for anyone. You *can* catch on a whole variety. On such stillwaters, I have taken fish on all types and sizes of fly, but the above are all you really need, though Daddy Longlegs, particularly fished just sub-surface, and leaving a wake, can be very effective, as can Vivas. For colours, I prefer black, followed by orange, yellow, olive and white. If nothing is happening, a frequent change of colour or size will often be rewarding.

While there are good reasons for the move to standardise certain aspects of well-ordered stocked fisheries, all the angler needs to know is what each has to offer. The argument about stocking big or small is equally sterile, as this should be a matter of choice. My own personal preference is for a relatively small average with a fair chance of an occasional big fish and a very reasonable charge. But I enjoy also the large fish still-waters, when I can afford an occasional day at Dever or wherever. Because of the vast proportional increase in cost in producing large trout, such fisheries are bound to be expensive. But the economics will prove whether there are enough who enjoy and can afford that type of fishing, rather than any moral arguments. The average fisherman is unwise to get completely hooked on big fish as it can be an expensive taste!

I also prefer, as a personal choice, the less organised and

wilder fisheries like Avington. It was amusing for me to see someone writing in the fishing press to complain because he had had to open two gates there to get to the lakes. Remembering I enjoyed walking four miles to get to a burn when aged 4 I wondered how precious the modern stillwater fisherman was becoming! My host in New Zealand had commented that, with so much fishing, most New Zealanders would not go more than fifty yards from a road to their fishing and they would probably be legless in the next generation. I trust our stillwaters won't go too far in encouraging a similar breed here!

As regards fishery records, it is true that Walton wrote of all anglers as 'very honest men', but they can be a bit fanciful at times. So don't give too much credence to numbers and flies in such records and follow your own judgement. I recall that inveterate leg-puller, Alan Pearson, catching four 'doubles' on a Midlands fishery using an assortment of large highly-coloured flies, which he entered in the book as 'Corixas'. The next thirty fish in the register were entered as caught on Corixas, presumably because everyone tried slavishly to follow the big trout man, and Corixas were the only flies on offer to the fish. Those anglers were as gullible as the ones who bought J. R. Hartley's book *Fly Fishing* in the belief there really had been such a book and that nice 85-year-old actor, Norman Lumsden, really was J. R. Hartley. As a result, a book rapidly cobbled together to take advantage of the Yellow Pages advert on TV became a best-seller. Well, if you believe television advertisements or fishery records you are certain to get the occasional surprise.

Instinct or experience can give the edge to the good fisherman. As with golf or cricket, or any sport, that is the vital X factor you will never learn from a book. Either you have the instinct or you don't. As for experience, the practical sort gained with other good anglers is the best, but you have to experiment all the time yourself until you are confident in your methods.

The retrieve can be vital as Jeremy Herrmann commented. You need to master variants for alternative use, but settle also on one basic method for standard practice until change becomes desirable. Before the retrieve you have to remember also that, in small stillwaters, particularly when nymph fishing, a high percentage of fish may be taken on the drop as the fly sinks before the first pull. Many anglers rise fish 'on the drop' without even knowing it, and you need to be as alert then as at the end when lifting slowly up before casting, which often induces a take. Sometimes the fish respond to a very slow retrieve, sometimes to a fast one. My own standard retrieve for sunk flies is a series of short jerky pulls which impart life to the fly. Again a contrast: John prefers a longer, steadier pull. Whichever suits you best, it is desirable to develop a natural rhythm as the basic retrieve, and be able to try many variants where necessary. In that video of the first stillwater championship, Moc Morgan comments, 'You get into a lifetime habit of a particular rhythmic retrieve and, as far as I am concerned, if on any one day the fish don't like it . . . too bad!' On that occasion, the trout did not appreciate his retrieve, even longer than John's. In the next such event, however, they did to the degree that we battled it out for second place, which went marginally to me. Certainly, I also adhere to Moc's philosophy of having confidence in your natural retrieve method and rhythm and only varying the speed and style when it isn't working.

When fishing sunk line blind I always watch the slight kinks in it, rather than the fly area. When these straighten, I strike at once, wishing I had remembered to do it sideways rather than my instinctive straight up. In that case, you strike before you feel anything. If, however, the first indication is a slight tug, *don't* strike. Rainbows will often nip the fly two or three times before taking solid hold. If you strike, the chance is gone. If you continue a natural retrieve and tighten as all goes solid you will hook the fish firmly. When you can see a fish following and not taking, speeding up or stopping the fly are two alternatives which can induce a take. If you see a rainbow doing an unusual dervish-dance all around your fly, be patient. He is certain to take, but only when his antics are over.

For me, stillwater fishing is relatively simple if you work

hard, have good basic technique and make sensible decisions about flies and depth at which to fish. As regards working hard, it is true that rainbows keep on the move most of the time and may come to you if you stay in one place. But I find that dull when nothing is happening and, anyway, stocked fish tend to congregate and circle in limited areas. So I always prefer to keep moving until I find such a hot spot. Having found it, a couple is the most I will normally take there, both for my own interest and to leave others the opportunity of trying it. To me, there is nothing more boring than staying in one place for hours on end, and nothing more tiresome than seeing individuals hog one spot all the time. But, again, it's a question of personal preference and personal choice.

John's preferences are different from mine in many aspects of stillwater fishing, but not in his enjoyment of it. These are his thoughts on fishing small stillwaters:

'A great help to my reservoir and lake results has been fishing on small clear stillwaters. Stalking individual trout in these is a delightful and entertaining form of fishing, and also one which teaches you a lot about trout behaviour. Some reservoir anglers scoff at such fishing saying it is easy to catch stocked fish in such conditions and, certainly, there are usually some easy fish, but those that aren't caught in the first couple of days have had as much fishing pressure and seen as many artificial flies as most Rutland stockies experience in a couple of months or wild browns in the Altnacealgach lochs in a couple of years.

There is nowhere for the fish to lose themselves as in the large expanse of Rutland, or even a reservoir of the Bewl or Grafham size, let alone huge natural loughs or lochs such as Corrib or Shin. So when you stalk individual fish that have been resident a few days in such waters you get a clear picture of how they react to various types of fly, what frightens them, and what turns them on, how they feed and how they behave. Storing that away in your mind can often be a great help when fishing sunk line blind in a reservoir.

You can never, of course, work out with certainty how any fish will react all the time, as their sometimes irrational behaviour is something which gives all fishermen hope all the

time. At Dever Springs trout fishery, I once spent over an hour
trying to coax an 8lb brown of beautiful colour and condition
to take any of a variety of flies cunningly and differently
worked in front of its nose. Having given it up, and seen
several try it with equal lack of success, I decided to have a
couple more casts as I was walking up to join my father for
lunch. Hardly had a nymph I had delicately presented to it
several times before hit the water, than it surged in as if it had
been waiting for it all its life. It was a beautiful fish indeed; but
what triggered that reaction after hours of indifference?

Spot fishing in pairs can be another enjoyable pastime on
such lakes. You can, for instance, find that a big fish's cruising
circle takes it into a dark corner overhung with bushes where it
is impossible for the angler to keep sight or spot the take. If
one spots for the other and directs the cast and tells when the
fish mouths the fly, a combined effort can often bring success.
Chris Howitt and I have often helped each other in this way
and, on one occasion at Rockbourne, Chris offered to show
my father how it worked, having spotted a large fish cruising
in a corner shielded from any caster's view. Dad did as
instructed and struck with a will when Chris said, "Now." A
9lb rainbow took off at speed stripping his line down to the
backing and only turned when he ran out of water at the far
end of the small lake. It was a long slow job working him back
but, long before the fish was netted, it was clear he was being
inched back tail first. Chris swore that the fly was in the mouth
when he called for the strike and that the fish was initially
properly hooked, only for the hook later to be shaken out,
then catch the tail. That sounded a fishy tale to me, but we had
both enjoyed the sight of father hemmed in by trees and
desperately trying to control the runaway rainbow.

Stalking fish in *small* stillwaters requires patience and good
vision. It also requires accurate casting and weighted flies
which will quickly reach the cruising depth of the fish. The one
technique you rarely need is long casting. But you do have to
remain aware always of fish hugging the bank while you are
looking further out, and be able to switch rapidly from casting
for those to dibbling for the one at your feet before it cruises
away. As you work at it, experience will also tell you when a
fish looks to be in feeding mood, even if not actively feeding,

and when even a disinterested fish may be teased or ambushed into taking your fly. Altogether, such stillwater fishing can be an absorbing challenge with the added pleasure of watching your fish.'

Tackle and Flies

John Ketley was my team captain when first I fished for England on Chew Valley Lake. We fished together on practice day, and his one instruction was to use Maxima nylon and have a cast one and a half times my rod length . . . 'if you are a proper fisherman'. Concentrating on the cast showed he had his tackle priorities right. As F. M. Halford pointed out, the leader is both the cheapest and most important part of your tackle.

When Lee Trevino holds golf seminars he is apt to ask his pupils, 'What is the most important aspect of the golf shot?' 'The backswing,' says one bright student. So Trevino whirls the club round his head and knocks the ball into the middle distance. 'The stance,' says another. So Trevino stands with his feet together and knocks the ball two hundred and fifty yards down the middle of the fairway. Finally he says, 'What really matters is how the club head is travelling an inch before and an inch after you hit the ball.'

It's the same with fishing; the key thing is how you present the fly to the fish, and how that last few inches of leader works it, how it looks to the trout, and how it takes the strain. Many different makes of leader have special qualities, but none can ever meet all you may require on strength-to-thickness ratio, pliability, or rigidity for droppers, or retention of strength when knotted. John introduced me later to Drennan sub-surface olive, similar to Maxima, but a colour less alarming for trout. Double strength Drennan followed as my ideal, particularly if you are using a single fly.

The other thing John Ketley said to me was, 'If you fish for

England once, that may be luck in a couple of qualifiers; if you fish twice, that may be fortunate coincidence; if you qualify three times you can consider yourself an England-standard fisherman.'

In an eight-year period, John has won a World Championship and made a major contribution to two World Cup-winning teams; he has been a member of no less than nine *winning* England teams at World and European and home international levels; he has won the national final and been runner-up; he has won the champion-of-champions match, and been three times runner-up, twice third, in French or Belgian Opens, and the first Englishman to qualify for both the boat and river international in the same year as well as being a runner-up in the small fisheries championship. Statistically, that rules out luck and points to more all-round technical ability than I could ever achieve. So hints on tackle and flies come best from John.

'There is much literature giving good technical detail on tackle, and it would be unrewarding and presumptuous of me to analyse tackle in detail and try to cover everything from salmon fishing to upstream dry fly. All I can usefully do is to describe what has worked well for me in the types of fishing in which I have had success, and some of the reasons for my choice.

Confidence is a key requirement for success in fishing. Unless you are comfortable with your tackle and your technique, you enjoy it less and do not fish as well as you might. So, when you have been fishing with tackle in which you have faith, it is usually best to stick with it rather than be forever chopping and changing in pursuit of some minor advantage, which may anyway not be as good as advertised. Once in a while, there are changes so dramatic that you have to become involved with them. The leader, for instance, is the most critical item in your tackle, and it would have been silly for father not to change from gut to nylon, or me not to make use of double strength nylon, which so greatly increases the strength-to-thickness ratio, particularly when fishing using single flies.

Once you start knotting double strength, that strength can
rapidly diminish. So you need to take special care in tying
dropper knots. To avoid breaks, I always wet the knots in my
mouth before tightening. Drennan double strength olive green
will then meet every reasonable requirement; provided, that is,
that you don't go down too fine at those knots. It is very rare
with double strength that you need to go below 5lb but my
normal cast is 7lb to the top dropper knot, then 6lb to the next
with 5lb for the final tippet, unless conditions make it
necessary to go even finer for the tippet. If you go finer at the
dropper knots, the flies won't stand out properly. The other
proviso is that you never mix double strength with standard
when tying on tippets. They have different stretch qualities,
and this puts avoidable stress on the knots.

Maxima used to be my first choice, because it had the right
elasticity and did not kink if you fished it properly. But the
colour was unsatisfactory as it stood out starkly under water.
That led to my changing, like most of the World Cup team, to
Drennan sub-surface olive, which otherwise had similar
characteristics. For double strength, Drennan is also my
favoured brand as it has all the properties you can reasonably
require. Others may be as good, but Drennan meets my needs,
so there is no point my changing.

Braided leaders are a recent development which some favour,
particularly in relation to the fast sink variety. Braided leaders
have for some time provided greater flexibility in river fishing,
though I have rarely found the need to use them except
occasionally, when desirable, to aid in fishing weighted
nymphs for trout or grayling lying on the bottom in deep
pools or fast runs. However, with a relaxation of rules in many
stillwater competitions now permitting them, there will no
doubt be interesting developments there too, as some
experienced anglers experiment to find if braided leaders can
prove more effective in some instances on stillwaters. What is
already clear to me is that such leaders must be used in
conjunction with non-stretch lines.

For the flies, gink is the best floatant provided you smear it
first between thumb and forefinger and don't put it on in
blobs. It is important, too, to have a fuller's earth or mud
compound to aid sinking the leader. This is especially
important when using double strength, as such leaders have a

shine which this tones down. Colour is of no real relevance to line or leader when dry fly fishing as, whatever the colour, it will look black from below when lying on the surface. There is an argument *against* using white lines on the basis that, on a bright day, they flash in the sunlight, and the flash may frighten the trout even before the line lands. Equally, there is a good argument *for* using white in late evening when it can help you know where your fly is as it grows dark, and you need to see the line as a pointer. Sub-surface colour can matter more, with green or brown both safe colours.

It does not pay to skimp on the cheapest item of equipment, but nor is it wise to skimp on the most expensive – and equally important – item, the rod. It pays to ensure you get full value, and that you have one which will give you control and distance without excessive effort. You need a rod powerful enough to give you distance without many time-wasting false casts, and light enough not to strain you on a long day's fishing. For floating line fishing from boats, I used to prefer an 11ft rod with a through action, which gave me distance and control and enabled me to work the dropper better. In one competition, however, the early takes on my intermediate line were nervous snatches, all of which I missed. I realised that that was because the soft action meant that reaction after the strike was very slow to transmit to the fly and, by the time the hook would have tightened into the trout, it was long gone. So I switched that day to using a stiffer action rod, which I had for Hi-D fishing.

One of the advantages of spot fishing on small stillwaters is that you learn about fish's actions and about tackle reactions as well. I have on occasions *seen* trout take the fly and move several feet sideways before I have *felt* anything, even though I was retrieving apparently in touch with the fly and with the rod pointing straight at the fish. So, unless there is a good take, you have no chance of catching the snatchers when fishing blind with slow-reaction rods. As a result, I now use either Loomis or Orvis 10ft rods, which are so powerful and so light they do as well for throwing heavy fast sink lines, or for more delicate top of the water fishing. And they are firm enough for quick transfer of the strike to movement of the hook. You do not want to waste money, but though they are expensive these rods are, for me, cheap at the price as they give me total confidence, maximum flexibility, and comfort over endless hours of fishing. In addition, they are all-purpose rods, saving me the need for two separate rods for sunk line and top of the water fishing.

The essential with lines is that you use the right balance for your type of rod and consider first what you want to achieve. If it is distance, then weight forward and the heaviest in your rod's range is likely to suit best. If it is to land lightly and cause the least disturbance on the water, as in upstream dry fly, then it is best to have the lightest in your rod's range and a double taper. Technical development has already been so good that there is little difference between good standard makes, and it is a case for personal preference, and not letting yourself be deceived by the hype of advertising for some new product. Indeed, when I was first given some of the heavily advertised Airflo lines I passed them straight on as not being as good as those I already had. Perhaps that reaction, which I knew was copied by a number of competent anglers at the time, helped in a rethink, because Airflo has since improved until it is now certainly among the best. With lines and leaders, don't worry too much about minor changes trumpeted abroad, and stick with those in which you have faith and on which you have caught well. Never forget that Walton and Cotton had no trouble catching on horsehair lines with the leader merely a reduction to one or two unreliable horsehairs, with no reel and with only a dozen or so different fly patterns. The trout are not all that much harder to catch now and their reactions have not changed significantly. By comparison, all modern tackle is good and it is how you use it which matters most. My father is always quoting the soccer tactical maxim which brought success to Spurs in their glory days: "Make it simple, make it quick." Part of that applies to fishing tackle. Don't get over-complicated. But, with tackle, don't be quick to change, unless there is some compelling reason to do so.

Reels are another main item of tackle for which there is really no need to agonise over minor differences or follow new fads. Expensive reels can be things of beauty and collectors' items. But, for practical fishing, all you require is a reel capable of holding the maximum amount of line and backing you need, which runs freely, and which has an adequate drag mechanism if you are going to require it. Particularly in bank fishing, I prefer playing fish by hand rather than off the reel, as it helps you to play them harder and gives you a better sense of touch, once you have become experienced with it. The one hazard to avoid when bank fishing for large trout is standing on the line retrieved on to the ground. I did that once with the first double I hooked at Aveley Lakes, and that meant a break instead of a fine fish netted. For salmon fishing, the chapter on Alaska (page 3ff) has already outlined my preferences there. For lake trout fishing, the reels I prefer are Bob Church Lineshoots or the Leeda LC range while, for general fishing, System Two reels are quite adequate. The Bob Church reels incorporate one highly desirable feature for sunk lines, that of a wide drum which avoids those tight curls in the line which narrow reels cause.

For lake fishing, I always take out six reels so that I have a full range of lines, which I stretch before starting. On each line I have a loop to facilitate changing reels. Using a long leader I reel this up to the dropper knot so that I can tie the cast straight on to the new line with the cast still threaded through the rings. This allows me to be fishing again in a minute or less and takes all the worry out of any decision to change. Trout often come up to the top for a short period, half an hour or less, which gives problems to those who take three or four minutes to change. First they delay the decision because of the hassle involved, then they waste further time in the change itself so that a splendid opportunity is largely squandered. If you are making the change from Hi-D to floater, for instance, it may be that your cast is now no longer an ideal length. But it is still best to make the change quickly and give your existing leader and flies a try until the results, or lack of them, force a change there too.

Most expert comment is about the need to balance rod, line, and leader. But that omits the most important item of all, yourself. For instance, in my own case I have a relatively weak wrist and forearm, so I need a light powerful rod which will do most of the work for me. If you are as strong in the upper body and forearm as Brian Leadbetter or Chris Howitt then you can manage a longer rod of a different type. Basically, I tend to strike quietly and merely tighten into fish. So I can use a stiff rod, a non-stretch Airflo line, and double strength leader. But, if you are an instinctive quick, hard striker, that set-up would be a disaster and invite a series of breaks. You can, of course, try to change your strike style but, if instinct and habit have trained you one way, change can be very difficult. In my case, I have to concentrate intensely to get the hard strike needed for Alaskan salmon or some "snatchers" on the hang. John Pearn, another successful lake angler with whom I have been teamed in European competition, had the reverse problem. With sunk line, his hair-trigger strike at the faintest twitch of the line is exceptionally effective, but it was a handicap fishing nymphs on a floater, so he has had to discipline himself in many a practice to improve to his present standard.

The first essential, then, in getting a proper balance of your equipment is an honest appraisal of yourself as an angler, your physical and mental attributes or lack of them, your eyesight, your striking instinct, and so on. Only then can a good tackle dealer help you find the ideal balance for yourself, and assess the total equation involved from hand to fly. That rarely seems to be pointed out in fishing literature, and I have seen competent anglers go backwards through trying to follow what some expert has written about tackle or technique which suits *him*. It rarely pays to mirror or mimic others without working out first whether that style or tackle suits someone of your build and characteristics. I was very lucky to be allowed to fish with practical experts from an early age. Brian Thomas taught me a lot early on, and then Bob Church and Brian Leadbetter took me in hand. That allowed me to cut many corners and accelerate my learning curve, but I would never have reached their standards had I not always tried to understand the rationale behind what they did, and then adapt and adjust to suit myself. In other sports, it is the same. The strongly built, powerful-driving Graham Gooch adds force to his shots with his heavyweight bat. If a small, quick-footed hooker, cutter and glider like my father had tried to wield that massive club, it would have made him late in his timing and undermined his effectiveness. Similarly, Nick Faldo and Ian Woosnam are among the top golfers in the world. Yet, if either tried to ape the other in his swing or choice of club for a particular shot, then their physical differences would merely ensure that it reduced his effectiveness.

Flies again are something in which the proliferation of patterns and developments can catch the fisherman, rather than the fish. That is another reason why it is best to learn to tie your own to good standard. I had been lazy about this until Brian Leadbetter showed me the way in preparation for the 1987 World Championship. He went through the many reasons why it was essential to be a good fly dresser if you wanted to be a self-sufficient all-round angler. Then he quoted to me his own learning experience. Spending time in hospital he had taught himself fly tying starting with Muddlers, and found increasing enjoyment as he became more proficient. Tying Black & Peacock Spiders had been the simple start for me, with Ray Cannon showing me the method. Like Brian, I have found fly tying an enjoyment in itself as well as an invaluable adjunct to my fishing ability.

It is particularly helpful to be able to tie up patterns quickly if you are fishing a strange water and find you lack those which the locals have found effective. Even more productive and more satisfying can be developing variants of your own. Apart from such variants, most of your fishing needs can be met by a fairly small range of flies without becoming bemused by the thousands of patterns on offer. In tying your own, hooks are of course a vital component. So far as I am concerned, it is best by far to use chemically sharpened hooks rather than machined ones. Charles Jardine was the first to point out the difference to me, showing under a powerful microscope that the machined ones are blunt by comparison. So I concentrate on the Kamasan range. If I was confined to one hook I would use their B175, which combines thinnish wire with a strong bend unlikely to straighten.

You may need different types for, say, fishing emergers dry. B405 is a good hook for this. However, for very lightly dressed flies, even gink cannot make them float unless they have a very light hook. So there are times when you need B400, but since this is likely to straighten, if you play a fish hard you have to adjust to giving the fish his head and playing him longer. Again, you need to know the exact qualities of what you are using and whether you have to make any adjustment to your natural style because of them.'

A great pleasure for me was that John and I used very similar flies in winning our World Championships, with the traditionals figuring largely; we both used a Bibio, while my second fly was a Black Pennell. The way the traditional and the modern can be effectively mixed was clear in John's other successful fly, the variant of a JK All-rounder and a Fiery Brown. There is always the publicity pressure to try something new, and some variants and some relatively new patterns are indeed highly effective. Yet never forget that the old favourites have caught well in the past and will go on catching for centuries to come. If I had to choose one wet fly to cover every type of fishing from river salmon to lake trout, the Black Pennell would be my first choice and black my first-choice colour. For a pattern which would be as good dry, the Greenwell's Glory is hard to beat. So don't accept the fallacy in relation to flies that 'new' is always 'better'.

PART 4

World Championships

Success in Spain

Making it into the *Guinness Book of Records* as the only father and son to win the same World Championship was more of a surprise in my case than in John's. By coincidence, he was practising and fishing in his first home international on Lough Conn on the same two days that I fished the 1984 championship on the Tormes River near Salamanca in Spain. While I was waiting for the final dinner there, John telephoned me in great excitement, and our conversation went roughly like this:

'How did you get on, John?'

'I came third out of the fifty-six, and our Confederation England team won in Ireland for the first time. I don't believe you ever did as well as that.'

'Son, you are talking to the world champion.'

'Pull the other one!'

While that was said jokingly it echoed my own astonishment at that result, which had been heightened rather than lessened by the fact that, earlier that May, I had won the first official French European Open at the Lac du Château. It did not seem possible that I could be that lucky twice.

The definitive assessment came four years later in a television interview and fishing sequence with the two of us after John had won his championship in Tasmania. He was asked what made me a world champion. There was a long pause while he considered that extraordinary event before he delivered his usual well-considered judgement: 'Well, of course, technically Dad is no great shakes, but he's very experienced and tremendously enthusiastic.'

There was a case for telling him to be more economical with the truth, but I was delighted with that exact summary! The important thing in my fishing is the enjoyment and enthusiasm, and the best result of my occasional competitions is that they have helped to keep that as fresh at seventy as at seven.

John's win in Tasmania was of a much higher order. Not only were double the number of countries involved, with sixteen participants, but the standard of the teams was much higher. Nor was his win a surprise to anyone who had fished with him. He, too, had just had outstanding success in the French and Belgian Opens, being in a winning team there as so often with the two Brians, Leadbetter and Thomas. *Plaisirs de la Pêche*, one of the many excellent French fishing magazines, had a detailed account of the Lac du Château event and prophetically captioned a picture of John as 'the son of a world champion and, who can doubt it, about to be world champion himself.'

The England team was greatly helped by being allotted Tasmania's two outstanding guides, Noel and Lois Jetson, to advise them in their week of practice. Before the championship began, Noel told me he was totally confident on what he had seen that England would win the team event and John the individual. As usual, he proved right though, as John was the first to say, such was the combined team performance in searching out the right methods and flies that individual placings owed most to the team's and the Jetsons' efforts plus something to the draw. But he was a true champion in the sense that, given the chance, he was good enough to take it.

My own involvement with these championships started close to their beginning. In 1981, I was finishing a book on competition fly fishing when I heard from the Northern Irish Tourist Board that something called a World Fly Fishing Championship had started that year. It had been held under the auspices of the freshwater division of the world body, the Confédération Internationale de la Pêche Sportive (CIPS). Poland originally offered to host it, but the political ructions there over Solidarity meant a late transfer to Lake Echternacht in Luxemburg. CIPS only accepts one organisation per country, so any entry had to be via the National Federation of Anglers, who were England's representative on the freshwater division, and by then had been involved in such world championships for some twenty years.

To include in my book something sensible about these championships I asked England's competitive body, the Confederation of English Fly Fishers, whether they would be entering a team and was told they were not interested in a new championship run by foreigners when, in England, we had fifty years' experience of fly fishing internationals. So I then asked Stan Smith, the NFA's international events manager, how English fly fishermen could ever enter a team when the only body empowered to do so only represented coarse fishermen.

'It's impossible. Forget it,' Stan told me. Then, just five weeks before the second World Championship was due to start in Spain in 1982, he telephoned me unexpectedly and said, 'I have a solution. The NFA will appoint you to take a team provided it does not cost us anything and provided you get backing from your governing body, the Salmon and Trout Association.'

The chairman of that association, David Swatland, promptly endorsed the project and agreed that he would come as non-playing captain with their field secretary, John Inglis, as a member of the team. To him I added three well-known anglers in Bob Church, Brian Thomas and Alan Pearson, who were happy to give it a try and bear the expenses involved.

As I had forecast to Stan Smith, once an England team appeared in the event and the championships had a successful start, everyone suddenly wanted to be involved. It had always been my aim to get the proper authorities to take an interest and immediately hand over to them and, not surprisingly, the Confederation officials now demanded to take it over. At a meeting with the Salmon and Trout Association, it was agreed that the Confederation should nominate an England team of four, but that the Association should organise the event and arrange any funding over and above what the participants paid. They were also to provide the non-playing captain. The Confederation officials then telephoned me to say that, had there been a fifth place, they would have invited me to fish again as I had been responsible for getting England involved, but there were four others they *had* to invite. Since no one had invited me to the meeting, though I was the only one who knew the organisational details of these championships, they were unaware that teams *were* five, nor four. So, tongue in cheek, I thanked them for having me as reserve and, a few days later, telephoned to say I had found out the teams were five so 'have rod, delighted to travel!' They then had no option but to include me, with the Salmon and Trout Association confirming I could go as their selectee.

In Italy in 1983, the fishing on the Sesia river was much better organised than it had been the previous year in Spain. As I was primarily a river fisherman, while the others were primarily lochstyle anglers, which was then the basis of all home international competition, it was not too surprising that by finishing in the top ten I was top rod of the England team. So, tongue in cheek again, I said firmly, 'By Confederation rules the top rod always fishes again the next year. So see you in Spain.'

This was the somewhat eccentric route by which I found myself in the 1984 England team to fish on the Tormes river near Salamanca in an event which was still in its early stages, but becoming better organised and more significant each year. The Confederation method of nominating their four was simply to take the top four from the previous autumn international, regardless of whether they had fished rivers or had any consistent record. This year, happily, that lottery came up with three who qualified under both heads: Bob Church, Dennis Buck and Mike Childs.

Spain had presumably been granted a second shot at running the World Championship partly because their president, Snr Joachim Diez y Diez, was a vice-president of CIPS, partly because they wished to improve on their first effort, in which competitors had been delightfully entertained but the fishing had been abysmal. That had been a misguided attempt to major on salmon in rivers which held few of them at the time. Indeed, the only person who hooked a salmon throughout the entire event was Alan Pearson. But as he had just decided that the only hope was to fish for trout instead, and had put on a nymph with a 3lb breaking strain tippet, he was not in contact for long. Alan was later invited to a drinking contest by the Bulgarian vice-president, General Christo Rouskov, who had come bearing Alan's book *Catching Big Trout*. They had formed an instant friendship, despite neither speaking a word of the other's language, and certainly no verbal explanation was needed as they drained glass after glass of a potent cocktail. It was clear that Alan was winning when the general summoned an interpreter to complain he was not consuming the pieces of fruit in each of the row of empty glasses, which would have absorbed some of the liquor, though Rouskov himself was not doing so. With more diplomacy than was usually associated with such a forthright character, and to avoid the general becoming entirely legless, Alan conceded. But that allowed me to comment on the loss of his salmon with a sub-head, 'Pearson smashed again!'

This time, the choice of the Tormes was much more sensible, since it has a good head of wild trout as well as some Huchen or Danube salmon. In normal conditions the Tormes fishes well but, when we arrived, the conditions were far from normal for the end of May. Instead of the hot sun to be expected then, which soon reaches such intensity that trout fishing is confined to the north of Madrid, the area was bitterly cold, with snow only just melting. The Tormes was naturally in flood and, in the Salamanca area, looking barely fishable. However, the river is controlled via a dam and the upper reaches, where the competition was to be held, were beginning to clear.

For once, we were allowed a day's practice on the actual venue, where we found stock fish had been liberally added again. We had formed a close friendship with an entertaining Spaniard, Rafael de Madariaga Giraldo, an expert angler whose many business interests include a fly-tying concern. Rafael is a keen naturalist who spends as much time studying the terrestrial and aquatic insects as he does casting. He therefore ensures that the nymphs his company produces are exact replicas down to the last leg or whisker, with his flies tied from the best of the famous cocks of Leon. He had strongly advised that, on the Tormes, it was essential to fish dry and match the hatch. So it would have been, had this been an ordinary May and the ordinary minimal stocking. In practice, however, Bob Church and I soon found that the water was so cold, and the fish so deep, that a sinking line and traditional wet flies brought large catches in some areas.

There was an amusing exchange between Bob and Rafael after Bob had tried his nymphs and his methods without success in a pool where I had already located some stocked trout. 'You never catch a trout on the Tormes by retrieving at the end of the cast,' Rafael kept telling him. But Bob finally put on two traditional wet fly patterns, and no sooner did he retrieve close to the bank than it was bang, bang, and two fish released in two casts.

As usual in Spain, the hospitality was overwhelming with a colourful opening ceremony in Salamanca's historic square and much other entertainment, the only drawback to which was that it reduced practice time! Our other main practice day turned out to be a brief morning's fishing on a very different part of this broad river before we were transported away for a prolonged lunch. That was followed by a visit to the local corrida to witness the running of the small bulls. These come into the arena with shaven horns and are therefore not lethal, though quite capable of injuring. Many of the locals jumped in to improve in relative safety their matador ambitions. After a time, a couple of French anglers joined in, and then a portly Luxemburger who was bowled over by the bull to general laughter. That changed to tumultuous applause when he sprang up, grasped the bull by its shaven horns and bowled *it* over. Mike Childs judged it time for the Brits to show a bit of spirit too and sprang lightly into the ring, from which he soon had to be helped out with fractures of ankle and wrist. His misjudgement was not of the power of the bull, but of the distance down to the floor of the corrida, some twelve feet below the wall over which he had vaulted so confidently.

That was a major concern for all of us and a sad blight on our eager anticipation of the match. He assured us, however, that he was comfortable and well looked after in the hospital and asked us to win for him. He was also a sad loss to our team but, fortunately, David Swatland was an experienced river fisherman who took his place, somewhat reluctantly but with considerable success.

The first look at the beat on which you are drawn is always an anxious moment. For me, there was a great lift of the heart when I saw it was of a kind which specially appeals to me. The main stream flowed fast towards the far bank while a smaller, quieter sidestream, divided from it by the little island above, rejoined in a quiet shallow run just below me. Between were inviting swirls and eddies and, below, a deep glide as the current steadied down. Whatever happened, I would enjoy the next three hours, but were there any fish there?

The best method looked obvious to me. Fish quietly down the streams, trying those near at hand from the bank, then return to the top to wade gently out covering all the other runs and eddies, searching the nearer ones first. An intermediate line in this cold water would be best for the shallower runs and might serve throughout. The flies would be two old favourites. For the point I tied on a Black Pennell size 8, for the dropper a Bibio size 10, both well hackled. In choosing I was careful that the Pennell had a well-formed golden tail as contrasting colour to the black hackles, and that the Bibio had a red body as its contrasting colour.

So far as possible I fished a short line bringing the dropper up quickly to bob on the quieter currents beside the main stream. That soon answered the query as to whether trout were present. Second cast I had one just below the 25cm limit, fourth cast and the first one to be *valido*. As others came at encouragingly short intervals, some taking the tail fly well below the surface, some slashing at the bobbing dropper, quite a crowd of spectators began to gather. The pool was close to the road and just below the main fishing lodge so that it was easy of access. With six in the first hour I thought I was giving them good entertainment value, but it was my seventh which really appealed to the gathering. By then I had covered the near streams and was up to the top of my chest waders in fast water fishing those under the far bank. When I netted that fish, it was clearly borderline for size and needing to be measured, as to keep an undersized fish meant disqualification. Keen not to waste time I set off too fast for shore. The toe of my waders caught a concealed rock, and I dived head first into the fast current. Worse, when I emerged, the trout on the point fly had come out of the net and the dropper had caught in its mesh. Happily, it was rapidly renetted, and the controller declared it *valido*, to the delight of myself and the watchers. By the end of the three-hour session I had eleven to count, by far the best catch on any of the top three sectors, though outscored by an Italian on one below. Dennis Buck, too, had eleven on that lower sector, so it was looking good for our team.

When my controller first met me, his quizzical gaze implied puzzlement that an elderly white-haired angler should be representing his country. Whatever he thought of my fishing, my deep wading in fast water and associated aquabatics must have impressed him for, when Rafael came down to congratulate me, the two had a jocular exchange in Spanish. 'What was he saying?' I asked.

'He says you have the balls of the horse of General Esparteros,' said Rafael.

'Is that sarcastic?'

'No, very complimentary about your unexpected energy. Esparteros was a fiery cavalry general whose horse was even fiercer, so that horse is regarded here as a symbol of virility.'

My next draw looked far less inviting. I was delivered there with only two minutes to go before the start, too little time to prepare properly. However, if you have only a small beat to work, there will probably only be a limited number of ready 'takers', and the essential is to fish well for them. So, with unusual patience, I made a careful inspection of the beat and also ensured the cast and flies were properly tested before beginning to fish some five minutes late.

That inspection confirmed my fears. The whole beat was a featureless rush of water with fine-looking pools above and below. Worse still, Bob and I had fished this very run in practice, catching only one apiece compared to more than a dozen in the pools above and below. So it was without great expectations that I worked down the quieter current right under the bank, and a pleasant surprise when a wild trout of around 1lb seized the dropper.

So far, my method had been unchanged. But, in the break between sessions, Dennis had told me that he had caught his eleven using a fast sink line, and this helpful information was to prove invaluable. We had been told in England that the only sensible method for this river was floating line and small dry flies matching any hatch. But previous experience had underlined to me the importance of being prepared for anything when tackling unknown water in foreign lands, and I too had brought a fast sink line. The only feature in my beat was right at the bottom, where the wide, even current suddenly dissolved into a broad, deep, swirling eddy that looked like a miniature whirlpool, which required a change in tactics.

Having fished down to it I changed to the fast sink line and quickly had three nice trout out of it. Then came a fierce take and, instead of another of the half- or three-quarter-pounders, it was soon clear that this was a fish of real substance. After playing it for more than five minutes, and making no impression on it, the fly came away. So I was left wondering what I had lost. Was it a large wild brown, for Rafael had talked of occasional three- and four-pounders, or a Huchen, which counted, or even a big uncounting bream, of which there were a number in the river? Not to know was the great disappointment. As this was the only hooked fish I lost throughout the event, there was no point thinking myself unlucky, heavily as it would have counted had it been a trout, as I believed.

To end that session with five was very pleasing after my

earlier experience there, and I was happy to find myself in the top five overnight. Once again, however, the draw was not promising. Hardly any trout had been caught on the top two sectors, and the two who had already fished my new beat had had little joy. So, as the bus took us down next morning, I had only in mind the hope of helping the team do well, and perhaps of finishing as top English rod again to ensure my place in Poland the following year. The beat did not look more promising than its reputation. The bank had trees and bushes close to the edge and, when tested, the water was too deep for wading except close to the margin. In the three hours I was able to try fast sink, intermediate, and floating lines but, again, the cold water made the fast sink invaluable. To me, the interesting aspect was that the trout did not take well down but followed the flies up from deep, then usually snatched the dropper as it surfaced. Such explosive rises are always exciting, but especially so in this tense situation.

Fishing quietly beneath overhanging bushes, and in the shadows of a large tree whose main branch hung far out over the water, I kept picking up fish to end with seven. Even so, it was a total surprise and a matter of intense pleasure to be told that I had won. That was enhanced by the team's performance in coming second, with Dennis finishing seventh, Bob thirteenth and David nineteenth. Dennis had epitomised the team spirit of such events. His advice to me proved a major factor in my win, yet it was given when he had an equal chance of ending as champion.

Indeed, his performance was almost certainly better than mine. He too had his first draw near the road and found the watching crowd a daunting experience. 'I had never been nervous in a home international but, with all those people watching my first session in a World Cup, my fingers were trembling so much I had difficulty tying on my cast. When I did start to catch well I was wading far out, and rather than waste time bringing fish to the bank I returned every marginal one rather than come back out to get them measured. On reflection, three or four more would probably have been *valido*, and the wasted effort was in returning them uncounted.'

His next session was on a beat where no one caught and which, in this high water, was virtually unfishable. His final draw was on Sector A, where no stocked fish had been introduced and the wild trout were scarce and shy. The twenty-four competitors who fished those eight beats during three sessions caught only ten between them. Dennis caught four of those, including a sizeable rainbow in what was probably the most skilful session of fishing in the competition, on a beat where two others had failed to catch. Bob Church was also unlucky enough to have a draw on that sector, but he too did well to catch a large wild trout there.

For me, it was particularly satisfying to have won on another country's waters, given that home advantage is important in fishing. It was also pleasing to have fished consistently throughout. On rivers, the draw can be crucial, and I was certainly fortunate to have three reasonable beats, though the results showed them not to be exceptional in any way. The other six who fished these same beats caught only nine between them compared to my twenty-three. So, fishing sometimes before, sometimes after me, they had each averaged one and a half per session to my seven and a half. Moreover, they were quality anglers, with a Spanish former world champion on his own water and three Poles, including Leslaw Frasik, who was to win the following year's World Championship.

The team were in happy mood as we flew back to Gatwick, with the huge cup strapped into Mike's seat and attracting many a curious glance. There we were met with a motorised baggage trolley for the corrida-damaged Mike, who caused quite a stir as he preceded us to customs, plastered arm sticking out one side and plastered leg the other, and clutching the enormous cup. Even the reserved English actually came up to ask about it. Bob Church had been taking colour pictures in Spain, but wanted a black-and-white of the team and trophies. He had been unable to get any such film in Spain, so I had phoned ahead to ask my wife to meet us with one. Once through customs we formed up on a patch of grass by the airport road and again attracted a curious crowd. There was some insignificant football match about to be played and, after much whispering in the background, we heard the usual loud-voiced know-all putting everyone straight: 'That's the European Cup, and those are some of the Liverpool team and staff taking it out for the final with Roma.' Fame at last!

There was a further bonus to come for me in the shape of an article by Hugh McIlvanney, so often sports-journalist-of-the-year, and the first sportswriter ever to win the coveted journalist-of-the-year award as well. As a colleague with whom I had shared the Wembley press box for many international games, including the 1966 World Cup final, it was natural that he should go over the top on my behalf, but it was delightful for me to have a record written in his mellifluous prose and with his inimitable insight.

However, I needed to employ a stratagem in order to be accorded such a distinction. Phone conversations in May with my sports editor at the *Observer* went roughly as follows:

'You will be glad to know your angling correspondent has won the European Open.'

'Well done, Tony. This is a busy sporting week, but perhaps David Hunn might fit in fifty words in his oddball sports column. Phone the details.'

Three weeks later:

'You will be glad to know your angling correspondent is now the world fly fishing champion.'

'Splendid, Tony. This is an exceptionally busy sports week. I will see if David can squeeze in a hundred words or so. Type him out the facts.'

That may have been a proper estimate of its lack of worth, but I felt the achievement was slightly undervalued. So I set myself up early on Saturday morning in the *Observer* sports office knowing that the staff would be arriving late, though staying even later. As I tapped away slower than usual with my one-fingered typing I had placed around me the vast trophy with its beautifully-shaped pewter fish on the top, another large cup for catching the most fish, and the special prize of a two-litre bottle of brandy in a commemorative cradle, which customs had passed untaxed as a sports trophy, and which seemed certain to appeal to newspaper persons even if the others did not.

The bait was quickly taken as the cup attracted many, the brandy others, until the editor himself joined the growing crowd. A hurried recap ended with pictures being taken and a brief article by David Hunn with a follow-up in much greater depth by Hugh himself. There was also to be a picture from Eamonn McCabe, so often sports-photographer-of-the-year that they had to put him on the selection committee to give someone else a chance. The following is part of Hugh's article, which is a treasured possession since it is like being able to read your obituary before you are dead. For Hugh was bound by a similar convention to that of 'de mortuis nil nisi bonum', having to go out of his way to accentuate the good and ignore the bad in his colleague.

The first fish Tony Pawson hooked was in the Nile and, since it gave convincing evidence of being the size of a small crocodile, Pawson was glad to be the one that got away.

He was 4 years old at the time and had been asked to take temporary charge of a line while his parents and some friends from the Sudan Civil Service organised the picnic lunches. It was when one of the monster perch that inhabit the old river decided on a midday bite that Pawson discovered what a violent pastime angling could be. The surging fish dragged him roughly over rocks towards the unfriendly waters of a dam and, although the competitive instinct was already noticeable in the boy, an instantly matured belief in the principle of live-and-let-live persuaded him to release the line. Had the ordeal occurred less than a year later, his reaction might have been dangerously ambiguous, for by then the young fisherman had been introduced (during his father's home leaves) to the thrill of yanking worm-lured trout out of Highland burns and over his head into the heather. He was so irrevocably addicted by the age of five that a 200-lb Nile perch could have tempted him to hang on just long enough to be towed to destruction.

That might have been a pretty good deal for the fish of the world because Tony Pawson was to pursue them so enthusiastically over the ensuing six decades that, as a 62-year-old on a very different river in Spain, he would emerge in May 1984 as the fly fishing champion of the world. But his loss would have been costly in the extreme for all those humans who believe that classic amateur values still have a place in modern life.

Pawson's special place in modern sport was pleasantly if superfluously confirmed last week when the people from the *Guinness Book of Records* contacted him with the news that they might be including his name in the section devoted to sporting performers of exceptional versatility. The suggestion that he could be entered alongside such as C. B. Fry and Babe Zaharias, the great Olympic athlete who went on to become easily the finest woman golfer of her era, elicits a familiar mutter of self-effacing protest, but the facts of his various careers are remarkable to say the least.

He was a genuine schoolboy prodigy as a cricketer at Winchester, subsequently a highly successful captain of Oxford University. And he might easily have been given the captaincy of England (only amateurs were eligible in his day) if he had not relinquished a secure position in the Kent First XI because of the pressures of earning a living and the conviction that too much cricket would make the game more of a slog than the joy it had always been to him.

Pawson had gone up to Oxford as a 25-year-old after serving through much of the Second World War as a front-line officer with the Rifle Brigade. Inevitably, many of his Army experiences were grim, but one of the happy bonuses towards the end of his service was the opportunity to play football in Italy alongside Tom Finney, who became an admired friend. As someone who could never be anything but an attacker on the field, the amateur was bound to learn from one of the supreme professional masters of forward play and, after surviving his own initial misconceptions about his capacity to be an inside-forward for Oxford, he became an excitingly productive winger in the University team.

But it was as one of the stars of Pegasus, the club formed in 1948 by combining the football resources of Oxford and Cambridge, that he enjoyed the most dramatic and satisfying phase of his career as a footballer. Pegasus flourished all too briefly in English football but it lit up the sky while it was around, and Pawson contributed significantly to the glow, figuring prominently in the winning of the Amateur Cup in 1951 and 1953.

He played a dozen times for Amateur England and, in three first-division appearances for Charlton, he was never on the losing side. On one unforgettable occasion at White Hart Lane he made himself the acclaimed executioner of a Tottenham Hotspur team that included, among other famous men, the future Sir Alf Ramsey.

Yet – while there is a hint of wistfulness as he acknowledges that his failure to develop fully his gift for scoring runs in cricket may represent serious neglect of a basic talent, and though he remembers the Amateur Cup victories before roaring crowds of 100,000 at Wembley as the most exhilarating peaks of his years as a games player – Pawson insists quietly that fly fishing has been the deepest, most abiding passion of his sporting life.

A day spent with him by the three small lakes set in the leafy parkland of the Avington trout fishery in Hampshire and on an idyllic stretch of the Itchen, a famous chalk stream running through the same county, did more than emphasise the strength of his attachment to the ways of Walton. In the few hours that it took to locate, tempt, strike, play and net a pair of 2lb rainbows at Avington, and a brown trout and another rainbow from the Itchen, there was about him a sense of pleasure as close to the ethereal as anyone so agelessly vigorous could convey.

He talked with an easy, enlightening authority about the subtleties and technicalities of the sport – the habits of the quarry, the precise relevance of different weights of line, kinds and colours of fly, and such arcana – but once he was going after a fish in earnest his non-angling companions felt themselves drifting out to the edge of his awareness. Along the Itchen, he was inclined to skip nimbly off the bank into the waist-deep water and wade comfortably upstream to make long, delicately accurate casts towards rising trout only he had spotted. By then he had entered that private place where, for real fishermen, the serene and the competitive mysteriously co-exist.

He has known it nearly all his life, and it has never been more attractive to him than it is now, though he has recently passed his 63rd birthday. Such a milestone need not mean a lot in the Pawson family. Tony's father is still healthily active at 96 and only gave up fishing two or three years ago because he decided that his years of working in a hot climate (he rose to be governor of the White Nile province in Sudan) had left him a touch vulnerable to the cold in this country.

Guy Pawson came of Yorkshire stock and, as an outstanding wicket-keeper, was offered the captaincy of that county after leading the Oxford cricket team of 1910 to victory over Cambridge by an innings, a triumph that Tony was to repeat in 1948. The only other father and son double-act as captains of Oxford was provided by the Pataudis.

Pawson has the fairly short, stocky, low-slung physique that often goes with well-balanced sprightliness, and the years haven't robbed him of the mobility that caused Sir Leonard Hutton to say he had never seen a better runner between the wickets. During the World Cup in May, fly fishermen half his age were liable to be unnerved by the sight of him wading so deep in the Tormes River near Salamanca that the ripples were almost lapping his shock of brilliantly white hair, or by his sudden headlong sprints, in full waterproof gear, towards a new casting position on the bank.

One younger rival in the sport who is never surprised by Tony Pawson's determination on the water is his 23-year-old son, John, who followed with impressive success the competitive route Tony had taken belatedly in 1976, when in his middle 50s. John, who works as an area representative for a paper company, has already fished for England. In the first European Open tournament staged by the French in 1982, he came third and, when Tony Pawson won that event this year as a prelude to his World Championship, John was in eighth place.

They often fish together for fun at Avington and elsewhere (Tony insists that competitions will never become more than a fraction of his commitment to the sport), and John was disconcerted recently to find that his father's habit of crouching low while netting a trout had proved contagious.

That crouch seemed to this outsider to originate in the same intensity of concentration that once made the senior Pawson a

hard man to discount on football and cricket fields. Such
concentration helped to give him an average of over 40 in more
than 100 first-class innings and a respectable 34 for the MCC
against South Africa at Lord's in one of his two representative
appearances. But he admits that on the way to the 34 sweat
poured from him, his muscles were painfully tense, his hands
bit into the rubber of the bat handle – and still he struggled to
middle the ball. 'Meanwhile, at the other end Denis Compton
was utterly relaxed, moving into his shots with all the time in
the world, the middle of his bat appearing to magnetise the
ball. As it happened, Denis got himself out for half my score,
but I had seen enough of him at close quarters to realise the
difference between the instinctive Test cricketer and one who
would have to fight for every run at that level.'

Despite his accumulating honours as a fly fisherman, he
recognises the same gulf between his own abilities with the rod
and those of the current captain of the England team, Bob
Draper. 'Bob is the equivalent of a Jimmy Greaves or Bobby
Charlton in football, a Denis Compton in cricket. He is
brilliantly consistent, has reduced luck to a marginal factor. I'm
a long way short of his standards.'

Of course, those of us who have come to know Tony rather
well through his many years as a lively reporter of football and
cricket for the *Observer* realise that his modesty can get out of
hand. The most admirable element of all in a lifetime of
amateur excellence has been the extent to which he has
remained a profoundly appealing and agreeable man while
beating so many opponents out of sight.

While Hugh was overkind to a friend, what astounded me
about him was that he had never fished or even interviewed a
fisherman before and yet, in a few hours of watching me, he
was able to make the most perceptive comment I have ever
read about the total absorption of an angler just fishing on his
own: 'By then he had entered that private place where, for real
fishermen, the serene and the competitive mysteriously co-
exist.' He had appreciated, too, that for me winning the World
Fly Fishing Championship was of much more importance and
gave much more pleasure than any other sporting achievement

of my lifetime. How greatly was that pleasure increased when John also won the championship only four years later.

With the event at such an elementary and formative stage in Spain, I was well aware that winning then was much less of an achievement than it was later to become. In Spain, only eight countries were involved; the number increased to twenty-one in England in 1987, before settling down to an average of seventeen. In addition, the standard of several of the teams was not up to the quality of later entrants. The Poles, however, were competing for the first time and, with their highly developed national river competitions they, as the Czechs later, were to enter a series of outstanding teams of river fishermen. Indeed, if grayling are involved, these two countries are virtually unbeatable. Under the guidance of the charismatic Jozef Jelenski, and later of Jerzy Kowalski, the Poles were to win two team golds and have three individual champions in the next six years.

Our friendship with them was further cemented when Poland hosted the next championship on their San river, full of grayling and with numerous trout as well. They won the team event there easily enough, catching the grayling in quantity on small dries when they were surface rising, on weighted nymphs when the fish were feeding deep.

For me, there was a nostalgic aspect to visiting a country whose people I had long admired. In another May some forty-one years earlier, I had had reason enough to thank the Poles. As my Sixth Armoured Division bridged the river Rapido and drove up Italy's Liri Valley to breach the Hitler Line, it was the Poles' storming of the dominant Monte Cassino towering above us which protected us. There those formidable fighters, the German First Parachute Division, had already repulsed three major attacks and endured two massive bombing raids before the indomitable Poles finally overcame them.

The close relationship which developed with the Polish anglers was extended in two ways. Their economic and currency problems prevented them acquiring the tackle they needed, and several of us left items behind for them. At Jozef's request I passed on my chest waders to a friend of his, Andrej Fox; his letter of thanks made it clear how highly English tackle and equipment has been prized.

> Please accept my sincere thanks for granting my request forwarded to you by my friend, Jozef Jelenski. Your chest-high waders were just fine and suits me very well. I should to thank you personally but circumstances prevented this, so I have written this letter.
>
> It was not my intention to bother you with such kind of request but simply no way of obtaining the body-waders exist nowadays in our country. I am definitely an amateur of fly fishing, being the third generation of fly fishermen in my family.
>
> Near hundred years ago my grandfather started to catch his fish with Hardy's fly fishing tackle. My father and I are still continuing the English fly fishing tradition – the best one in my opinion, in the world. Therefore it was a true pleasure for me to observe you and your colleagues fishing the San river last May.

As soon as the Poles knew that the team championship in England two years later would be fished on lakes, they set about learning all they could of what was for them a new fishing experience. I sent Jozef books and videos to help in their trials, and we invited Jerzy to come and stay with us and fish with our team to help their preparation. A happy outcome was that Poland began to take seriously the possibility of stocking their lakes and developing lake trout fishing in its many aspects. That is useful supplement to their wealth of trout and grayling river fishing freely available to all. The intense interest in the World Championship, and their exceptionally thorough approach, led to this pleasing result as foreshadowed by Andrej in another paragraph of that letter: 'I hope you will be pleased to hear that I have read your book which I borrowed from Jozef. It deals with topics less known in Poland, and I will come back to it after creating trout lakes near Krakow.'

So keen were the Poles that they practised on a thousand-acre lake stocked with just one thousand rainbows and enjoyed the experience. They actually caught a few of them, too, which was some performance with only one fish per acre! Not surprisingly, they finished fifth in the team event in England in 1987, as the leading team from continental Europe, after England, Australia, New Zealand and Wales.

The Confederation's method of selecting the England team had so far simply taken a soft option which avoided argument, but also denied any hope of success. Nor had their officials been at all interested in the results, or concerned at poor performances. That was understandable, since their first priority was the home internationals and, at that stage, their constitution in fact related solely to the organisation of these matches fished under IFFA (International Fly Fishing Association) rules which concentrated on Scottish lochstyle fishing. The result of such slipshod selection was natural enough. For the four years during which the Confederation had supplied four of the five team members, the top rod on all four occasions had been the sole Salmon and Trout Association's selectee. Moreover, except for the happy chance of their lottery method throwing up Bob Church and Dennis Buck in the same team, and a second Salmon and Trout river fisherman coming in after Mike's accident to help claim second place, team results were abysmal compared to England's potential. The nadir was in 1985 when we could beat only one of the ten full teams entered.

Not surprisingly, the National Federation of Anglers who had to take official responsibility for entering the teams were making it clear they were not prepared indefinitely to support such poor performances in England's name when the potential was so much higher. For myself, I had to endure embarrassing conversations with overseas anglers on these lines:

'Your country has a great reputation for fishing. Why does your team not do better?'

'Well, we do have many better river anglers, but we only select lochstyle fishermen for river events.'

'Ho, ho, you droll Englishman. You cannot expect us to believe that you are as stupid as that.'

'We *are* as stupid as that, but I don't expect you to believe it. I can hardly credit it myself.'

My own view was quite different. If you enter a World Championship you have a duty to your country to select the best team you can, whatever the difficulties or the inevitable controversies. With the publicity attending such events, it is not only the country's fishing reputation which is directly in the balance abroad, but indirectly that of its tackle-makers, its writers, and all others concerned with the sport as Andrej Fox's letter underlines. For 1987 we were going to be very much in the public eye as hosts for the event. We had to raise some £150,000 in cash and kind for staging the event, which was a main responsibility of mine as organiser. We therefore owed a duty also to the main sponsors, the Sports Council and the National Westminster Bank, as well as the hundred or more volunteers who so generously assisted at great expense of time and effort to make the event a success. So it was imperative that we did our best to show the true strength of English angling and to take selection seriously.

Happily, the organising committee took the same view and, for the first time, the Confederation readily agreed to make its selection on the best estimate of consistent performance, known ability, and all-round skill, since the individual event included also river and stillwater fishing. The Salmon and Trout Association further agreed to nominate only an angler who had also fished at least twice in home internationals to ensure that he, too, was a Confederation member and had proved himself more than a 'oncer' in international events. The nomination of son John brought inevitable comments about nepotism, which he soon silenced by winning the individual runner-up trophy in the team event and finishing third in his Test session in the individual and then first by a mere 7000 points in his Avington Lakes session. His was the best performance in the two individual events and he ended with 44,300 points to winner Brian Leadbetter's 44,760, though the complex scoring method did not fully reflect his performance in the final placings. The team as a whole won by a margin never likely to be equalled. They scored more than double the points of runners-up Australia, and triple those of third-placed New Zealand. In the team event, Brian Leadbetter was a worthy winner and went on to be an even worthier champion, while the team filled the first four and sixth places. You cannot get a much cleaner sweep than that. The same straightforward system applied when England won again in Tasmania and, though some limitations were then introduced to try to compromise with the different Confederation practice, the results remained much improved.

My other concern as organiser was that this was a chance to make the event a genuine World Championship, rather than a European event masquerading as a world one. In Belgium the year before, the number of countries had risen to thirteen, with an exceptional Czech angler, Slavoj Svoboda, winning as a start to a long run of top-class performances. But the thirteen entrants were all European. So I went off to Australia, New Zealand, and Canada to try to persuade them to join in. In relation to Australia, Andrew Fink soon proved an enthusiastic organiser. Yet addressing the somewhat sceptical Australian Freshwater Fishing Assembly proved something of an ordeal as I was faced, among others, by the representative of the Native Fish Society, to whom trout are anathema. They have still not accepted them as naturalised and view them as interlopers snapping up native galaxids and the like.

Earlier, I also had to listen to an erudite talk indicating that one of the problems for Australian trout fishing was that part of the population perceived it as the imported sport of wealthy, privileged Poms, unsuited to such a socialist environment! Happily, four million of Australia's sixteen million participate in fishing, and as natural competitors the Australians quickly took up the challenge and, indeed, were hosting the event themselves a year later. The professional guides in New Zealand proved equally enthusiastic, and New Zealand too were to stage a successful championship later. In Canada, Jack Simpson invited me to attend the main meeting in Toronto of the countrywide Izaak Walton League and to speak at their dinner afterwards. I had found that dealing at a distance with official bodies resulted in inertia, inaction, and failure. It was necessary to find someone of standing in the country, who was enthusiastic and energetic enough to get things moving there. Jack certainly comes under that heading. He brought Canada in and will be staging the championship in style in 1993 with the World Championship on the Kamloops Lakes, where the world record rainbow of 48lb was caught long ago, and the Commonwealth event nearby. Kamloops fish include landlocked salmon, kokanee, and a species of rainbow trout called kamloops. It was no surprise therefore that, when the world body formalised a new federation for fly fishermen (Fédération Internationale de la Pêche Sportive à la Mouche), Jack should be elected president.

With the late King George VI having been England's first captain-elect for the 1928 home international, it was an especial privilege to have the Queen Mother as patron of the 1987 World Championship. Her foreword to the championship programme was also much appreciated:

> As patron of the Salmon and Trout Association and, in particular, patron of the World Fly Fishing Championship, I take much pleasure in welcoming those who have come to take part in the competition.
>
> Fishing is assuredly the most popular of sports and to its devotees the most enthralling; it can provide days, or perhaps even only a snatched hour, of relaxation in improbable, but often beautiful, places and no fisher should travel without a rod.
>
> Of all the forms the sport can take, fly fishing is pre-eminent. It calls for a deep understanding of fish and their habits, a knowledge of water conditions and much weather lore, great skill and, finally, infinite cunning.
>
> I hope the championship will bring together friends, old and new, sharing a common interest and that you will all go back to many days of enjoyment on your home waters.
>
> Elizabeth R
Queen Mother
Patron
>
> May 1987

We were all happy that the team did their immensely popular patron so proud.

Triumph in Tasmania

My own involvement with FIPS had been as a minor technical representative. However, when Australia hosted the championship in Tasmania in 1988, I found myself as the only official prepared to accept the effort and expense of attending, so I received a message that I was now the official in charge of the championship on FIPS behalf. But officials are of no importance compared to participants. That delightful friend of mine, the late John Arlott, was a typical propounder of that principle. At his memorial service both the addresses emphasised this, with the Bishop of Basingstoke quoting another writer's view of John that he had never had any truck with that spurious sentiment that the game is greater than the players. For me, too, the performers are all-important. In Tasmania, son John was one of the most important of them. This was to be his triumph and has to be his story.

'The great success of our team and of the championship in England had caused quite a stir. So it was a great privilege for us to be seen off to Tasmania by the minister for sport and an even greater one when a well-signed Parliamentary motion was passed later complimenting the team on its performance. We were confident we could do well again. Less confidence was expressed elsewhere, with the media rightly emphasising that it was one thing to win with ease at home in a style of fishing which particularly suited us, quite another to do well fishing for scary wild trout on strange waters.

At the end of a flight of over thirty hours, it was difficult for us to look suitably alert and assured as we faced the inquisition by television in a noisy airport lounge immediately on landing. When queried on how we would cope with Tasmania's trout, Brian Leadbetter at least was awake enough to reply that Tasmanian fish were descended from English stock and that he hoped their memory was good. Tasmania was, in fact, the place to which the first successful shipment of trout ova was made with some of the browns hatching out in the Pools of Plenty near Hobart, after an extraordinary ninety-day voyage before the days of refrigeration. The trout ova had nearly been dumped into the sea at London Docks because it was salmon which the authorities hoped to naturalise in Australia and they feared the trout would hatch out first and eat the salmon eggs. In fact, it was only the trout which survived to be the progenitors from which all Australia and later southern New Zealand were to be stocked. So the browns, though not the rainbows, for which we were to fish were descendants of trout whose ova had come from the Test and the Itchen, the Wick and the Wey. That in itself made this an exciting challenge.

We were a very happy team with only one change from England. Chris Ogborne's business commitments prevented him from coming, so Brian Thomas was promoted into the team, having been the reserve before. An Australian speciality when fishing their shallow lakes is spot fishing, in which you wade far out looking for individual trout through your polaroids before any spot you. You then fish for that specific trout. On the assumption that this would be the only successful method, one of the angling journals criticised Brian's selection because he was "too small to spot fish well". Brian was to prove that a very wrong estimate, but what needed no proving to us was that he is an outstanding team man as well as a good all-round angler. You can rely on him to give total effort and to help the whole team in any way he can, even if he thereby diminishes his own chance of winning. Nothing typified that spirit more than when we both fished Bronte Lagoon in the final session. It was soon clear that he and I were the only ones in contention to be champion, and one of the flies I was using had been tied up for me by Brian.

We had more than a week to prepare, and that allowed several mentally relaxed days. We could fish intently, yet enjoying the experience and the new surroundings. Then, gradually, the championship itself with its pressures, hopes and doubts began to take centre stage in our minds, concentrating thoughts and tautening nerves. But those early days were pure pleasure, as we explored two competition lakes, Little Pine and Bronte Lagoon, in the clear air and untouched countryside of the central highlands. Our prospects and our enjoyment were vastly enhanced by having Noel and Lois Jetson as guides, advisers and friends. They showed us their special skills on these waters without ever trying to persuade us to abandon our own methods and our own flies, with which we also experimented.

With their wealth of available free fishing, many Tasmanians only go out when the conditions suit their preferred style. So stalking trout in the tussocky margins, or spot fishing, were their specialist and very entertaining standard tactics. But that demands sunny weather, and we were faced with wind, cold and driving rain. On Bronte we did find some fish rising to duns in a calmer spell, but even these took wet flies better than dry, though we practised with both. Little Pine was the chilliest and most exposed lake, with cold water pouring in from the high mountain streams and the wild winds sweeping across it. The fish were scattered and deep-lying, hard to locate, even harder to catch. Yet they were also exceptionally exciting to hook, the thrill enhanced by their rarity value. Particularly was that the case with "tailing" trout in the margins. Robert Sloane of the Tasmanian Inland Fisheries had written books on how to catch them, since this is a phenomenon much commoner, it seems, in Tasmania than elsewhere. No sipping rises, but large tails suddenly breaking surface as the trout turn down for food lying on the bottom in the shallows. The technique is to spot them, estimate their cruising path, drop the fly well ahead preferably with a bit of a splash to draw attention, then leave it lying motionless on the bottom.

The first time I tried the method was when Brian Thomas and I suddenly stopped in our tracks as we spotted several large tails intermittently surfacing close to the far bank of Little Pine. I cast in front, not really believing in this tactic and certain that, even if it did mouth the fly, I would not feel the take. I need not have worried. As if it had touched an electric wire my rod was almost jerked from my hand, and the line raced out to the backing as a torpedo-shaped four-pounder sped off at incredible speed heading for deeper water with myself in hot pursuit. Both Brian and I had one of those superb fighters and another memorable fishing experience to store away.

Little Pine was soon established as the problem lake, with Bronte having areas where we caught more freely. The London Lakes, Samuel and Big Jim, were barred for practice, though we went and studied them carefully with Noel pointing out the best places and tactics. The first spot to which he guided us was designed to show that some of the most difficult places were also the most productive, if you could cast accurately and play big fish hard. The approach to the water was through a tangle of coarse grass tussocks and fallen logs, and in the margins was a further tangle of tussocks and rotting gum tree branches. "Trout often congregate where they get shelter and food, as here," said Noel, kneeling behind a bush with yards of line stripped off at his feet to be ready to cast short or long the instant a cruising trout was spotted.

The ubiquitous Australian TV had trailed us here and requested an interview with Brian as current champion. As usual, their interviewers were unversed in fishing and an easy target for a leg-pull. "Now that you have studied these delightful lakes, what decisions have you taken about equipment and tackle?" Looking dead-pan at the camera Brian responded, "Two items are essential: a lawnmower and a chainsaw."

That left the interviewer confused and incoherent, much as John Sautelle senior had done the previous year in England when interviewed at Rutland in his Aussie hat. "How do you go fishing in the wilds of Australia?" he was asked.

"We are lucky to have all these 'roos . . . kangaroos to you. We saddle one up and hop off to the river after stowing our tackle in its pouch."

We enjoyed coming across old friends and rivals in the Australian team, particularly John Rumpf and Terry Piggott. John is the Hardy representative in Sydney and has been Australia's casting champion. He was my boat partner in my first World Cup session on Rutland the year before, and a delightful partner too. Terry Piggott was another who had done well in England, but we were pleased to note young John Sautelle was helping to organise rather than being in the team, since he was established in our minds as an outstanding fly fisherman. John Sautelle senior, one of the great characters of Australian fly fishing who is now no longer with us, also enlivened things when he appeared on the scene accompanied as usual by crates of whisky and a fund of fishing stories. We were intrigued, too, to meet Mrs Jan Spencer, who had been selected as one of Tasmania's outstanding anglers and was catching well in practice.

As we began to know the lakes better from our shared experiences we became more confident about tactics and flies. Provided the weather remained wet and windy, we would wade deep and search blind using a continuous fan-shaped pattern in our long casting and methodically covering the maximum amount of water. We practised also stalking the margins and using dry flies, but that was a fall-back method if it turned sunny. Dennis Buck was particularly helpful in locating effective fly patterns, and we now produced our own special version. We code-named it a Fiery Brown, but it was a mixture of several successful patterns and was more like a JK All-rounder tied with a fine wing of grey mallard flank, a gold body, plus a hackle of soft-dyed brown cock. That proved a splendid point fly, but a traditional Bibio was also serving me well, and I agreed to keep that for the dropper.

The speed of the retrieve also seemed important. A fast retrieve brought more takes, but very few hooked on. I began to appreciate the reason for this when, under Noel's guidance, I spent most of a day fishing dry flies. When a rise came I waited longer than I usually did, even when delaying the strike fishing small dries on an English reservoir, and I still missed. "Too slow?" I queried Noel.

"Too fast. You must be more patient."

Next rise I waited, and waited, and waited, and it was then with total disbelief that I found I had struck home. Never had I encountered before such slow risers.

When we were taken back to Hobart for the opening ceremony, it was the last time we could relax and enjoy ourselves chatting with friends in the Belgian, New Zealand, Canadian and other teams we had met before. Among the new teams, the Americans were a flamboyant addition. At the formal dinner, I had to listen to father responding to the Minister on behalf of CIPS. He ended by wishing the teams good luck in what he imagined were their own languages, but they probably thought he was speaking in Esperanto. When he wished the Swiss live lines rather than dead ones, it was a reminder of how challenging the fishing had been, for none of their team of five had yet caught a fish (and in the championship a combined total of ninety hours' hard fishing netted them just two). Between us, however, with Geoff Clarkson fishing as well, we had caught and returned around a hundred already. So we were feeling reasonably optimistic about our chances.

Now only the formal practice for all teams remained, and the tension began to mount. The Bronte Park Village complex of huts grouped around a hotel restaurant suited us admirably, except that our huts tended to be crowded.

Most pleasurable of all was the happy atmosphere, with the fraternal feelings between teams and the shared excitement reminiscent of father's comments on his experience with the Great Britain soccer team in the Olympic Village in Helsinki more years ago than he cared to remember. Several supporters had made the long trip with us, and one who was lodged in our hut was Ray Cannon, who did sterling work in helping during the many fly-tying sessions. This activity now reached a crescendo and, as usual, many more were tied than we needed.

Sleep was soon to be a problem, for the three lake venues were all to be fished at different times. Fishing on the London Lakes started at 5:30 a.m. with a 3 a.m. bus departure. The Little Pine sessions were 10 a.m. to 4 p.m.; Bronte Lagoon from 2:30 p.m. to 8:30 p.m. So there was constant coming and going as well as the bustle of preparatory work, and little chance of undisturbed sleep.

My first draw was on London Lakes with Dennis Buck. So it was the early start for us and then a torchlight briefing in front of the lodge before my controller, David Imbar, took me to my beat. The London Lakes are two separate lakes, so the six-hour fishing session was broken in half by a stop for breakfast and a switch to the opposite lake. We had had no chance to practise there as it had been barred to competitors until the event, and since I was the first of our team to fish it, we had no prior feedback. The early start I knew was because the big trout tended to work the margins at dawn, and it was a case of creeping along trying to spot the fin of a fish in a few inches of water.

So I tiptoed towards the margins, since trout can be as susceptible to noise and vibration as to seen movement. Behind me, however, my weighty controller, laden with equipment, crashed noisily through the undergrowth in a way that sent shock waves through my taut nerves. For once, there was no wind ruffling the water and, with its surrounding gum trees, the lake was breathtakingly beautiful as the light brightened. More to the point, and less beautiful, was the apparent absence of trout. At last I spotted one, held my breath as the fly landed right and the fish cruised up to it. A solid take, a splashing fight as I held hard a fish of 4lb-plus to prevent it running into a snag, and then the supreme relief of my first good fish netted.

Carefully as I worked my whole long beat, there was nothing else to be seen until, at the very end, I noticed a good fish cruising easily in range, but an infuriating couple of yards beyond the line of my marker post. I tried casting delicately as close as permitted and getting the fly to drag with a slight wake to attract it across. I tried landing the fly with a hint of a splash, but still it cruised just out of my permitted water. "I'm watching you," said my alert controller, so I had to be careful too not to overshoot the imaginary line. That fish disdainfully refused to cruise the few feet my way, and nothing else showed.

Still, we had a cheerful breakfast for Dennis, too, had a fish and had been broken in a snag by another. With few being caught, we had made a fair start. It was obvious that Big Jim Lake, where Dennis had been, was fishing much better than Lake Samuel, where I had started. I was not surprised to find that expert angler, John Rumpf, had had four good browns as he stalked the margins of Big Jim and dropped his Red Tag in front of their noses. "The Australians will probably walk away with it," I thought to myself. How were either of us to know that, with four in the first three hours, Rumpf would have only one more in the next fifteen? Nor could we imagine that the equally expert Jan Spencer was, like several others, to have the nightmare experience of remaining blank throughout the eighteen hours.

At that stage, however, I was hopeful that there were plenty to be caught in Big Jim, even though the witching dawn hours

13. *Dual concentration as young John eases an Onny trout to the net.*

14. *Playing a salmon in a productive pool on the Avon, a tributary of the Spey.*

15. *John plays a rainbow from Rutland Water watched by Australia's John Rumpf as he heads towards the runner-up individual trophy in the 1987 World Championship team event.*

16. *Watched by controller Chris Howitt, John plays a large trout on his way to a runaway win in the session on Avington Lakes, near Winchester, of the individual event in the 1987 World Championship.*

17. *John fishing the first European Open Championship on the Lac du Chateau in 1982 in which he finished third.*

18. *John prepares by torchlight for his dawn session on Tasmania's London Lakes at the start of eighteen hours of fishing to become the 1988 World champion.*

19. *Brian Thomas brings in a Bronte trout for measuring as he finishes as runner-up in the 1988 World Championship.*

20. *John with Brian Leadbetter* (centre) *and Dennis Buck after they had finished as the top three in their river Test session of the 1987 World Championship individual event.*

21. *The top five in the 1991 National River final.* From left to right: *Tony, John Lindsey, Martyn Adams, Ian Greenwood and John. Standing at the back, between Martyn Adams and Ian Greenwood, is the representative of the sponsors, Yorkshire Electricity.*

22. *The 1987 World Cup party at Rutland.* From left to right: *Bob Morey* (reserve), *John, Tony* (organiser), *Bob Church, Brian Leadbetter, Geoff Clarkson* (captain), *Brian Thomas* (reserve), *Chris Ogborne, Dennis Buck.*

had passed. After an hour's fruitless stalking I found that my beat included a small underwater channel, no doubt where a stream had once flowed into the bay in the middle of my area, or where it had dredged out before the man-made lake had been formed a few years earlier. Reasoning that some trout must congregate there, I fished it carefully from well back, only allowing the long leader to alight in the channel. Less pleasing was the presence of one of the two TV teams covering the event; a posse of cameramen, however careful, are apt to scare ordinary fish, let alone these very wild ones. Happily, they gave me up for useless after nearly an hour, and no sooner had they moved off than the line tightened and another thrilling fight ensued, after which another large brown went into the measuring tray and back into the water. Twenty minutes later, there was a repeat performance and another 50cm trout to record.

By now I was full of confidence that the channel would yield me more. It nearly did, too, for there were two more strong pulls as I searched it with the Fiery Brown and the Bibio. Perhaps because the clear shallow water now had the strong midday light playing on it to make the fish even more cautious, perhaps because it was just one of those things, neither caught on. Still, three browns averaging well over 40cm was an encouraging start, though Dennis had had no further luck. The catch was good enough to put me in second place, and back at the camp there was better news to come. Team manager Geoff Clarkson had asked Brian Thomas to make sure he avoided a blank on the dreaded Little Pine. Brian responded with a remarkable four-fish total. As the other twenty-five competitors caught only five between them, that ranked as the outstanding performance of the day.

On the more prolific Bronte, Bob Church also had a good catch, his four trout proving the best bag of the twenty-seven anglers there. Brian Leadbetter had been less fortunate, ruefully commenting that he had probably blown his chance of retaining the title. He had rises enough, but around a dozen fish either failed to hook on or shook themselves free. But, great competitor that he is, Brian's concentration never wavered despite five and three-quarter hours of total frustration. With just five minutes to go he was rewarded with one in the net. What a relief!

Next day it was the midday shift on the inhospitable Little
Pine for me. The rain drenched, the wind howled, and I was
drawn in an area we had found unproductive even by Little
Pine's standards. So it was a case of grit your teeth and keep
casting, reminiscent of a wet and chilly opening day at
Rutland. Well used to many hours' continuous fishing in such
conditions back in England, that at least gave us some
advantage over our fellow-sufferers. Nothing stirred as I
diligently searched the barren-looking water in front of me
throughout the first three-hour session.

The change then was to a beat close by, just hammered
unsuccessfully by a Frenchman. According to my controller,
he and the two anglers fishing there on the previous day had
fished close to the bank without getting an offer between them.
There was, however, a more hopeful-looking area some 100
yards out where a couple of mud banks had built up just below
the surface where a stream flowed in. They were just visible
from the bank, but my controller said, "It's too deep. You
cannot get within fifty yards of them without going right over
your chest waders." My own thought was, better be wet and
cold than blank. So out I waded, pushing on slowly even when
the water began to trickle over the top of the chest waders.
Finally, I reached the near bank with a wader full of icy water,
but more promising water to fish either side of the banks.

Searching it quietly and carefully, I had a take at last.
Happily, it was a small fish and came quickly to the net to
boost my confidence. Soon another seized hold, but perhaps I
was too eager in playing it hard. Inches short of the net it
dropped off. It's always a desolate feeling when the line goes
slack but, at this stage of a World Championship, there is a
special sense of depression which has to be quickly shaken off
by intense concentration on getting another. After two small
ones the next took me by surprise. It was a four- or five-
pounder, and again there was the sickening sense of loss as the
fly pulled out on the first run.

Still, I had avoided a blank and, by coincidence, every
member of the team had just one fish that day. So we kept our
lead, but the French and Australians closed up a little on us.
The first two sessions on the final day settled the team event
beyond any doubt. Bob Church had a good fish on London
Lakes where very little else was caught. Then two Frenchmen

blanked on Little Pine along with many others, but both Dennis and Brian Leadbetter had two there. No team could catch us now, but I was more than two hours into my own session on Bronte before the news reached me.

For the first time the wind had dropped to a gentle breeze, there was a glimmer of sun and a welcome warmth in the air. Brian Thomas had started with five fish to my four, but was not many points ahead as mine had been larger. Brian was drawn on the Redrock Shore in an area known as Rainbow Bay and very productive in practice. My draw on the left side of Woodwards Bay also looked reasonably promising. On the other two venues we had each had an individual beat, then changed to another after three hours. Here we were allotted over a kilometre of bank to three anglers who could fish where they pleased for the whole six hours, provided they did not encroach within fifty metres of each other. That gave us water to spare, for you could wade out over a hundred yards from the shore in this shallow lake, or stalk the many little tussocky creeks indenting the shoreline. John Rumpf was one of our trio and he chose the stalking method, while I stayed true to our own tactical plan. I was pleased to be lined up by my controller close to the wide river which flowed quietly in, cutting a deep channel. As I waited for the start I remembered a comment of Dennis's when he was fishing this area: "The only rise to which I cast looked like a big trout, but I was shaken rigid when a platypus surfaced and looked indignantly at my flies."

The water level on Bronte was controlled by a dam, and the Australians had deliberately lowered it in advance of the competition. Their belief was that, when they raised it again just before the event, the trout would be enticed into the new margins searching for the good food usually associated with recently flooded areas. That would put a premium on stalking amid the tussocks or spot fishing, the two techniques in which the Australians specialised and felt appropriate to their waters. In fact, we found in our final practice that the reflooded areas had not been dry long enough for any real hatch of terrestrials or for other trout delicacies to gather there. Most of the trout remained well beyond the old shoreline.

That had been further confirmed by the earlier experience in the competition of Dennis, Bob and Brian, with the unusual fishing pressure on Bronte having driven the trout even deeper. With conditions so promising, I reasoned I had a real chance of doing well if I could wade out some 200 yards. That meant pushing on, even when the water was up near the rim of my chest waders. Much of the time I fished perched on underwater tussocks to try to keep dry. Even so, there were occasions when the wavelets lapped over and my feet were soon swimming in water again. But that, and the waste time of walking so far back with the trout in the net being kept from injury, were soon forgotten in the pleasure of catching well.

By now I had perfect confidence in the refinements I had made in method. Because even the ripple of a line hitting the surface and being retrieved would scare the trout, I used a leader some seven yards long. Having cast long I inched the flies back very slowly over that seven or so yards then immediately retrieved fast again, wasting no time on the disturbed and fishless water. Confident as I was, a rise first cast was so surprising and unusual that I missed a fish I should have caught. That sharpened my concentration and, a few casts later, the rod bent and before long I was wading out with a fish to be measured.

Fishing steadily on I kept picking up the odd fish and missing the occasional one. After four and a half hours, I had five and was told that Brian had five also, but larger ones, which would have extended his lead. Suddenly, it dawned on me that he or I must win it now. An hour later, I had no doubt who that would be, having played and lost no less than five more trout which had appeared well hooked. The fifth was clearly a very large and powerful one. With confidence disturbed by these previous losses, I may have played it too carefully, too desperate to take a fish which looked around 6lb as it came to the net. It was agony as the fly again pulled out just when it appeared beaten. Rafael was fishing nearly a mile away and, when I mentioned this loss to him later, he said, "I know. I heard it." Perhaps I said, "Bother," or whatever, rather louder than I intended.

At that stage I thought to myself that, anyway, Brian was a close friend, a great team man, and I would be delighted if he won. So why bother to concentrate more? Then I knew instinctively that the only sensible response was to relax the tension, but intensify the effort and keep fishing in the same

methodical way. Whatever the result, I could now be happy
with it provided I had given of my best. But if I threw away
what might be my only chance of winning a World
Championship what would I think in later years? Inevitably, I
would be nagged by the uncertainty of whether I could have
won or not, and by the stupidity of perhaps throwing away a
golden chance for lack of concentration. So I fished on with
heightened awareness, but able to accept with equanimity
when another trout shook loose.

As so often in fishing, the luck suddenly changed. With less
than half an hour to go, another came to the net. With a
quarter of an hour left, I was wading out again to my
controller, who had been kindly and supportive throughout
and was now in a fever of excitement, as if he was himself
winning the championship. All the time I had been wading out
to the limit of my chest waders with the water sometimes
slopping over unnoticed. That meant a long trek back each
time a fish was netted, and I could not believe there was time
for another. But, with under five minutes left, the line
tautened, the strike was true, and the fish came safely to the
net.

John Rumpf had only had one fish in the margins and lost
one, while the third angler had stirred nothing. John and I
walked back in friendly companionship, each knowing we
would have finished well up (John in fact was fifth just behind
Bob Church). I couldn't help wondering how Brian had
finished and which of us had won. Even when I heard he had
six to my eight, the result was not certain because he had
several big fish and had started ahead. It was midnight before
my father came to announce the results that I had won and so
had the team. Congratulations and the interviews with
Australian TV kept me from appreciating just what it meant to
me. There was also the profound fellow-feeling for Brian
Thomas, who had fished so well and come so near, and for the
poised Jan Spencer who had endured with great dignity the
pressures and the bitter criticisms of an Australian press
expecting and demanding victory. My first reaction was to seek
her out to express our great respect for her composure and to
give her the rod with which I had won the event.

The following day came the prize-giving by Tasmania's
Governor. The most important to me was the guides' special

prize for the best performance on any day which Lois Jetson, as president of their association, handed to me. From the first day I saw it on display I had coveted it as the trophy I really wished to win.

Ahead were a couple of days of total happiness as Noel Jetson took us to fish the Western Lakes, wading the shallows and spot fishing as the weather turned to sun so bright that Bob's hands were badly blistered in this high area where the ozone layer is no longer so protective. There was also a Commonwealth match to enjoy on London Lakes though, after those three days of such intense effort, we were all too drained to do more than enjoy our fishing. The championship had been a memorable experience, but just as memorable for me was the fishing with Noel whose lifestyle, whose companionship, and whose fishing I so admired.

Bob Church recorded his own view of one day with the Jetsons on the Western Lakes. "It was sunny, ideal for the polaroiding technique we had heard so much about from the expert, Jim Allen. The method can get in your blood, I imagine, for Jim seemed to love it more than anything else. At his bar Jim's photo looks down on you as he displays a brace of double-figure browns caught in one day on the Western Lakes with this method. Noel at last did some fishing and soon spotted two big trout. He flicked his Red Tag with deadly accuracy into their paths and hooked a good brown which he released. He found another for our new world champion, John Pawson, who promptly caught it and proudly commented, 'Now I've done the lot.' He had, too.'"

That brace of doubles in Jim's bar were only half the 40lb-plus total of four fish he had caught when I was out there to meet the Australian Assembly a couple of years earlier. I had spent several days in a car camper (which creaked and leaked equally badly) with Australian World Cup anglers Terry Piggott, Andrew Fink and Owen Nuttridge. Jim displayed his catch the night before I was due to leave, and this caused great excitement to the trio. They kindly said they would be sorry to see me go, even if my snoring had kept them awake most nights. They added that I was unlucky to miss the expected bonanza the following day, as they knew where Jim had caught them. Later I telephoned Fink to hear about the magic day. 'How did it go?' I asked. 'Not well. With more space in the camper Nuttridge rolled out of his bunk and pinched a nerve so that he could not fish. I caught nothing. And you may have noticed by now that you packed Piggott's trousers so he couldn't leave the camper.'

In the real post-championship bonanza for the team and Noel I was indeed unlucky to be left out as I couldn't be fitted into Noel's camper. Instead, I was driven back to Launceston by John's controller, who contrived to hit two large boulders and splay out the wheels of the hired car so that descending the steep escarpment with a dozen hairpin bends was a shattering experience in all ways. By the time I reached Launceston I was suffering from a bout of bronchitis through being silly enough to have joined the team in practice inadequately clad on one of the wetter, colder Little Pine days. The championship had been massively covered by Australian TV, at times even taking precedence over a Test match against West Indies, perhaps because their team had been doing much worse on the cricket field. Feeling too ill to go out of the small hotel into which I had booked I sat in the lounge watching continuing disasters befall Australian cricketers in the next Test just started. All round me sat formidable beer-drinking Aussies with large bellies and forearms. As another Australian wicket fell, one of them said, 'It's bad enough being beaten by West Indians, but I couldn't – stand being beaten by a load of bloody Poms.' I made no mention of my nationality or the fishing championship! But it had been a truly remarkable performance to finish 1, 2, 4, 12 and 13 when the second-placed French had a team score adding up to 136, four times as much, and the Australians to 150.

I at least could appreciate how John felt. Winning that World Championship had been more important to me and brought a greater lift of the spirit than twice winning before a full house at Wembley, or batting with Denis Compton before a packed Lord's crowd and helping to beat the South Africans. His win, too, gave me even greater pleasure than my own and was so much better deserved and achieved.

Before the event some of the media had been in pessimistic and critical mood about the England team and its chances but, after the championship, made amends with generous appreciation of such a decisive win. Peter Gathercole had come with us and been active in his photographing, as indeed in fishing himself to test out these challenging waters. This was how he concluded his account in *Trout Fisherman*:

With the team competition well and truly decided in England's favour, it was left to Bronte Lagoon to sort out the individual placings. Favourite for the title was Brian Thomas of England, who had not only done well in his previous two sessions but had also drawn a very productive beat known as the Redrock Shore where some of the best catches from Bronte had already been made.

It seemed that this prediction could only be fulfilled as he picked up three good rainbows, all measuring over 45cm. The effective fly which produced many of England's fish was a home-tied Fiery Brown. Or at least that was the code-name. It was in fact a version of the All-rounder, tied with a fine wing of grey mallard flank, a gold body, plus a hackle of soft dyed brown cock.

With John Rumpf and John Pawson on only one fish each, and Brian picking up three more good fish, the seal appeared set – but that was without reckoning on the sheer tenacity of John Pawson.

Situated on the left side of Woodwards Bay, John waded out to the very extent of his chest waders. Bobbing along with water almost up to his armpits he began to hit fish again on the Fiery Brown but also on the Bibio. Takes came thick and fast and, as the final minutes of the competition slipped away, his total reached a magnificent eight fish, not only enough to ensure him the prize for top rod of the championship but enough, too, to give him the title of world fly fishing champion.

In both points, and ranking, as well as total fish caught, England were clear winners, having taken thirty-seven fish to second-placed France's sixteen and Australia's fifteen.

Finland is the venue for the IXth Championship in 1989, and the question of course has got to be, can England take the title for a third year in succession?

Bob Church was as consistent as ever, finishing fourth a few points behind Terry Piggott, whose six fish totalled a few more centimetres than Bob's six. In his own reviews in *Angling Times* and *Trout Fisherman*, Bob was later generous to both John and Brian, and also described the special attraction Tasmania had for him.

Top marks to John Pawson. By winning the world individual title he has proved what most of us already knew – that he is a superb angler.

I say 'most of us' because John's selection was criticised in some quarters. It was said he was too young and lacked the experience to succeed at world level.

I'm delighted that he well and truly buried that criticism.

He took his chance on Bronte Lagoon where he was drawn on the same beat as a top Australian, who knew the venue better than John.

John netted eight fish to the Aussie's one. Need I say more?

Brian Thomas is also worthy of the highest praise. He was kept out of the team by Chris Ogborne last year, and didn't grumble.

But, when his chance came this time, he took it superbly, finishing runner-up. That's exactly the attitude and ability that has put us on top of the world.

Wild and wonderful – that's Tasmania

Although I've travelled extensively I've never seen a place like it. I thoroughly recommend it for a holiday, even if you are not an angler.

The air is exhilarating, the scenery breathtaking, the flowers beautiful and the wildlife fascinating.

I'm not after a job on TV's holiday programmes, but I reckon they should give Tasmania a try.

Our guide, Noel Jetson, is a man of nature. He has his own log cabin high on the plateau where he has a golden touch with animals.

221

VIIIth World Fly Fishing Championship

Final Individual Scores: Top 16 out of 80

Team Name	Individual's Name	Code	Total Catch	Total Length (cm)	Total Points
England	John Pawson	I1	12	452	692
England	Brian Thomas	I5	11	401	621
Australia	Terry Piggott	O3	6	243	363
England	Bob Church	I2	6	220.5	340.5
Australia	John Rumpf	O1	5	231	331
Wales	Raymond Jones	D5	5	215	315
France	Jean L. Dauchin	G5	5	211.5	311.5
Scotland	Sandy Forgan	M1	5	189.5	289.5
France	J. P. Guillemaud	G1	5	186	286
Italy	V. Davighi	H2	5	161	261
Luxemburg	Remy Lanser	A2	4	164	244
England	B. Leadbetter	I3	4	162.5	242.5
England	Dennis Buck	I4	4	157	237
USA	W. Ungermann	N5	4	151.5	231.5
Canada	Phil Kettle	J3	4	137.5	217.5
Canada	Paul Marriner	J5	3	152	212

Team Scores

Rank	Rank Score	Team's Total Catch	Total Fish Length (cm)	Total Points	Team Code	Team Name
1	32	37	1393	2133	I	England
2	136	16	625	945	G	France
3	150	15	673.5	973.5	O	Australia
4	169	11	459.5	679.5	C	New Zealand
5	191	12	465.5	705.5	M	Scotland
6	192	11	452.5	672.5	J	Canada
7	193	11	466	686	D	Wales
8	208	11	354	610.5	H	Italy
9	214	8	367	527	P	Finland
10	215	9	360	540	L	Norway
11	237	7	306.5	446.5	F	Spain
12	247	8	305.5	465.5	N	USA
13	256	7	304	444	A	Luxemburg
14	269	6	228.5	348.5	E	Belgium
15	305	4	169	249	K	West Germany
16	358	2	69	109	B	Switzerland

After a day's fishing, he would barbecue steaks for us and have wild possums coming into the cabin to take bread from his hands.

We also saw four breeds of wallaby, wombats and deadly poisonous tiger snakes which are 4ft long. If one of them decides to sink its fangs into your legs, you had better be wearing tough waders.

The plateau is just about the last unspoilt wilderness in the world, but the pure air does carry one nasty problem.

Even though it wasn't sunny, I suffered painful ultra-violet burns. Huge water blisters appeared on the back of my hands, and when the blisters burst they left raw flesh.

However, the pure air, which blows straight from the Antarctic, does wonders for the flowers which are incredibly colourful.

Incidentally, the locals are more like Norfolk or Fenland folk than Aussies. Their accent is remarkably similar.

Bob had in fact beaten a hasty retreat from the water when a couple of tiger snakes headed towards him during practice after initially giving the Welsh team a scare. Noel Jetson was also given a fright when from a distance he saw Geoff Clarkson holding up a snake. To catch a tiger by the tail is an expression for unnecessarily endangering yourself; to hold a tiger snake by the tail may well be lethal as it can still climb up its own body to bite you. So Noel dashed towards him yelling to drop the tiger. Geoff held on . . . the one he had picked up was long dead.

Administration is always too dull a subject for fishing magazines to tackle, or to be much debated at meetings. So it is not surprising that the vast majority of Confederation members have remained in ignorance of basic facts about World Cup selection, notably that the Confederation itself has never been, and can never be, the body with ultimate responsibility for entering a team, or that the Confederation's early contribution to teams, based on one eliminator, was a disaster. Nor do they appreciate the Sports Council's role in helping to fund travel and monitoring performance, or that the National Anglers

Council had, and the new Angling Council may have, a similar monitoring function. Nor are they made aware of the dramatic change in performance once selection became a genuine attempt to pick the five best anglers based on their consistent perform-ance, proven ability and mastering of the particular technique needed at the current venue.

That is not to criticise the eliminator system for the home internationals, where there are vast differences. The twice yearly teams automatically picking themselves from the top twenty in the previous year's national boat final, plus the top four in the previous international, works well in these totally different circumstances. All will have shown themselves com-petent lochstyle anglers in events which are solely lochstyle. With fourteen in a team and results on total points, a few poor performances or fortunate inclusions can be covered by excel-lent performances of others. The rival teams are selected in the same way, and the reputation of British fishing is not at stake. So it is a pleasant feature of these internationals that many get the chance to participate even if the vast majority turn out to be 'oncers', and very few manage to qualify four or more times.

The World Championship is vastly different. The team is only five. The results are determined on individual placings, not total team points. Therefore a runaway win by your top angler counts very little compared to a blank, or very low placing by your fifth team member. One bad individual per-formance destroys the team's chances of winning. The pressures are greater, the standards much higher, the competitions much longer, the techniques required are more varied, the results much more important for the reputation of English or British fishing and tackle. So, however difficult – and it is exceptionally difficult – the effort has to be made to pick the five best to represent the country. Systems can be refined and amended, but that principle is immutable.

Some Confederation members are apt to advance nostalgic arguments for the return of an eliminator system under which every team seemed to have one or more 'Eddie Edwards', unversed in the required type of fishing. The trouble was, of course, that in this case other countries laughed at, not with, them. The improvements in selection were clear enough from the results. Those *nominated* via a single eliminator never achieved any success in the five years to 1986 inclusive, except in 1984 when the team came second. But, on that occasion, there were two Salmon and Trout selectees among the five, and it was one of them who won the event, not a Confederation nominee.

In the next five years to 1991 inclusive, a real attempt at selection resulted in dramatic change with three individual and two team wins, two individual silvers, and a team and individual bronze. Moreover, that was achieved against an average of eighteen countries entered as compared to an average of ten, and with the general standards vastly higher.

The same applied even more markedly in coarse fishing, where the NFA has more complex problems with up to a quarter of a million taking part in formal competitive events. In *their* World Championships, England faces an average of twenty-six countries, nearly all with highly professional teams of great expertise before crowds of up to 15,000 or more. With more complex problems the selection system is now even simpler and goes a stage further than in fly fishing. Until 1984, England, in twenty-three years of competition in the World Championship, had never won the team event. Dick Clegg was then appointed as manager and sole selector with the brief of picking the best team. His method is also to choose anglers of proven ability and competitive consistency in good current form and with exceptional skills in the technique required on the particular venue, be it expertise in pole, or waggler, or whatever. Having picked his squad he then makes a final selection after practice on the championship venue. He is always prepared to back his own judgement of class. Tom Pickering, for instance, won the World Championship in Bulgaria in 1988, but dropped his team to second place the following year in Yugoslavia by blanking in both sessions. Dick stuck by him for Hungary, and the team was back to gold again. By then Dick had indeed put them on the gold standard.

In that eight-year period, England has won four team golds, two silvers and a bronze plus four individual golds, four silvers and a bronze. The statistics also make it clear that the closer you come to the Clegg selection system, the greater your chances of success, while the closer to the eliminator 'nominations', the greater your probability of failure. However, any such selection system also depends on two other variables: first, a selector or selectors of the good judgement and personal competitive skills and knowledge of a Clegg; and second, that you have anglers of the potential to win. On lakes England unquestionably has that ability. For rivers, the potential is improving, but still with much room for improvement.

Whatever the future holds, John and I have had immense pleasure from our involvement with these championships and happy memories to treasure. As climax there was the invitation to the Queen's July 1992 anniversary garden party at Buckingham Palace for the sporting champions of her reign. Apart from John, myself and double world champion Brian Leadbetter, these included team winners Dennis Buck, Bob Church, Chris Ogborne and Brian Thomas.

It was that exceptionally kindly and thoughtful man, Brian Thomas, who suggested we present the Queen with a box of all our favourite flies. Geoff Clarkson also contributed salmon flies more suitable to fishing at Balmoral. Bob Church organised a splendid box inscribed, 'A Fortieth Anniversary Tribute to Her Majesty from her Fly Fishing Champions', and I was deputed to confirm its acceptability. After I had delivered the box to the Comptroller of the Lord Chamberlain's office, Colonel Ross, the following letter was received:

Dear Mr Pawson,
    I passed to The Queen the beautiful fly box which you gave to Malcolm Ross yesterday as a present for Her Majesty from her Fly Fishing Champions. Its acceptance gave The Queen a rare moment of unalloyed pleasure in her all too busy summer.
    The box will be borne away to Balmoral early next month and will be put to good use, I suspect without delay, by members of her family and her guests at the Castle. Her

Majesty asked me to thank you and all those associated with the gift for a good idea and a charming and generous present.

Yours sincerely,

Robert Fellowes

What better ending could there be to our World Championships?

PART 5

The Master Angler

Celebrating Walton

My first meeting with Dora Oliver was in 1982 in connection with preparations for the tercentenary of Izaak Walton's death the following year. Fortunately, eleven years later, that kindly and charismatic man has left us the chance to celebrate the quatercentenary of his birth in 1593. This son of a Stafford alehouse-keeper lived to the age of 90 and made a profound impression on English history. But, like many prophets, Walton is now even more honoured outside his own country, and the most active Izaak Walton leagues and societies are in America and Canada. The main collector of Waltoniana is Rodolphe Coigney, an American, who claims the *Angler* is the most popular book worldwide after the Bible, and that includes Shakespeare. Well, it has run to well over 400 editions and reissues.

My historian cousin, Dame Veronica Wedgwood, wrote of Walton as 'perhaps the most sympathetic character in English history'. Certainly, that was how he appeared to me as I researched his work and his fishing when, having offered to help something calling itself the Izaak Walton Foundation because I liked its aims, I made the mistake of not attending its first meeting but found I had been put down to write about him and arrange a commemorative party. So far as I know, the Foundation has still not founded itself, but I forged ahead with the tasks assigned to me in my absence.

The party started as tea at home for a few friends before the commemorative service in Winchester Cathedral and the Salmon and Trout Association dinner at the Wessex Hotel in

Winchester. Somehow it ended as arranging local fishing for sixty followed by drinks at my home in Chilcomb for eighty! For that party Charles Jardine kindly embellished the programme with a special drawing featuring the watervole, his personal signature, converted into a 'Waltavole' character. The rations for the day were also in true Waltonian tradition, and there were many celebrated anglers joining in the spirit of a very happy party. The special programme for the day included two Jardinc drawings, and the cover of it is reproduced on the opposite page; the rest read as follows:

PROGRAMME OF EVENTS

0900   Fishing starts at Avington. Elsewhere as advised.
1600   Refreshments available at Manor House, Chilcomb.
1900   Izaak Walton Service in the Cathedral.
2030   Dinner at the Wessex Hotel (for those who have reserved places).

NOTE: Throughout the day there is an exhibition of old fishing tackle and of Waltoniana (including a first edition of *The Compleat Angler*) in the Silkstede Chapel of the Cathedral where Walton is buried.

FISHING HOSTS:
At Avington . . . . . Barbara Holland and Roy Ward
   Handicapper for the 9 a.m. dash . . . . . Tony Pawson
At Nythe Lakes . . . . . David Reilly
   Chilcomb Guide . . . . . John Pawson
At Ladywell Lakes . . . . . Beadon Dening
   Chilcomb Guide . . . . . Philip Pawson
At the Arle Fishery . . . . . Jack Sheppard
At Itchen Abbas . . . . . Peter Kane
At Ovington . . . . . Roger Harrison
At 'Old Barge and Logie' . . . . . Michael Baron and Winchester College anglers
For Segars and Itchen-Test beats . . . . . Ian Hay and Tim Healey arranging

Izaak Walton Commemorative Day
FRIDAY 8th JULY 1983
at *Chilcomb and Winchester*

*IZAAK WALTAVOLE welcomes you to a Fishing Party
at Chilcomb in memory of the Master Angler*
(*born in Stafford Aug. 9th 1593; died at 7 the Close, Winchester Dec. 15th 1683*)

The Manor House, Chilcomb, will be open all day for any guest who may wish to look in. The Cast of Anglers, in unknown order of appearance depending on speed out of bed and driving ability, is set out in the separate insert.

THE REPASTS
'too good for any but anglers and very honest men'

'WALTON' PICNIC:
Your packed lunch is a 'brave meal of beef and radish', with a bottle of Whitbread's Barley Wine. There are two bottles for Alan Pearson for endorsing Izaak's view of the best barley wine as 'this good liquor that our honest forefathers did use to drink of; the drink which preserved their health, and made them live so long, and to do so many good deeds.'

PISCATORIAL PICK-ME-UP AT CHILCOMB:
Various small offerings and a plentiful supply of strawberries and cream. 'We may say of angling, as Dr Boteler said of strawberries, "Doubtless God could have made a better berry, but without doubt God never did"; and so God did never make a more calm, quiet, innocent recreation than angling.'

To refresh the thirsty anglers there is a supply of: Vin d'Izaak (sparkling white wine); Chateau Chilcomb (red); Pawson's Plonk (white); Walton's Wallop (more barley wine and Hampshire ales); and sundry less potent beverages.

'"Tis the company and companionship that makes the feast.'

THOUGHTS FOR OUR COMPLEAT ANGLERS

'No life so happy and so pleasant as that of the well-governed angler; for when the lawyer is swallowed up in business and the statesman is preventing or contriving plots, then we sit on cowslip-banks, hear the birds sing and possess ourselves in as much quietness as these silent silver streams we now see glide by us.'

For those who find it difficult to possess themselves in as much quietness there is an alternative text for the day from *The Angler*: 'There may be many that have forty times our estates, that would give the greatest part of it to be healthful and cheerful like us who have eat and drunk and laughed and angled and sung and slept securely; and rose next day and cast away care and sung and laughed and angled again; which are blessings rich men cannot purchase with all their money.'

All the Pawsons wish all their guests a happy day and a 'leash of good trouts' on their 'jury of flies'. Should you have a blank, and come in 'clean', we hope you will be able to say with Walton that your angling 'has been so pleasant it has proved to be, like virtue, a reward in itself.'

The Continental interest in Walton was well demonstrated two days earlier in a commemorative tournament I organised at Patshull Park. Bertrand Kron's French team won this twenty-one-team event, with Sid Knight catching the largest trout of 8¼lb on one of those flies he ties so well.

Francis Lodge, president of the Fly Fishers' Club, described the highlights as follows:

Patshull Park was, until recently, the home of the Duke of Dartmouth. It lies in the beautiful country to the west of Wolverhampton. Developers have built a comfortable, ranch-style hotel overlooking one of the many lakes on the estate. The hotel is backed by a well laid out golf course.

I arrived at the hotel on the afternoon before the event to find the place swarming with golfers taking part in a pro/am competition. It had been a blazing hot day, and the lake lay like a mirror broken only by the wake of coot and duck.

During the afternoon, teams started to arrive from France, Luxemburg, Spain, Ireland and Wales with club teams from many parts of Great Britain. A convivial dinner that evening enabled them to meet each other.

The Fly Fishers' Club team were due to assemble at 9 a.m. on the following morning, so I was up early to meet the five other members for the first time.

Team A, captained by myself, included Reggie Rigby and 'Tam' Chambers. Team B, captained by Hugh Keep, included Ian Hall and Chris Patrick.

Tam Chambers, who is the local vet, had acted as my spy in finding out the best flies and the best areas of the lake. He had provided a marvellous selection of highly coloured lures recommended by the locals which were distributed to the members of our two teams.

The contest started at 10 a.m. with a blast on a horn at which all thirty-eight boats rowed as rapidly as possible to their chosen positions on the lake where competitors considered that most fish would be found.

It was a hot, thundery morning with a threatening orange-coloured overcast sky and a glassy calm over the lake.

As for myself, with slow sinking line and traditional loch flies, I began to feel that I was not representing the club very adequately. However, I now had time to deliberate upon the conversation that I had overheard at dinner the previous evening when Maggie Vaux, representing the Salmon and Trout A team, had remarked that she was going to spend the day 'stripping'. To which her companion John Inglis had replied, 'You'd better look out. I'm a judge tomorrow and I'll certainly put a stop to such unladylike conduct.'

By lunchtime, my companion had landed four fish and was beginning to express concern at my lack of success. Even our gillie was saying that I should fish nearer the bottom but, without a 2lb weight, I did not see how this could be achieved.

I was aware that, in an adjoining boat, Maggie Vaux had by judicious stripping already landed six fish. The horn sounding for the luncheon break saved me from further embarrassment.

The teams came ashore for a gargantuan al fresco lunch lasting two hours.

At this stage, not one member of the Fly Fishers' teams had caught a fish. Fortunately, Tam Chambers came to the rescue. He had come prepared with a great collection of reels with various weights of line, and I was able to borrow a lead-cored line from him.

The horn sounded for the commencement of the afternoon session, and a rather less athletic start was made by the various teams.

During the afternoon, my companion had rather lost touch with the fish and had only managed to catch one more.

At 6 o'clock, the horn sounded for the end of the match and under darkening skies we rowed ashore for the weigh-in and prize-giving.

The contest was won by the French team with a total weight

of over 13lb, followed by Salmon and Trout A team with 10lb. The Fly Fishers' Club was well down the list. Our A team weighed in at 5lb 4oz and the B team close behind with 5lb 2oz.

Immediately after the prize-giving, which had taken place on the lawn overlooking the lake, the heavens opened and the thunder rolled: the air cooled, and fish began to show on the surface of the lake.

The day ended with a prolonged drinking session at the expense of the Irish Tourist Board, followed by an excellent dinner with speech-making and a further award of prizes.

Walton would have thoroughly approved of that convivial evening.

The day at Winchester was chronicled by 'Grey Duster' in the *Fly Fishers' Journal* as follows:

Our sport affords an intriguing little contradiction. On the one hand, anglers set great store by companionship; on the other, fishing is a singularly individualistic – perhaps even an isolationist – pursuit. Certainly, we gather together for purely social purposes, as is evidenced by the very existence of the Fly Fishers' Club and, more and more nowadays, some fly fishers gather to compete, but it is rare to see the social and the piscatorial facets of our pastime blended into a single, perfect day.

It is for this reason that so much credit is due to Tony Pawson – a respected club member and a renowned angler and writer – for his initiative, his imagination and for the sheer hard work that he put almost single-handedly into organising a tribute to Izaak Walton in July to mark the 300th anniversary of Walton's death.

The day started with a splendid and suitably light-hearted fishing party for sixty invited guests on an assortment of stillwaters and on various lovely stretches of river in and around the Winchester area. The piscatorial proceedings were notable for the extraordinary warmth of the hospitality extended to all those present by their hosts at the various fishings, for the quality and numbers of the fish taken at almost all the venues in almost ridiculously hot, bright and sultry conditions, and for the overall sense of fun. Do we not perhaps lose sight too often of the fact that the sole purpose of our going fishing is that we may relax and enjoy ourselves?

The kindnesses of those who hosted the fishing were well matched by the generosity of the Pawson family as a whole. Their house at Chilcomb was thrown open to us all for the day, and it was here that we foregathered at teatime to eat more strawberries and cream than we should have, and to tidy up prior to the service at the Cathedral. The trout taken during the course of the day were gathered together to be sold to raise a contribution towards the restoration of No. 7 The Close, the house almost adjacent to Winchester Cathedral where Walton spent his last few years and where he eventually died.

Most of us know Walton only as the author of *The Compleat Angler*, but his claims to fame go far beyond that. A man of considerable achievement, and a force for peace when peace was something that most men only dreamed of, he was . . . much respected by the Church. It was through his friendship with George Morley – established in the 1630s when Morley was at Oxford and consolidated in the 1660s when he was made Bishop of Worcester prior to being appointed Bishop of Winchester in 1662 – that Walton became associated with the Cathedral in particular.

The service, led by the Dean of Winchester, the Very Reverend Michael Stancliffe, with lovely singing by the Cathedral choir and with a most aptly chosen reading by Sir Michael Hordern from *The Compleat Angler*, was an entirely fitting celebration of and thanksgiving for the life of a very great man.

At least the demand that I write about Walton stimulated my research into the 'father of fishing' and first sent me to walk the Dove. Inevitably, I spent time also in the Silkstede Chapel of Winchester Cathedral which houses his tomb and has the stained glass window donated by American fishermen, depicting the many saints involved with fishing. The chapel was much in need of refurbishment and was cluttered with cupboards and the like, since it served also as a vestry. Happily, the celebration of his birth in 1993 has stimulated the fund-raising to restore this chapel to prime condition in a cathedral where Walton's figure is on the Great Screen along with that of his relation, Bishop Ken. Reading more widely about Walton I came on a perceptive article by Sidney Vines debunking some of the mystique of *The Compleat Angler* and deploring its emphasis on quietness in such an active sport, as well as highlighting its obvious attractions. Izaak might have appreciated that article, but not the one by A. G. Marshall in an old issue of the *Hampshire County Magazine*. Headed 'Father of Fishing or Fraud?' it made an entertaining case that Walton had never fished himself, but was merely a journalist who had cleverly cobbled together the ideas of others. There is indeed much in the *Angler* that is cribbed, such as the format of the book and the twelve flies, which derive straight from the *Boke of Fysshynge with an Angle* of some 150 years earlier. And there is indeed very little direct evidence from Walton himself about his own fishing. There is enough, however, to refute Marshall's tongue-in-cheek theory, since Sir Henry Wotton made it clear he fished with Walton, as did Charles Cotton (who was much too good an angler to have accepted as 'Master' a fishing 'fraud'), and Izaak in a letter to Colonel Venables wrote that he practised the sport for thirty years.

That puts the start of his fishing about 1630, when he was getting on for 40. That was a surprise to me. So too was finding how much of his fishing must have been in the Thames or Lea or other London rivers, and how little in the Dove, with which legend associates him. My only copy of *The Compleat Angler* had been the 1899 Temple Classics edition, given me by my father. It is based on the fifth edition of 1676, the last of Walton's lifetime, and his final revision and expansion of his work. But where was the famous Dove, the Temple Fishing House, and all those trout and grayling in its clear stream? Nowhere in the text so far as I could find. Desperate rereadings confirmed just one passing reference to the 'delicate Dove'. It was with relief that I discovered Part II, devoted solely to the Dove; but that is all Cotton's work, with minor amendments only from Walton. And it was produced to be sold separately, or together with Walton's fifth edition, or with a book of

Colonel Venables's as well. For most of the fairly brief time that Walton can have fished the Dove he would have had to ride over from London or Winchester when of advanced age. And though at 83 he was offering to jump on a horse and dash down to Dovedale if Cotton took offence at any minor alterations in his text, he can't have made that taxing journey too often!

No wonder, then, that the *Angler* is set round London or that Cotton in detailing his own inventive fly patterns comments that Izaak's standard twelve weren't good enough for the Dove, though they might be all right for London rivers where Walton had done most of his fishing. Walton's other traditional rivers such as Trent, Stour, Darenth, Meon, Hampshire Avon, Test or Itchen are more guessed at than verified. Living so long in Winchester he must have fished the Itchen, and I did at least come across some new evidence of that. The Canon Librarian of Winchester Cathedral wrote to me in his beautiful copper-plate handwriting: 'You will know, of course,' (which, of course, meant that neither I nor anyone else knew) 'that Walton had a little Fishing Hut in the garden of 1 The Close which only fell into disrepair in recent years in Dean Selwyn's time.'

The then Bishop of Winchester's wife, Mrs Taylor, kindly showed me all that remained of this hut, though I also discovered an earlier drawing of it. Now only the round stone floor remains in the garden close to one of the little tributaries of the Itchen. But it is Cotton's 'Poor Fishing House' on the Dove that was such a pleasure to visit. It is privately owned now, as is the stretch of water round it in Beresford Dale where Cotton and Walton fished. And the person to show me round was the remarkable Dora Oliver, now in her 70s, and river-keeper there for over thirty years, having returned from being a sergeant in BAOR to take over duties from her father. Though Beresford Hall has long disappeared without trace, the Fishing House is little changed from when it was finished. The Walton–Cotton initials are still entwined in cipher, the 1674 date and the Piscatoribus Sacrum are also as clear as when cut in the stone. The siting is quite beautiful as it nestles in a sharp bend of the river protected from viewers on the public footpath by its screen of trees. In front of the Temple is a stone trestle on which trout have been gutted for over 300 years, with the scour marks of the knife having cut a small channel.

Nearby in a lovely setting, in a dip surrounded by trees but with a view of a long quiet stretch of the Dove, is their round stone table for outdoor meals. Did they boil trout in a fish kettle on a fire by the Fishing House to Walton's recipe and eat them there?

For the jacket of the book I was asked to pose as 'a mysterious Walton-like figure' in the background of the Fishing House. I had indeed borrowed a Walton-type 18ft reelless and ringless rod from Peter Stone, and a Walton hat from Winchester College Drama Society. But, at the last minute, the local costumiers failed to produce the rest of the promised costume, and an overnight search of home cast-offs found me driving to Dovedale in the early morning attired in a black polo-necked sweater of my wife's, my daughter's discarded school cloak, and my black tracksuit trousers. A mysterious figure indeed, crouching by the waterside!

The greatest pleasure for me has been in finding what a well-rounded and charismatic character Walton must have been in all aspects of his life. Indeed, Veronica Wedgwood has also commented on this remarkable man that, contrary to popular myth, he exemplifies the fact that in his age the English class system was less rigid than anywhere else in Europe. It was nothing unusual for an alehouse-keeper's son with a good education to rise to the heights as Walton did. He was a highly successful businessman who acquired properties in London, Hampshire and Stafford. He was soon the favoured acquaintance of poets, prelates and princes. He was the most outstanding of early historical biographers, winning praise for his lives (of the likes of Sir Henry Wotton and George Herbert) both from contemporaries and later from Samuel Johnson, who rated this his favourite work. What a pity Walton left no autobiography to tell us how he shot up the social scale from such humble beginnings, or how he helped save King Charles's garter jewel, the lesser George, after the disastrous defeat at Worcester by Cromwell's army or, more importantly, where and how much he fished himself.

With his royalist and high church sympathies, well might Walton have followed his philosophy of 'Go a Angling. Study to be quiet', as he kept a low profile in London, the Puritan power centre in the Civil War. But he was clearly a born reconciler acceptable to all parties, and his will, with its kind words for Catholics as well as the affirmation of his Anglican faith, confirms him as a remarkably broad-minded and tolerant man for those times. It confirms him, too, as a generous and kindly one with his gift of a cottage (now his museum) to the town of Stafford and of money to 'buie coles for the poor' in the most 'pincing' times of the year. His writings confirm that from all his many qualities and activities he would be satisfied that it is his fishing for which he is remembered.

The special attraction of Walton's writing was well summed up by Lord Grey when analysing fishing literature:

> It is worth while to consider some of the different ways in which authors of repute have written about angling. Walton, of course, stands first; his book has become a classic, and has been read and remembered now long enough for us to be sure that it will remain so. This, no doubt, is due to his literary skill, and to that distinguished something called style, which Walton had, and without which no book lives long. There is no definition of style which is satisfactory, or which tells how it may be acquired, for when a man has it, what he has is his own and no other's: without him that particular style would never have been, and no one else can produce the same effect of imitating it. It must, therefore, in some way be the result of the man's personality; and the charm of Walton's *Compleat Angler* is at any rate partly due to the simplicity and purity of nature, which find expression in his book. There is a quiet and benign light in his writing, which draws us to it, and makes us choose to linger over it. It must not, however, be forgotten that Walton wrote other books not about angling: these, too, are of literary excellence, and we still have to account for the

fact that it is by the *Compleat Angler* that Walton is best remembered. It may be that the others would not have been forgotten; but unless he had written the *Compleat Angler*, Walton would never have been as well known as he is. It is his best book, and I like to think that it is so, because the happiness of the subject was specially suited to his kind and quiet spirit. Walton took a wide view of the pleasures of angling; he was of too sensitive a nature to neglect what was to be seen and heard around him, and the object of Piscator is at least as much to teach his scholar to enjoy the spirit of places, times, and seasons, as to catch fish. None the less is Walton careful of instructions in the art of angling. In imparting these he had at any rate the advantage of believing that what he had to teach was new, and he enters into details of baits and tackles and methods, with a zest and confident interest which are hardly possible now. There is an impression of freshness and leisure which never leaves us as we read Walton. The delight of days spent by the river is described as if he felt himself to be the teller of good tidings, in which whosoever wished might share. There is a detachment of mind about him, a sense of freedom and length of days, to which it is less easy to attain in these times of trains, letters, telegrams, and incessant news. There were years in Walton's life of civil war, of great disturbance, public misfortune, and excitement, but it was nevertheless more possible in that age to have long intervals undisturbed and to feel remote. With the exception of Gilbert White's *Selborne*, I know no book in which it is so easy for a tired mind to find refuge and repose as in the *Compleat Angler*.

For me, the essence of *The Compleat Angler* is contained in three brief extracts:

No life so happy and so pleasant as the life of a well-governed angler; for when the lawyer is swallowed up with business, and the statesman is preventing or contriving plots, then we sit on cowslip-banks, hear the birds sing, and possess ourselves in as much quietness as these silent silver streams, which we now see glide so quietly by us. Indeed, my good scholar, we may say of angling as Dr Boteler said of strawberries, 'Doubtless God could have made a better berry, but doubtless God never did;'

and so, if I might be judge, God never did make a more calm, quiet, innocent recreation than angling . . .

But for the practical part, it is that that makes an angler. I once heard one say, 'I envy not him that eats better meat than I do; nor him that is richer, or that wears better clothes than I do: I envy nobody but him, and him only, that catches more fish than I do.' And such a man is like to prove an angler; and this noble emulation I wish to you and all young anglers . . .

I tell you scholar, it is an art to fish or, at least, it is an art to catch fish.

The charm of Walton's book was enhanced by his judicious selection of verse. Even so, it is probable that Cotton's addition to the fifth edition in 1676 was necessary to revive flagging interest and ensure its immortality. For it was Cotton who had the real technical expertise, and his Part II is the one which gives a true feel of dedicated fishing to supplement Walton's exquisite enjoyment of the sport. The two men need to be recalled as contributing equally to the lasting success of the *Angler*. Theirs was an ideal partnership of opposites. The alehouse-keeper's son, who was happy-go-lucky fisherman, but serious man of religion and business and who died extremely wealthy, found an affinity with a high-born spendthrift, who had to hide in caves from his numerous creditors, but was a dedicated and expert fly fisherman. They complemented each other, as closely linked as the entwined initials above the Temple.

For some, Walton and Cotton are still living presences. Chatting with Dora Oliver inside the Temple, Deindorfer recorded this conversation:

'Come along inside,' Miss Oliver said, unlocking the double oak door. We passed under a heraldic-looking crest: Piscatoribus Sacrum, the initials CC and IW entwined in a cipher. Miss Oliver offered me a chair, and a sandwich she extracted from a canvas bag strapped round her worn mackinaw. She offered everything except a log fire in the ample hearth behind me, which would have been nice on that chill

December day. Even a shrew that squirted across the floor while we talked looked cold.

'Sometimes I sit in here by the hour,' she said. I must have registered surprise. 'Oh, I read some, the papers, a magazine, a paperback, and I think a lot. I often think of the two of them.'

Miss Oliver unwrapped a sandwich for herself but made no signs of piling wood onto the fireplace. 'I am fond of Charles, you know, of both of them, as a matter of fact, Charles and Izaak Walton. It warms me just to think of them. Charles is a nice man, a very nice man – kind, generous – a proper gentleman for all his financial problems.'

All of a sudden I experienced a spooky feeling. All of a sudden I realized that she occasionally used the present tense in discussing two men who had been dead and gone for nearly three centuries. But I didn't even consider editing her lapse. Given the mood, the sweet music of the Dove washing outside, and the fact that this had once been their most favourite water, time was beginning to blur for me, too.

Surely it was easy to picture the two of them still, yarning, reciting remnants of verse, fishing what the old boy described as 'the strongest swifts of the river,' Walton soaking a few lobworms or a penk, Cotton casting an antique fly with a fourteen-foot greenheart rod, fishing until they killed enough not only for themselves but also for some resident milkmaid who forever seemed the beneficiary of Walton's kindness.

APPENDIXES

Appendix I

Extract from 'Angling for Safety'
Tasmania's guide to water safety for
freshwater anglers

Know your Boat
Ask yourself these questions: Is the boat suitable for where I plan to go fishing? Does it have enough buoyancy? Is it seaworthy when fully loaded? Is the outboard reliable? Is there enough fuel for the trip and any unforeseen change in plans?

Do I have these on board:
  Anchor, chain and line
  Oars or auxiliary outboard
  Bailing bucket
  PFD (life-jacket or buoyancy garment) for every person
    on board
  Fire extinguisher
  Flares, torch, first-aid kit
  Waterproof matches.

Make sure you can answer 'yes' to all of these – one day your life might depend on it!

Clothing
Appropriate clothing can not only make your day's outing more pleasurable, but can also prolong your survival time if you end up in the water.

Wear protective warm clothing. Wool or approved thermal clothing is the most preferred material for cold climates. Make sure your head and neck are covered.

Wear a buoyancy aid. The thermofloat jacket not only acts as a wet weather jacket, but also provides flotation and prolongs survival in the water.

Alcohol

The old story about having a sip of rum to warm you up is false. In fact, in cold climates, alcohol actually does the reverse . . . it causes your body to cool even quicker!

If you accidentally fell in the water, those few drinks could be fatal.

Why not take a thermos of coffee, tea or soup instead. Save the alcohol for when you are telling those 'fishy' stories around the fire, *after the trip*.

Weather

'Some people are weatherwise. Most are otherwise.'

Check the weather in advance if fishing on big waters where rough weather can cause problems. Keep an eye on it, take the necessary precautions and don't take risks if it does get rough.

Hypothermia

When the *Titanic* sank, hundreds of people were found floating dead in their life-jackets. They didn't drown, they died of hypothermia.

Hypothermia has already claimed victims in the Tasmanian Highlands. Both anglers and walkers have been killed by the wet, cold and windy conditions that are common to this area.

What is hypothermia?

Your body core contains all the vital organs needed to maintain life, and is normally kept at 37°C. When the core temperature falls below 35°C, hypothermia has set in. If nothing is done to prevent the loss of body heat, a person will progress from intense shivering to a loss of co-ordination, unconsciousness and ultimately death.

However, as a person can lose body heat twenty-five times faster in water than in air, a person in cold water has a shorter survival time. In fact, in a water temperature of 19°C, a normally dressed angler has only a 50 per cent chance of surviving one hour. Water temperatures in our lakes can plummet to 3–4 degrees or less!

How to increase survival time

Obviously, if you have properly prepared and planned your

fishing trip as explained earlier, you have already greatly reduced any risk of hypothermia.

Accidents do occur, however, and the risk of capsize or falling in is ever present. If this happens there are many things that you can do to expand your survival time. Remember, rescue is not always immediate; by increasing your survival time you improve the odds of being found alive!

Keep your clothes on. They will help to trap some heat.

Wear a buoyancy aid, preferably one which offers thermal protection, e.g. a thermofloat jacket.

Keep movement to a minimum. A buoyancy aid will help you to do this.

Keep your head out of water. If possible, climb aboard your overturned boat. This will also help you to be spotted by searchers.

If alone, adopt the H.E.L.P. position – cross both arms, put hands under armpits and raise legs to cover the groin area.

If in company, huddle in a group and maintain the maximum amount of chest contact as possible.

(Both the H.E.L.P. and HUDDLE positions can more than double your normal survival time.)

Don't try to swim for it unless you are absolutely certain of reaching shore. You lose heat 35 per cent faster when swimming.

Don't take alcohol while boating. Alcohol increases the cooling rate by 20 per cent. You would die happier, but sooner.

Treatment

The hypothermic victim must always be handled very gently and rewarmed slowly. The following procedures should be observed:

Remove the victim from the water.

Shelter from wind and rain immediately.

Create a sheltered dry and warm place.

Put the victim into dry clothes between blankets, space blankets or a sleeping bag.

Cover all the victim's body, except the face.

Huddle together for warmth, so body temperature can rise gradually.

Give warm sweet drinks.

The unconscious victim will need the usual first-aid care of airways, breathing and circulation.

Don't move the victim unnecessarily.

Don't apply excessive external heat such as fire, electric blankets or hot water bottles.

Don't rub arms and legs.

Don't give alcohol.

Sudden cold water immersion

In some cases, cold water can kill instantly. The shock of a sudden plunge into cold water can cause heart attacks and rupture blood vessels, especially in older persons. It can also cause hyperventilation (over-breathing) which has killed even capable swimmers!

Wader safety

'Have Waders, Gone Fishing.'

Waders are considered by anglers as an essential piece of equipment for keeping the person dry in a wet environment. They are mandatory for the shore-based angler, and are often worn when fishing from a boat.

Waders also are potentially the most lethal piece of equipment used by the angler. It is widely known that if you fall in the water, the likelihood of drowning is high if you are wearing waders. This is because they can quickly flood with water, and drag you under.

Even the shore-based angler can misstep, overbalance or be swept by fast-flowing water into deeper waters.

Both fresh- and saltwater anglers have been advised for many years not to wear waders when in a boat and, over those years, this advice has generally been ignored.

As a result, Bill Stewart of the Tasmanian Water Safety Unit has developed a technique that will help keep a person afloat while wearing waders.

Belt up to buoy up and stay afloat!

To restrict the flooding of water into your waders, simply

fasten a belt around your waist. This practice will also trap air inside the waders, giving the wearer some buoyancy that will help keep them afloat.

To be effective, the belt must be as firm as possible, but always comfortable to the wearer. The drawstring found on most waders will not keep the water out.

Although any belt will be adequate, divers' belts or velcro-fastened belts are recommended.

What to do if you fall in

Immediately tuck up! In a tuck position, less water will leak in, and the air in your waders will be trapped, buoying you up and also keeping you drier. Roll on to your back, keeping your knees tucked. You will need to put your arms in the water to balance yourself. If close to shore, you can use a backsculling action to get back.

Don't panic! You must not try to swim, tread water or float in an upright position.

It is advisable that you master this technique in a pool. It will give you confidence if ever an accident does occur.

If swept into fast-flowing water, face downstream and go with the current, feet first. Use your feet and hands to push away from rocks. Try to stay on your back and in the tucked position.

Remember

Always prepare adequately before you go fishing.

Check the weather
Know the area
Tell others, where and when!
Know your boat's capability
Know your equipment
Wear suitable clothing
Wear a buoyancy aid in the boat.

Don't have alcohol before or during your fishing trip.

Survival in the water

Keep your clothes on
Keep still as much as possible

Keep your head out of water
If alone, H.E.L.P. position
If with others, HUDDLE position
Don't try to swim to shore unless certain of making the distance. Otherwise stay with your boat.

Wader safety
Belt up and stay afloat!
If you fall in:
Don't panic
Immediately tuck up
Roll on to your back
Keep your knees tucked
Paddle to shore, or the boat.

Appendix II

Extracts from the submission to the Review on Angling
by Mrs Llin Golding
Member of Parliament for Newcastle under Lyme

Angling is a fine sport which provides recreation for millions of our people. The only hooliganism it attracts is from those opposed to the sport. Its big advantage as a sport is that it can last for a lifetime; participation is not confined to the young and fit. It brings as much pleasure to the disabled pensioner as it does to the 10-year-old. It provides not only fresh air and exercise, but also the mental therapy which so many of us need.

As a sport and recreation, therefore, it deserves to be encouraged much more than it is at the present time. Anglers face problems in the pursuit of their sport which they are powerless as individuals to solve, e.g. the 'antis', availability of water, pollution, costs. If angling is to flourish, there has to be a collective approach not only to protect the individual angler but also to ensure that the rare resources on which angling depends (e.g. water, fish) and affects (e.g. birds and countryside generally) are conserved.

This requires a more coherent institutional structure than we have at the present time. As a Member of Parliament who has taken a great interest in the problems of anglers, I have been surprised at the lack of influence of such an important group. This is partly because when issues arise it is sometimes not simple to get a clear and concise briefing from anglers or know where best to process them in Whitehall.

Angling needs a stronger voice to a more readily identifiable ear in Whitehall.

*

It is, of course, not only Whitehall that is important. Increasingly, decisions that affect anglers are being taken by the EEC in Brussels, and we would hope that any British Minister responsible for angling matters would also keep an eye on European law and regulations to help protect the British angler.

Governmental decisions are extremely important for the angler. One that was of very great significance, of course, was the setting up of the National Rivers Authority. Anglers expect much from this body, including much stricter control of pollution than has occurred in the past.

Indeed, anglers look to the National Rivers Authority to ensure, either directly or by assisting the multitude of clubs, that there is clean water containing fish at a reasonable cost for all those who wish to fish . . .

The fishing licence should not only give a general right to fish. The issuing authority would also have a responsibility to ensure that it permitted the holder to fish some free water. It cannot be stressed too strongly that angling must be available for all.

In return for the licence fee, this and other obligations have to be accepted by the National Rivers Authority. These include not only the prevention of pollution and excessive abstraction but also the maintenance of adequate stocks of fish in all of our main rivers and lakes. This should be achieved not only by direct provision but also by assistance to the many clubs and associations who do so much for the sport.

In this short submission I have argued that, in the interest of the sport and recreation of angling,

(i) Government should give more consideration and support to the sport;

(ii) the National Rivers Authority should be more vigilant than the old water authorities in the protection of our water and more conscientious in the maintenance of our fish stocks; and

(iii) we need the creation of a new central body to improve, protect and speak for angling as well as providing education and training for anglers.

In making these suggestions for community action, however, I have not forgotten for one moment that the enjoyment of angling will continue to be, as it has always been, totally dependent on that sublime sense of individual freedom and self-fulfilment which it brings.

Llin Golding
24.9.90

This submission is available in full for inspection by the public as are the more than 500 other submissions to the Sports Council's Angling Review Body. The submissions are held in the Sports Council Offices, 16 Upper Woburn Place, London WC1H 0QP.

Appendix III

Advertisement placed by the
League Against Cruel Sports in the *Angler's Mail*,
Wednesday 20 October 1982

THE TRUTH IS,
WE OPPOSE
BLOODSPORTS
NOT ANGLING

A lot of wild words and accusations are being bandied around by the fox hunting fraternity, stating that the League Against Cruel Sports is opposed to angling. These are stupid and ridiculous charges. They represent false propaganda of the worst kind.

The League is opposed to the pursuit and destruction of wild animals by the use of dogs and packs of hounds. This does not include angling.

If you have ever witnessed the death of a stag, which has been pursued over country and through villages for twenty-five miles, for seven hours, by a pack of hounds and horsemen, you will realise why the League Against Cruel Sports exists.

The ultimate death of the stag is barbaric by any standard. It is sickening, immoral – and utterly unsportsmanlike.

The League has a clear-cut policy. It seeks the abolition of hunting with hounds of Britain's wild animals.

We wish to make our position unequivocally clear both to squash these vicious rumours and to clarify our policy. The League is not opposed to angling. Angling for consumable fish is more humane than trawling, and responsible coarse anglers put the fish back in the water unharmed.

Appendixes

Finally, we would ask all true sportsmen to join the League and to speak out in our favour. Do not let the huntsmen hide behind Britain's anglers as a tactic to preserve their cruel 'sport'.

The League Against Cruel Sports Ltd.,
83–87 Union Street
London SE1
Tel: 071-407-0979/071-403-6155

The Game Angling Code:
a guide to good practice

The Hirsel
Coldstream
Berwickshire

Angling is all about good manners, and I commend the principles and the spirit of the code to all who share with me a love of fishing and a proper regard for the fish, the environment and for others.

Some may put one emphasis or another on particular proposals, but the principles expressed in the Code are exemplary and should command general approval. I congratulate the authors.

Home

The Principles of the Code

Environment
All anglers should be actively concerned in protecting the environment.
Conservation
Fishing, and the management of fisheries, should be conducted so that healthy fish populations are maintained.
Behaviour
Moderation, courtesy, and consideration for others are the marks of a sporting angler.
The Sport
There is more to fishing than catching fish.

Appendixes

Introduction

Rod fishing is a traditional and pleasurable pastime. As more people take up the sport of game fishing, there is increasing pressure on wild fish stocks and more demand is put on the limited space on rivers, lakes and lochs; at the same time there is increasing public concern for the environment and for wildlife.

The purpose of this Code is to encourage proper standards of sportsmanship among game anglers and those who manage and regulate game fishing and to help them show regard for the environment, the sport, their quarry and for each other. All involved with game angling are expected to obey the relevant laws and fishery regulations, and to avoid any behaviour which might bring the sport into disrepute. In this Code, Game Angling covers fishing for salmon, sea trout, trout, grayling and char.

Fishery Owners and Managers

Standards

The Code expects that all owners, managers, associations and clubs will set and maintain high standards of sportsmanship and encourage mutual courtesy among rods fishing their own and adjacent waters.

Conservation

Wherever there are wild fish, angling pressure should be regulated to ensure that the natural stock can regenerate and be preserved. Where there is any danger of over-fishing, owners and managers of fisheries should control catches by adopting some of the following measures:

by limiting the use of certain baits or methods of fishing
by voluntary alteration of the number of days fished
by introducing catch limits daily, weekly or annually
by discouraging the sale of rod-caught fish by anglers
by limiting the number of rods or fishing effort.

Fishing Methods

This general Code cannot attempt to define the proper use of all legal fishing methods in every locality, and in varying water and weather conditions. Appropriate fishing methods are established by regulation, and often by tradition. Where particular baits or methods of fishing are unreasonably damaging to fish stocks or to the interest of other anglers, or are seen locally to be unsporting, they should be prohibited.

Stocked Fisheries

Many fisheries, both stillwater and river, depend on regular stocking. Stocking should take account of the ability of the water to support, in a healthy condition, the number of fish introduced.

Natural populations of wild fish need to be preserved. Stocking policies should take account of the risk involved by the introduction of conflicting species. To avoid genetic change through interbreeding, local broodstock should be used wherever possible.

Fishery managers should set catch limits (in size and numbers) and have a clearly understandable policy on fish to be returned. They should keep, and are encouraged to publish, accurate records of numbers and weights of fish stocked and caught.

Competitive Game Fishing

Rules for fishing competitions should comply with the principles of this Code.

Responsibilities

Owners or managers are encouraged to:
draw up and publish fishery rules based on this Code
provide adequate supervision to ensure compliance
co-operate with adjacent fisheries in implementing this Code
make provision for local anglers.

Owners and fishery managers should call for the introduction of by-laws or regulations by the relevant authority wherever this is necessary to ensure that the principles of this Code are applied.

The Game Angler

The Environment

Good anglers are the watchdogs of the water and its environment. Any sign of deterioration must be reported immediately to the fishery manager and the appropriate authority in the area. The report should include:

'what' has been noted

'where' the occurrence was seen

'when' the event was noticed

'the extent' of any pollution.

Anglers should take great care to avoid damage to the waterside or disturbance to wildlife. No tackle or litter must be discarded, and particular regard should be paid to the hazards to wildlife from monofilament nylon.

The Fish

Fish retained for food should be promptly and efficiently dispatched. All other fish should be released as quickly as possible. Fish should only be handled with wetted hands; they should never be thrown back in to the water but held facing upstream in running water until they swim free. Where 'catch-and-release' is practised, barbless hooks are recommended.

Fishing Conduct

Angling as a sport and recreation is a fragile and personal experience, which can so easily be disrupted by external interference. However, water space is in great demand both from anglers and other activities and therefore its enjoyment has to be shared. The following points should be observed by every angler:

ensure you have permission to fish and a rod licence where appropriate

observe the bounds of any beat to which you have been assigned

be prepared to give way after you have fished a drift or pool and never fish too long in one place

never crowd or obstruct an angler near to you on the bank or in a boat do not walk into or cut across another person's fishing and avoid unnecessary wading

give consideration to anglers on the opposite bank

make sure you can distinguish between takeable and not takeable fish

where there are no bag limits, exercise restraint in the number of fish taken, particularly when fish are easily caught

accept that the 'blank days' are part of the experience of fishing

acknowledge considerate behaviour by other legitimate water users

follow the Country Code particularly in relation to control of dogs, the risk of fires and fastening gates

wear unobtrusive clothing and respect the peace of the countryside

do not park vehicles so that they obstruct gateways or cause a hazard on the road

support the organisations which safeguard your sport.

Safety

All anglers should be aware of the inherent dangers of fishing not only to themselves but to others. They should:

wear head and eye protection particularly when casting in windy conditions

look behind before casting

keep rods and lines away from overhead electric power lines

in an electric storm cease fishing, put the rod down and move well away from it

when wading in difficult conditions use a wading stick and always have one foot firmly on the river bed before moving the other

wear personal buoyancy aids wherever appropriate and be familiar with the location and use of any other buoyancy or life-saving equipment provided by fishery owners

be prepared to help anyone in difficulty.

Prepared and produced by the following organisations:

Association of Stillwater Game Fishery Managers
Packington Fisheries, Maxstoke Lane, Meriden, Coventry CV7 7HR

Association of Scottish District Salmon Fisheries Boards
Lachlanwells, Forres, Morayshire IV36 ORA

Atlantic Salmon Trust
Moulin, Pitlochry, Perthshire PH16 5JQ

British Field Sports Society
59 Kennington Road, London SE1 7PZ

Central Council of Physical Recreation
Francis House, Francis Street, London SW1P 1DE

Confederation of English Fly Fishers
Troutbourne, Wotton, Abinger Hammer, Dorking, Surrey RH5 6QL

Country Landowners' Association
16 Belgrave Square, London SW1X 8PQ

Game Conservancy
Fordingbridge, Hants SP6 1EF

Grayling Society
10 Park Road, Salford, Lancashire M6 8HG

National Anglers' Council
11 Cowgate, Peterborough, Cambridgeshire PE1 1LZ

National Federation of Anglers
Halliday House, 2 Wilson Street, Derby DE1 1PG

Salmon and Trout Association
Fishmongers' Hall, London Bridge, London EC4R 9EL

Scottish Anglers' National Association
5 Cramond Glebe Road, Edinburgh EH4 6NP

Scottish Landowners' Federation
25 Maritime Street, Edinburgh EH6 5PW

Sports Council
16 Upper Woburn Place, London WC1H 0QP

Ulster Angling Federation
6 Beech Green, Doagh, Ballyclare, County Antrim BT39 0QB

Welsh Salmon and Trout Association
Swyn Teifi, Pontrhydfendigaid, Ystrad Meurig, Dyfed SY25 6EF

Index

Aasleagh House, 71
Abu, 73
Adams, Martyn, 51, 57
Aelianus Claudius, 137
Aigle, 67
Airflo, 176–7
Allen, Jim, 218
Altnacealgach Lochs, 116–7
Amoco, 104
Angling Times, 32, 221
Aniwhenua Lake, 23
Ashness, Adrian, 131
Australian Freshwater Fishing
    Assembly, 204
Aviemore, 73–5
Avington Lakes, 104, 165–7, 197–8, 232
Avon River, Scotland, 73–5

Bachman, Bill, viii
Bailey, Trevor, 67
Ballynahinch Fishery, 102–3
Baron, Michael, 232
Barratt, Erskine, 129
Bath & District team, vii, 39, 59
Bayham Abbey Fishery, 110
Beauly River, 127
Benson & Hedges UK Championship,
    58–9
Bethel, 3
Bewick, Mickey, vii, 54, 116, 163
Bewl Water, 35–7, 154, 156, 158
Big Jim Lake, 209, 212
Blagdon Reservoir, 59, 154, 160, 164
Blunden, Edmund, 6
Bobin, David, 77
Borolan Loch, 116–8

Boyce, Max, 106
Bridge Hotel, Huntingdon, 114
Bristol Reservoirs team, 59
Brooker, Gary, 53
Bronte Lagoon, 208–9, 215–6
Bronte Park Village, 211
Brora Loch, 115
Brora River, 72–3, 104–5
Buck, Dennis, vii, 23, 25–6, 28, 43, 49,
    186, 190–3, 202, 210–5, 222, 226
Burr, M. I., 84

Cama Loch, 116–8
Canning, Paul, 25, 54
Cannon, Ray, 70, 179, 211
Carron River, 65, 112
Carron Loch, 69
Chambers, Tam, 235
Charles, HRH The Prince of Wales, 109
Charlton Athletic Football Club, 197
Charlton, Bobby, 194
Château, Lac du, 115–6, 183–4
Chaytor, A. H., ix, x
Chew Valley Lake, 124, 131, 154, 162,
    172
Childs, Mike, 42, 59, 131–2, 186, 188,
    193, 202
Chosen River, 3–13
Church, Bob, vii, 23, 38, 43, 51, 54–5,
    155, 160, 177–8, 213–5, 217–8, 221,
    226
Church Hill Farm Fishery, 83
CIPS, 184, 210
Clarke, Jeremy, vii, 39–41
Clarkson, Geoffrey, vii, 43–4, 148, 155,
    160, 211–3

Index

Clegg, Dick, 255–6
Clervaux, 52
Cockwill, Peter, vii, 3, 7, 10–2, 52–3, 116, 165–6
Coigney, Rodolphe, 231
Collee, Dr John, viii, 83–5
Collins, Jim, 33–4
Colorado, 76
Compleat Angler, The, 150, 232–40, 242–5
Compton, Denis, 198, 219
Confucius, 85, 100
Conn Lough, 183
Corrib Lough, 127–8, 109
Cothi River, 76, 90, 101, 121–3
Cotton, Charles, 135, 149, 176, 239–40, 244–5
Coulags Burn, 112
Cowdrey, Sir Colin, 40
Craigellachie, 120
Cribbins, Bernard, 109–10

Daltrey, Roger, 111–2
Darenth River, 240
Dart River, 46
Dartmouth, Duke of, 235
Darwin, Charles, 63, 78
Dauchin, Jean, 222
Davighi, V., 222
Dawrus river, 69
Dee River, 47, 51, 56
Deindorfer, Robert, 149–50, 244–5
Delsnahaugh Hotel, 74
Denning, Beadon, 232
Dever Springs Trout Fishery, 55, 108, 165–6, 170
Diez y Diez, Joachim, 186
Douglas, Lewis, 93
Dove River, 149, 238–44
Draper, Bob, 199
Drennan, 18, 44, 56, 58, 172, 174
Drummin River, 70
Duncan, Brad, 12

Echternacht Lake, 184
Edwards, Gareth, 107–8
Edwards, Oliver, 49
Erriff River, 70, 119
Esparteros, General, 190
Eton College, 130

Faldo, Nick, 178
Farmoor Reservoirs, 163
Fellowes, Robert, 227
Field, The, 116
Fink, Andrew, 204, 218–9
Finney River, 70
Finney, Tom, 196
FIPS, 206
Fly Fishers Club, The, 235, 237
Forgan, Sandy, 222
Foster an Angler, 82–3
Fouvez, Christian, vii, 53
Fox, Andrej, 201–2
Francis, Francis, 97–8, 116, 136
Frasik, Leslaw, 193
Friedman, Erika, 85
Fry, Charles, 196

Gathercole, Peter, viii, 220–1
Giraldo, Rafael de Madariaga, viii, 187–8, 190, 216
Golding, John, 86–9, 109–11
Golding, Llin, 82, 111, 255–7
Gooch, Graham, 178
Gorm Lochs, 96
Grafham Water, 43, 57, 99–100, 114, 154, 169
Grantown-on-Spey, 74
Greaves, Jimmy, 199
Greenwood, Ian, 50, 57
Grey, Lord, ix, 30, 172, 242–3
Grey, Zane, 14
Grove, Dave, 33, 45, 54
Grove, Lucy, 45
Guillemaud, Jean, 222
Gwilym, Vince, 57

Halford, F. M., 172
Hall, Chris, 235
Hardy Bros., 201, 209
Harrison, Roger, 232
Hartley, J. R., 167
Hay, Ian, 232
Hayes, Tony, 128
Hayward, Alan, 54
Headland, Gareth, 59
Healey, Tim, 232
Heinz, Dr, 141
Henfrey, Lee, 39

Index

Herbert, George, 241
Herrmann, Jeremy, viii, 160–3, 167
Heusden Lake, 54
Hintz, O. S., 14
Holland, Barbara, 232
Holland, Sam, 164
Home of the Hirsel, 260
Hordern, Sir Michael, 238
Howitt, Chris, vii, 49, 51, 170, 177
Hughes, David, vii
Hunn, David, 190
Hutton, Sir Leonard, 198

Imbar, David, 211
Inglis, John, 185
Irish Tourist Board, 237
Itchen River, 106, 207, 232, 240
Iveagh Club, 59

Jardine, Charles, vii, 54, 76, 179, 232
Jelenski, Jozef, viii, 141–4, 200–1
Jetson, Noel, viii, 184, 208–10, 218–9, 221–2
Jetson, Lois, viii, 184, 208, 218
Johnson, Samuel, 241
Johson Smith, Sir Geoffrey, 110
Jones, Raymond, 222

Kamasan, 179
Ketley, John, 59, 172
Kettle, Phil, 222
Kipling, Rudyard, 137
Kite, Oliver, 48, 146–7
Kowalski, Jerzy, 195, 200
Kron, Bertrand, viii, 52, 235
Knight, Sid, 232

Laerdal River, 110
Lakedown Fishery, 112
Lancing College, 130–1
Lang, Andrew, 64, 83, 144–5
Lanser, Remy, 222
Laxa River, 105
Leadbetter, Brian, vii, 43, 52–3, 55, 129–30, 155–8, 184, 203–4, 207, 209, 213, 215, 222, 226
League Against Cruel Sports, 80, 258–9
Leeda, 177
Leenane Hotel, 69

Leven Loch, 116
Lewis, Emyr, 59
Lindsey, John, 49, 51, 57
Little Pine Lake, 208–10, 214–5, 219
Llanilar Club, 59
Lodge, Francis, 235–6
London Lakes, 209–10
Loomis, 175
Lucas, Jeremy, vii, 35, 37, 158
Lyons, Lindsay, 25

Malloch, P. D., 116
Marcus, Rixi, 38
Marshall, A. G., 239
Mason, Lord, 83, 109–10
Maynard, Marguerite, viii
McCabe, Eamonn, 195
McIlvanney, Hugh, 194–9
Medway Report, 80
Meehan, James, 69–0, 127–8
Meon River, 240
Merkland Loch, 113–4, 132
Morecambe, Eric, 110
Morey, Bob, 87–9
Morgan, Moc, vii, 168
Moynihan, Colin, 44

National Anglers Council, 224
National Federation of Anglers, 185, 202, 225
National Fishing Licence, 109
National Rivers Authority, 109, 256
National Westminster Bank, 202
Neville, Patrick, vii, 16–20, 24–5
No Lake, 68
Northampton Town Football Club, 160
Nuttridge, Owen, 218–9

Observer, The, vii, 108, 194–9
Ogborne, Chris, vii, 38, 41, 43, 49, 51, 54, 154, 207, 221
Okataina Lake, 27
Oliver, Mike, 28–9
Onny River, 72
Orvis, 175
Overscaig Hotel, 96, 163
Oykel Bridge Hotel, 118, 123, 125
Oykel River, 103, 123

Index

Patrick, Chris, 232
Patshull Park, 104, 110, 235
Pawson, Dr Anthony, 67, 76–7
Pawson, Guy, vii, 67–70, 92, 100–2, 112, 117
Pawson, Helen, vii, 68
Pawson, Hilarie, vii, 72, 92, 96, 193
Pawson, Peggy, 98–9, 123–4
Pawson, Sarah, 72, 75, 96–7, 114–6
Pawson, William, 123–5, 132
Pearn, John, 54, 178
Pearson, Alan, 104, 167, 185–7
Pearson, Graham, 34
Pegasus, 196–7
Perkins, Clive, vii, 54
Perry, Mike, 57
Pickering, Tom, 225
Piggott, Terry, 209, 218, 222
Platts, Carter, 137
Player, Gary, 32
Preston, Bob, 45, 47, 57

Queen, HM The, 226
Queen Mother, HM The, 205
Quinn, David, 30
Quinn, Pat, 30–1

Ramsey, Alf, 197
Rangitaiki River, 21–2, 28
Ranjitsinhji, K. S., 102
Reese, Terence, 38
Reeve, Chris, 37
Resch, Reinhard, viii, 101, 135
Rigby, Reggie, 235
Rifle Brigade, 196
Robinson, Tim and Elva, 17
Rockbourne Lakes, 126, 170
Ross, Malcolm, 226
Rotoma, 23, 28
Rotomahana Lake, 25
Rotorua Lake, 15, 22, 27
Rous, Sir Stanley, 161
Rouskov, Christo, 187
Rumpf, John, viii, 209, 212, 217, 220, 222
Rutland Water, 32–5, 38–43, 131, 153, 153, 157, 160, 169, 209, 212, 217, 220, 222

Salmon, Lord, 125
Salmon, Lady, 125
Salmon & Trout Association, 89, 185–6, 202, 205, 225, 231, 236–7
Samuel Lake, 209
San River, 140, 145
Sautelle snr, John, viii, 209–10
Sautelle jnr, John, viii, 209
Saville, Tom, 80
Scourie Hotel, 132
Sesia River, 90, 186
Sheppard, Jack, 66
Shin Loch, 96–7, 162, 169
Shipman, David, 41, 50
Simpson, Jack, viii
Sloane, Robert, viii, 208
Spencer, Jan, 210, 212, 217
Spey River, 72, 83, 120
Sports Council, 203, 257
Stack Loch, 132
Stewart, Bill, 252
Stone, Peter, 107–8, 241
Stour River, 240
Svoboda Slavoj, viii, 204
Swatland, David, 109, 185, 189, 192
Sweet, Lionel, 67

Taillandier, Robert, viii
Tarawera Lake, 24–5, 28
Tarrant, Chris, 3–4, 8, 109
Taylor, Jeanette, 16, 24–5, 54, 115–6, 166
Taupo Lake, 14, 27
Te Wairoa Village, 25
Tegelaar, Gerard, 101
Teign River, 45–6
Teme River, 72
Test River, 147–8, 240
Thomas, Brian, vii, 25–6, 38, 53–4, 148, 178, 184–5, 207–9, 215–7, 220, 226
Thomas, Dave, 153–4
Thomas, Peter, 91
Tongariro River, 128
Tormes River, 183, 186–7, 198
Traun Gmundener, 101, 138–40, 147
Trent River, 240
Trevino, Lee, 172
Trout Fisherman, 220–1
Tullich Burn, 17, 63

Index

Ungermann, Walter, 222
Urigill Loch, 116–9
Usk River, 67, 129

Valentine, Bryan, 100
Vaughan, Frankie, 106, 110
Vaux, Maggie, 236
Vekemans, Paul, viii
Venables, Colonel, 240
Veyatie Loch, 116
Vinck, Guido, viii, 66
Vines, Sidney, 239

Waikaremoana Lake, 26
Walton, Izaak, 107, 135, 145, 149, 197, 207
Walcott, Clyde, 67
Ward, Roy, 107–8, 164, 232
Wedgwood, Dame Veronica, 68, 231, 241
Weekes, Everton, 67

Weiss, Paul, 3
Weiswampach Lake, 52
Wellington, Duke of, 109
Western Lakes, Tasmania, 215
Westwood, Roy, viii
Wey River, 207
Whaeo Canal, 23, 28
Wharfe River, 44, 47–51, 148–9
White, Gilbert, 243
Wick River, 207
Wilcon Classic, 55
Wilshaw, John, 51
Winchester, Bishop of, 238
Winchester Cathedral, Dean of, 238
Woodwards Bay, 215, 220
Woosnam, Ian, 178
Wotton, Sir Henry, 239, 241
Wye River, Derbyshire, 149
Wye River, Wales, 68, 135–6

Zaharias, Babe, 196